Credits

Author
Andriy Lesyuk

Reviewers
Ludovic Gasc
Lester Martin
Mykhaylo Sorochan
Giovanni Toraldo

Acquisition Editors
Pramila Balan
Wilson D'souza

Lead Technical Editor
Arun Nadar

Technical Editors
Sharvari Baet
Kaustubh S. Mayekar
Kirti Pujari
Devdutt Kulkarni

Project Coordinator
Abhishek Kori

Proofreaders
Mario Cecere
Claire Cresswell-Lane

Indexers
Rekha Nair
Hemangini Bari

Graphics
Aditi Gajjar
Sheetal Aute
Valentina D'souza

Production Coordinators
Shantanu Zagade
Conidon Miranda

Cover Work
Shantanu Zagade

About the Author

Andriy Lesyuk is an open source evangelist, an enthusiastic, and passionate developer with more than 14 years of experience. He is skilled in Ruby, PHP, Perl, C, and more. His primary areas of interest are web development and Linux system development. He is also the author of more than 20 open source plugins for Redmine. He lives and works in Ivano-Frankivsk, Ukraine. His website is www.andriylesyuk.com.

Andriy started his career as an engineer in Ivano-Frankivsk National Technical University of Oil and Gas, where he grew to be the Head of the Software and Networking Laboratory. For some time he worked as a freelancer developing custom Redmine plugins for companies world-wide, the most famous of which is oDesk. Recently, he joined the Kayako team which develops the world's leading helpdesk solution.

First, I would like to thank my wife, Lena Lesyuk, for support and patience. Special thanks to the Packt Publishing team, who assisted me in creating this book, especially to Sayama Waghu, Wilson D'souza, Pramila Balan, Abhishek Kori, Arun Nadar, Sharvari Baet, Devdutt Kulkarni, Kirti Pujari, Kaustubh S. Mayekar, and many others (Sorry, guys, I don't know all your names). And very much thanks to Redmine developers for their great work, especially to Jean-Philippe Lang, Eric Davis, and Toshi Maruyama.

About the Reviewers

Ludovic Gasc is a senior software integration engineer at Eyepea, a highly renowned Open Source VoIP and Unified Communications company in Europe.

Over five years, Ludovic Gasc has managed more than a hundred projects using Redmine in a number of different fields (telephony, webapp development, education) and for a wide variety of purposes (support, coaching, development and so on).

He is also the author of one Redmine plugin and has published several patches.

Lester Martin's 20 year career showcases his accomplishments as a software development manager, architect, and programmer. His skills and experience are centered on Java, .NET, and e-commerce/web technologies. A self-described player/coach, he enjoys helping others grow in their software development careers while continuing to learn himself. He holds Sun Certified Java Programmer and Enterprise Architect credentials.

Mykhaylo Sorochan, PhD, has wide experience in Information Technologies ranging from software development to project management. He started from working on C++ console applications for Unix and now develops web applications in Ruby with Ruby on Rails framework. Besides professional interests in computer aided software engineering, domain specific languages, metaprogramming, and software transformation, his personal interests include such as science fiction, psychology, cycling, reading, and continuous acquiring of new knowledge. Currently holds a project manager position at the Sphere Consulting, Inc. – www.sphereinc.com. In his free time, he supports Russian-speaking Redmine community – www.redprojects.net.

Giovanni Toraldo started to mess around with Linux and free software during his early years at school, developing hobbyist websites with free CMS and maintaining the official Italian support site of PHP-Fusion. After a few unsatisfactory years at university, he decided to start working as a System Administrator and Web Developer. Nowadays, he has developed skills in Linux systems administration, and has taken part in development teams actively using Redmine for years. He is also the author of the *OpenNebula* book released in mid-2012.

www.PacktPub.com

Support files, eBooks, discount offers and more

You might want to visit www.PacktPub.com for support files and downloads related to your book.

Did you know that Packt offers eBook versions of every book published, with PDF and ePub files available? You can upgrade to the eBook version at www.PacktPub.com and as a print book customer, you are entitled to a discount on the eBook copy. Get in touch with us at service@packtpub.com for more details.

At www.PacktPub.com, you can also read a collection of free technical articles, sign up for a range of free newsletters and receive exclusive discounts and offers on Packt books and eBooks.

http://PacktLib.PacktPub.com

Do you need instant solutions to your IT questions? PacktLib is Packt's online digital book library. Here, you can access, read and search across Packt's entire library of books.

Why Subscribe?

- Fully searchable across every book published by Packt
- Copy and paste, print and bookmark content
- On demand and accessible via web browser

Free Access for Packt account holders

If you have an account with Packt at www.PacktPub.com, you can use this to access PacktLib today and view nine entirely free books. Simply use your login credentials for immediate access.

I dedicate this book to my lovely wife, Lena Lesyuk.
Her support and patience made it possible.

Table of Contents

Preface

This book describes the functionality and capabilities of Redmine, reveals its secrets and gives tips on how to use it. The book contains all the information needed to install, configure, use, and master this application. Redmine is a very powerful and an extremely flexible project management tool and an issue tracker. It's free, open source, built on the popular Ruby on Rails framework and has a strong community.

What this book covers

Chapter 1, Getting Familiar with Redmine, prepares us for the next chapters by briefly going through the Redmine interface concept and reviewing pluggable components of the application.

Chapter 2, Installing Redmine, guides on how to install Redmine in four different ways, each of which is suitable for different purposes.

Chapter 3, Configuring Redmine, reviews the configuration options, which are available in the Settings section of the Administration area and covers the advanced options obscured behind them.

Chapter 4, Issue Tracking, reviews what makes Redmine one of the best issue trackers, also giving heed to the configuration options related to issue tracking.

Chapter 5, Managing Projects, covers the major part of Redmine functionality, which is related to projects, and shows, why this is one of the best applications for project hosting.

Chapter 6, Time Tracking, describes time tracking capabilities of Redmine and guides how to generate time reports.

Chapter 7, Text Formatting, is a comprehensive tutorial for the Redmine rich text formatting syntax, which is based on Textile and gives formatting powers to Redmine's Wiki.

Chapter 8, Access Control and Workflow, is aimed at enlightening the permissions system and the issue life cycle by explaining what is the role, the tracker, the issue status, and how are they connected.

Chapter 9, Personalization, gives hints on how to make Redmine more comfortable for users, and helps users to ensure that important and interesting information will be delivered to them.

Chapter 10, Plugins and Themes, guides on how to find plugins for a particular Redmine version, covers installation of plugins and themes and reviews some interesting plugins.

Chapter 11, Customizing Redmine, shows the power of custom fields and guides how to customize Redmine without breaking upgrade compatibility.

What you need for this book

For this book, you need to have access to a Redmine installation (or you will need to install it). It's better (but not required), if you are an administrator of the installation.

The book describes Redmine 2.2.x. However, versions from 1.4.x to 2.1.x should be fine (they just miss some minor functionality).

Who this book is for

This book is for anyone, who already uses or plans to use Redmine. But readers should consider, that most reviewed topics are specific to the software industry (while Redmine can be used for other industries as well). As the book also reviews topics, which require privileged access, it will be especially useful for project managers and Redmine administrators. No prior knowledge of Redmine is required.

Conventions

In this book, you will find a number of styles of text that distinguish between different kinds of information. Here are some examples of these styles, and an explanation of their meaning.

Code words in text are shown as follows: "We can include other contexts through the use of the `include` directive."

A block of code is set as follows:

```
<VirtualHost *:80>
        RailsEnv production
        PassengerAppRoot /opt/redmine/redmine-2.2.0
        DocumentRoot /opt/redmine/redmine-2.2.0/public
        <Directory "/opt/redmine/redmine-2.2.0/public">
                Order allow,deny
                Allow from all
        </Directory>
</VirtualHost>
```

Any command-line input or output is written as follows:

```
$ RAILS_ENV=production rake db:migrate
$ RAILS_ENV=production rake redmine:load_default_data
```

New terms and **important words** are shown in bold. Words that you see on the screen, in menus or dialog boxes for example, appear in the text like this: "clicking the **Next** button moves you to the next screen".

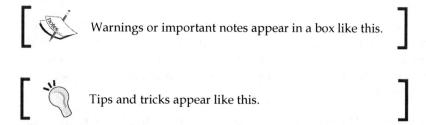

> Warnings or important notes appear in a box like this.

> Tips and tricks appear like this.

Reader feedback

Feedback from our readers is always welcome. Let us know what you think about this book—what you liked or may have disliked. Reader feedback is important for us to develop titles that you really get the most out of.

To send us general feedback, simply send an e-mail to feedback@packtpub.com, and mention the book title via the subject of your message.

If there is a topic that you have expertise in and you are interested in either writing or contributing to a book, see our author guide on www.packtpub.com/authors.

Customer support

Now that you are the proud owner of a Packt book, we have a number of things to help you to get the most from your purchase.

Errata

Although we have taken every care to ensure the accuracy of our content, mistakes do happen. If you find a mistake in one of our books—maybe a mistake in the text or the code—we would be grateful if you would report this to us. By doing so, you can save other readers from frustration and help us improve subsequent versions of this book. If you find any errata, please report them by visiting http://www.packtpub.com/support, selecting your book, clicking on the **errata submission form** link, and entering the details of your errata. Once your errata are verified, your submission will be accepted and the errata will be uploaded on our website, or added to any list of existing errata, under the Errata section of that title. Any existing errata can be viewed by selecting your title from http://www.packtpub.com/support.

Piracy

Piracy of copyright material on the Internet is an ongoing problem across all media. At Packt, we take the protection of our copyright and licenses very seriously. If you come across any illegal copies of our works, in any form, on the Internet, please provide us with the location address or website name immediately so that we can pursue a remedy.

Please contact us at copyright@packtpub.com with a link to the suspected pirated material.

We appreciate your help in protecting our authors, and our ability to bring you valuable content.

Questions

You can contact us at questions@packtpub.com if you are having a problem with any aspect of the book, and we will do our best to address it.

1
Getting Familiar with Redmine

When we are about to try a new web application we ask experts, who are familiar with it, what would they recommend us to use, for example, which database backend, which platform, and many more. That's what this chapter will try to do, it will help you learn what options are available and which one fits your needs better.

In this chapter you will also find a very short description of the **Redmine** interface. It's described in short because I believe it is easy to learn. You will be able to play with it more in the next chapters where we'll discuss how to install and use Redmine. So why this chapter should be of interest to you? The power of Redmine is in its components; some components influence performance, others influence functionality. I'm quite sure that even experienced users will discover new options in this chapter and may decide to switch to or utilize them.

In this chapter, we will cover the following topics:

- What is Redmine?
- Walking through the Redmine interface
- MySQL, PostgreSQL, or SQLite
- Textile or Markdown
- Selecting a **Source Control Management (SCM)**
- Selecting a web server and an application server
- Redmine or ChiliProject?
- Recent versions of Redmine and ChiliProject
- Helping Redmine

What is Redmine?

If you search for a free project management tool most likely you will end up with Redmine. This is an open source Ruby on Rails web application, which can be considered to be the de facto flagship of project management solutions in the open source world. It supports all you need for effective project management: member roles, permissions management based on roles, Gantt charts, scheduling, calendar, roadmap, versions management, documents management, news delivery, files directory, activity view, and more. With third-party extensions, you may also get invoice management, Scrum backlogs, Kanban board, burndown charts, and more. But it's not only a matter of project management.

No one can tell whether Redmine is more a project management tool or an issue tracker. Ideally, a good issue tracker must have some project management features. In Redmine these two components are combined flawlessly. But what makes it a perfect issue tracking application is the fully-configurable workflow, which lets defining issue status change permissions for each role and tracker (issue type). As an issue tracker, Redmine also supports such essential features as priorities, sub issues, watching, comments, custom fields, listing filters, and more. Anyone who has ever worked in a team understands the importance of project documentation. For this purpose, many teams establish Wiki sites. Redmine ships with its own per-project Wiki system supporting the Textile markup syntax and source code syntax highlighting. The staggering thing is that this Wiki syntax is supported all over the Redmine that is in issue descriptions, comments, news, and so on. The syntax also allows you to have cross links to other issues and projects.

For public projects support, Redmine comes with a simple bulletin board module, which allows you to have as many forums as you need. Each forum can have an arbitrary number of threads. Forums and threads can be also watched.

Having read the above paragraphs one may think that the only missing feature for making Redmine host one's projects is some support for version control systems. But such support is also available. Redmine can be used as a repository source code browser. The repository component also integrates flawlessly into other Redmine components such as issue tracker and Wiki. For example, an issue can have list of revisions related to it, a Wiki page can link to a revision, a commit, a source file, and more. With some additional extensions, Redmine also can be turned into a repository manager or even play like Github. The list of supported version control systems is also impressive. They are **Subversion (SVN)**, Git, CVS, Mercurial, Bazaar, and Darcs.

All the things mentioned above make Redmine a perfect application for project hosting. Many individuals and organizations use it for this purpose. But it's not limited to a single project – it is multiproject and each project can have subprojects to any nesting level. Many companies utilize Redmine's collaborative capabilities for forge or labs sites. However, it is not even limited to software development. Other companies use Redmine for customer support, order fulfillment, task management, document management, and more.

I cannot describe Redmine without mentioning the people who created this fabulous software. As soon as you open Redmine, you see the name of its primary author at the bottom of each page (near the copyright section), Jean-Philippe Lang. A huge contribution to Redmine was also made by Eric Davis who then forked Redmine into ChiliProject.

Why does Redmine succeed

The previous topic makes Redmine sound like some all-in-one software. To some extent it is. It was the evolution of Redmine that made it look like this. It is extremely popular these days and that's why it constantly gets new features. But what makes it so popular?

Having first seen Redmine I got the impression that it was a very easy-to-use and friendly application. It is not overloaded with design and UI elements and everything seems to be in its place. This makes users get used to Redmine and like it on first sight. The very first time I saw Redmine I also thought that perhaps it was too limited for my needs mainly because it looked too simple. Both impressions were wrong; it's not an easy-to-use software and it's not limited. The easiness of the look and feel however does its job. If you need only basic features you are ready to use Redmine right after you have seen it for the first time. When you need more advanced features you need to spend some time learning them. That's the main thing that makes Redmine so popular I believe.

The right tools are built with the right technologies. What make Redmine so "right" are Ruby and Rails. **Ruby** is known to be perhaps the most modern metaprogramming truly object-oriented language. This programming language is very flexible and is considered to allow building powerful applications fast and easily. All this can be said about Redmine. This all can be said about Ruby-on-Rails as well. **Rails** is a web framework similar to Symfony and Zend Framework but unlike the others it is the de facto standard for Ruby. Treat Rails as a construction set for building web services like Redmine. The names are so closely associated that many people believe they are about the same language. Ruby-on-Rails also became the source of inspiration for many frameworks and libraries such as CakePHP and Grails. Redmine is built on these technologies and this is the thing that makes it so good.

Of course, you can wonder what exactly is in Ruby-on-Rails that makes it good? The first thing is that Ruby (and therefore Ruby-on-Rails) supports metaprogramming. It's the technique which allows an application to modify its code (that is itself) at runtime. This means that there is almost nothing in Redmine that cannot be altered programmatically. Usually API of an application is limited to some functionality but there are no limitations in Ruby thanks to metaprogramming. What a good feature for plugin API, isn't it? The second thing is that Ruby-on-Rails establishes plugin API, which is used to develop Rails plugins called **engines**. So as you see Redmine does not actually need to provide plugin API to be extendable but it does. Redmine plugin API is built on top of the Rails engine API.

Thereby we come to the next thing, which makes Redmine so popular—its plugins. If you are familiar with Ruby and Ruby-on-Rails, you need to learn a little to start developing Redmine plugins. Taking into account that Ruby-on-Rails is very popular nowadays, Redmine has a huge amount of potential developers. Therefore it has a large variety of plugins. With its plugins you can even turn Redmine into a CRM or help desk. Some of the plugins will be reviewed in *Chapter 10, Plugins and Themes*.

The known issue is (at least partial) Redmine versions incompatibility. Redmine plugin API used to be changed from version to version without good backwards compatibility. It's even more critical as many plugins use metaprogramming for altering non-API (core) functionality. But in fact it's impossible to preserve full backwards compatibility in such cases. The same compatibility issue affects the Rails API that is especially seen in Redmine 2.0, which switches from Rails 2 to Rails 3. Hence, when selecting a plugin you should always check if it is compatible with the Redmine version you are using.

And last but not the least important benefits are that Redmine is cross-platform open source and freely available. Open source code and GPL license makes any modification possible. Nothing limits you in making Redmine better fit your needs.

Walk through the Redmine interface

It's always better to meet than to only hear about. I cannot imagine a reader who is familiar with Redmine but has never seen it. So let's start with checking the Redmine interface.

As mentioned earlier, Redmine has an easy-to-use and simple interface. The following screenshot shows its **Home** page:

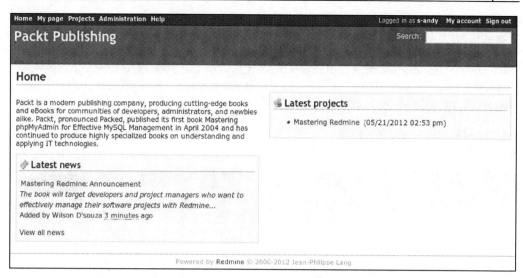

On the top-left of the page, we have the global menu (**Home**, **My page**, and so on). To the right-hand side of the page, we have the account menu (**Logged in as**). The blue area below these menus contains the site title. And finally the content area contains site introduction, recent news for all projects and recent projects.

Actually any page in Redmine can be either a global page (the previous screenshot) or a project page:

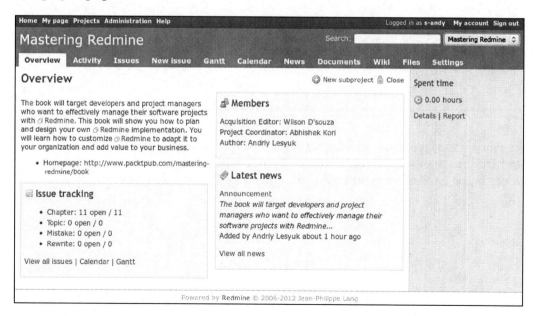

This is the start page for a project or the project home page. Most of the time when working with Redmine, you will be interacting with project pages. The blue top area on a project page contains the project title. The project menu is displayed below the title. The project home page contains a description of the project, issues summary, members summary, and the latest news about the project. Most project pages also have the sidebar with contextual information, such as links and forms.

As one of the primary features of Redmine is issue tracking, let's check the issue list:

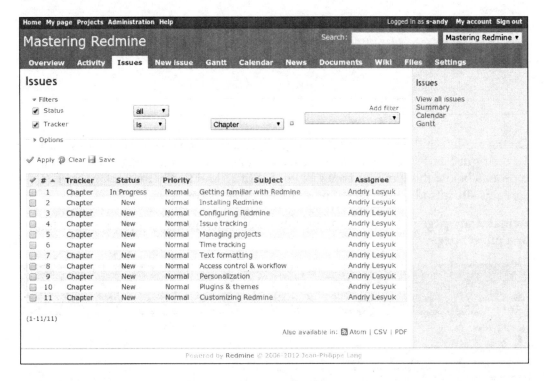

As you see the layout is quite simple and friendly. Collapsible boxes such as **Filters** and **Options** are used all over Redmine to hide rarely used elements. The order of issues in the issues-listing table can be changed by clicking on a header.

The following screenshot shows how an issue page looks:

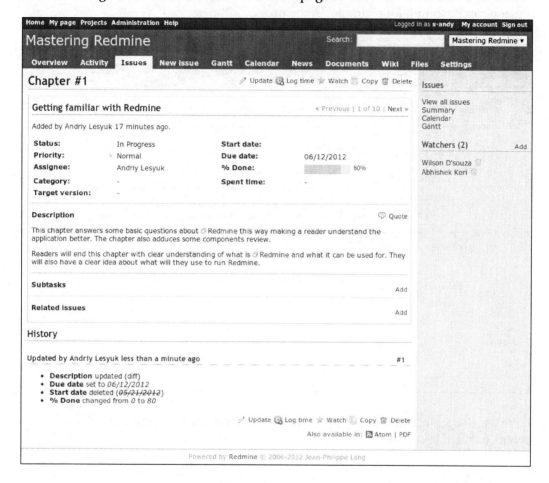

In the top-right corner of the content area we see the contextual menu, which is duplicated at the bottom of the page. A similar type of menu is used for other Redmine *objects* such as projects, Wiki pages, and more. The big yellowish box contains issue details. Below this box, there is the changes' history.

Another UI element, which is intensively used in Redmine is the tabular menu. Such a menu can be found, for example, in the project settings:

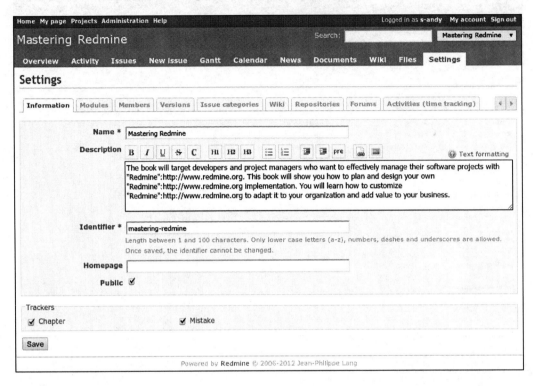

Here we also see another UI element, which is widely used in Redmine - the Wiki syntax enabled text area.

The following screenshot shows how administration settings are implemented in a similar way:

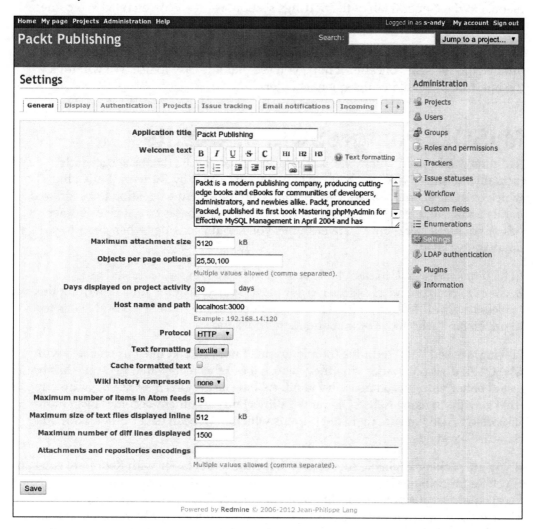

This is another global page (similar to **Home**). Administration sections are available on the sidebar. Currently, we are in the **Settings** section, which also utilizes a tabular menu. On the **General** tab of the **Settings** section, we see Wiki-enabled **Welcome text** field.

This was a short walk through the Redmine interface to let you get used to it and understand its basic concepts. I hope you see that it is easy to use. We will review the interface in detail in subsequent chapters.

MySQL, PostgreSQL, or SQLite

Redmine can be used with MySQL, PostgreSQL, or SQLite database backends (actually the same backends that are natively supported by Ruby-on-Rails). But which of those should you use? It's perhaps too important a question to be ignored in this book. No, I'm not going to praise one of the databases or criticize another (it's out of scope here) but I'll cover things you should consider when choosing a database backend.

In its *Installation Guide* in the Database section (`http://www.redmine.org/ projects/redmine/wiki/RedmineInstall#Database`) at the time of writing this book, authors of Redmine added (recommended) to the right of **MySQL**. Let's try to understand why they recommended this backend.

Having worked with Redmine for a long time I noticed that most users use it with MySQL. It does not matter why they choose it but this means that Redmine has been tested better with this database backend. As long as plugins may use SQL directly (that is without using Rails SQL query builder) this argument becomes even more important. Also I'm sure there are plugins which have been never tested with other database backends.

If you are seeking a reliable source on what database is faster with Redmine, you can check Redmine build logs at `http://www.redmine.org/builds/index.html`. These logs contain results of tests for different versions of Ruby and different databases. Thus at the moment of writing this topic the latest revision r9739 in the latest stable branch 2.0-stable contained the following timings (showing only ruby-1.9.3-p194):

	mysql	postgresql	sqlite3
Tests run 1	304.131903s	320.018676s	276.440358s
Tests run 2	308.206684s	311.683513s	283.817843s
Tests run 3	112.832042s	105.113524s	94.457021s
Total	725.170629s	736.815713s	654.715222s

According to these data, SQLite is fastest and PostgreSQL is slowest. You can check new data or take several revisions into account to make sure.

You can ask: Why not SQLite then, if it's the fastest? SQLite has scalability issues (you can't put it on a separate server) and can potentially have problems with concurrent access. So, MySQL looks to be the optimal backend.

Textile or Markdown?

Good readability helps achieving perception. Rich formatting is very important for issue tracking software as it allows you to distinguish and highlight more important things thus drawing special attention to them. In Redmine, rich formatting is done using **Textile** syntaxes, which is supported almost in every text area. In addition, Redmine provides formatter API, which means that the default Textile formatter can be replaced.

There were attempts to add different syntaxes to Redmine Wiki but the only successful and still active non-native Wiki syntax plugin is the Markdown Redcarpet plugin (`https://github.com/alminium/redmine_redcarpet_formatter`). This plugin replaced the default Redmine formatter with the Markdown formatter, which uses the Redcarpet library. This is the same library that is used by Github. Therefore the syntax provided with the Redcarpet plugin is compatible with Github's **Markdown** syntax.

If you asked what formatter I recommend, I would answer *Textile*. The Textile formatter is native, well supported, and well tested. However, when choosing a formatter you should consider your audience; if your audience is mostly Github users you should perhaps try Markdown but still remember that the majority of Redmine installations use Textile and users may expect your Redmine to use Textile as well.

But let's not be too verbose and compare basic rules of these syntaxes:

	Textile	Markdown
Bold text	`*Bold*`	`**Bold**`
Italic text	`_Italic_`	`*Italic*`
Underline text	`+Underline+`	`<ins>Underline</ins>`
Inline code	`@inline code@`	`` `inline code` ``
Preformatted text	`<pre>`	Text which starts with spaces
	`....`	
	`<pre>`	
Syntax highlighting	`<pre><code`	`` ```ruby ``
	`class="ruby">`	`...`
	`...`	`` ``` ``
	`</code></pre>`	
Bullet List	`* Item 1`	`* Item 1`
	`* Item 2`	`* Item 2`
Numbered list	`# Item 1`	`1. Item 1`
	`# Item 2`	`2. Item 2`
Headings	`h1. Heading 1`	`# Heading 1`
	`h2. Heading 2`	`## Heading 2`
	`...`	`...`
	`h6. Heading 6`	`###### Heading 6`
Links "Anchor":http://link	`[Anchor](http://link)`	
Images	`!image_url(Title)!`	`![Title](image_url)`
Tables	`|_.Table|_.Heading|`	`|Table|Heading|`
	`|Cell    |Cell     |`	`|-----|-------|`
		`|Cell |Cell     |`

Selecting a Source Control Management (SCM)

Source Control Management (SCM) is better known as Revision Control Management. Revision control systems currently supported by Redmine include Subversion (SVN), Git, Mercurial, Bazaar, Darcs and CVS.

As mentioned, Redmine integrates SCMs nicely using them not just as source code readers but making more use of them. In Redmine, we can do the following: Associate a revision with issues (having revisions listed on issue pages). Automatically close an issue and/or change its done ratio when an appropriate commit has been made. Use Wiki syntax in commit messages. Refer a revision, a commit, or a file from a Wiki syntax powered content, which can be a Wiki page, an issue description, a project description, or a forum message and much more

But all this makes Redmine a source code browser not a SCM manager (that can be done with plugins however). So why is choosing the right SCM so important?

Unless you are fine with having SCM and Redmine integrated visually most likely you will want a deeper integration when you know the options. Three levels of Redmine and SCM integration can be distinguished as follows:

- Redmine as a source code browser
- Redmine as a SCM authenticator
- Redmine as a SCM manager

The basic browser level requires SCM clients to be installed on the same server Redmine is running on so you may want to use only some of the supported SCMs. Also the basic support of SCMs is not equal: revision graph (similar to one on Github) is supported only for Git and Mercurial, however, these two SCMs can be only local (*repositories should be on the same server, where the Redmine is*).

Revisions

Revision: master   OK

#	Date	Author	Comment
fb7abea9	03 May 2012 15:41	José Valim	Merge pull request #6139 from pwim/extract_options-actionpack use extract_options!
54174b5f	03 May 2012 15:26	José Valim	Merge pull request #6141 from mhfs/mailer_tweaks Minor ActionMailer tweaks
e821611c	03 May 2012 15:21	Paul McMahon	use extract_options!
5f2f9b57	03 May 2012 15:11	Marcelo Silveira	No need to force conversion to Symbol since case ensures it's already one.
3d021951	03 May 2012 15:10	Marcelo Silveira	No need to work around 1.8 warnings anymore.
ab7b5501	03 May 2012 14:59	Vijay Dev	Merge pull request #6137 from FLOChip/cache_documentation cache_store has an extra option of :null_store.
e608588d	03 May 2012 14:58	Oscar Del Ben	Update command line guide
5c0cbb3d	03 May 2012 11:50	José Valim	Merge pull request #6138 from bogdan/routes RouteSet: remove some code dups
7273adab	03 May 2012 11:28	Teng Siong Ong	cache_store has an extra option of :null_store.
c9e809c8	03 May 2012 11:20	Paul McMahon	I found it strange that this guide is redirecting questions to a specific person. Heiko Webers' (@hawe) last blog post is a year and a half old, so it's not obvious that he's still active with Rails security. If he is, feel free to revert.
3e541799	03 May 2012 10:53	Jon Leighton	Merge pull request #6134 from carlosantoniodasilva/ar-relation-kernel-private-methods Fix issue with private kernel methods and collection associations
5d26c8f0	03 May 2012 05:23	Carlos Antonio da Silva	Fix issue with private kernel methods and collection associations. Closes #2508 Change CollectionProxy#method_missing to use scoped.public_send, to avoid a problem described in issue #2508 when trying to use class methods with names like "open", that clash with private kernel methods....

Redmine comes with `Redmine.pm` — a Perl module for Apache web server — which can be used to authenticate Subversion and Git users against Redmine. If the `Redmine.pm` tool has been integrated, you can control who has access to project `Subversion/Git` repository and what kind of access (read and/or write) they have by simply managing project members (and roles). Something similar (with additional changes made to Redmine and/or system) can be done for Mercurial and Bazaar. Nevertheless Subversion and Git SCMs are best supported by `Redmine.pm` and their support is out of the box. Most likely you will have problems configuring other SCMs to authenticate against Redmine.

The only missing functionality for Redmine to become a full-featured SCM manager is the ability to create repositories. And such functionality also comes with Redmine and is provided by the `reposman.rb` command-line tool. This tool supports Subversion, Darcs, Mercurial, Bazaar, and Git (all except CVS). The problem is that in order for it to work you need to create a cron job executing it periodically. Luckily alternative solutions exist and are provided by third-party plugins such as SCM Creator, Redmine Git Hosting, and Redmine Gitosis.

When choosing SCM, you should also consider your requirements, your experience, preferences of your team or audience, easiness or complexity of use and so on. However, the best integratable SCMs seem to be Subversion and Git.

Selecting a web server and an application server

Redmine as a Ruby-on-Rails web application should be run under a web server. This can be an independent web server such as Apache, Nginx, or Lighttpd running Ruby-on-Rails using either Passenger, FastCGI, or a dedicated Ruby web server such as Unicorn or Thin.

A big options list, isn't it? Actually these are not all the possible options. Redmine can also be used with JRuby under a Java virtual machine, can be run under standalone Passenger, under Mongrel, under WEBrick, and more. But the above options were *chosen* by practical use and, therefore, are most commonly used. So we review only them here. They can be divided into three categories:

- Dedicated Ruby web server
- Dedicated Ruby web server plus for example, Nginx as a load balancer
- Separate web server with for example, Passenger module

Ruby often gets compared to PHP but actually these technologies are very different. For a PHP guy, which I am as well, using a web server written in Ruby for running a Ruby application can be weird. But in fact Ruby, like Java, also runs under a virtual machine. Therefore, for example, Apache in order to run a Ruby application needs to run a Ruby virtual machine as well so in total these are at least three processes: a web server, an application server, and an application itself. For this reason running a Ruby application under a Ruby server seems to be reasonable because in this case we get only two processes namely an application server and an application.

The lack of good multithreading support is a known problem of all Ruby virtual machines. This is the main reason why when running Ruby applications on production they usually use a Ruby application server in conjunction with another web server. As Ruby does not play well with multiple connections they run many instances of Ruby application server and use for example, Apache as a load balancer for forwarding requests to those instances and as a web server for giving static content (images, CSS files, and so on). The most documented option for this category is Apache plus Mongrel, the combination which, for example, was used by Twitter before the company moved first to Unicorn and then to Java. But the best combination, according to many benchmark results, is Nginx plus Thin or Unicorn.

But in fact this configuration uses not only a web server and an application server but also a load balancer. A web server needs to support the reverse proxy mode to be able to act as a load balancer. For Apache, this mode can be provided by mod_proxy, Nginx, and Lighttpd have built-in proxies. In addition, a good idea is to use some software for monitoring Unicorn/Thin instances, for example, Monit.

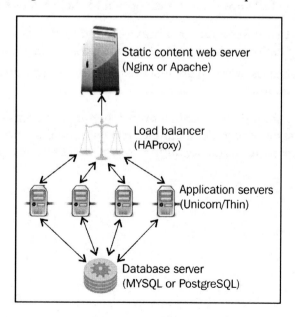

You perhaps got the feeling that the just discussed category is for advanced usage and for high loaded services? Yes, it is in a way. The most commonly used, easy-to-install and best documented is the third category: a web server running a Ruby application using the Passenger module (also known as **mod_rails**) or the FastCGI module. The **Passenger module** is in fact another Ruby application server. The difference between it and Unicorn/Thin is that it usually runs as a module of a web server and not as a standalone server (while the last is possible). The problem with the Passenger is that it does not work with Windows. Also, the Passenger module is not available for Lighttpd. Thus, Lighttpd uses FastCGI for running Redmine instead. FastCGI, which is actually a protocol name, can be also used under Apache and Nginx.

However, the Passenger is more popular. It is used, for example, by BitNami Redmine stack and TurnKey Redmine appliances (systems for easy deployment of Redmine). In addition it is suitable not only for small and middle-sized websites but can be used for high-loaded web services as well. Thus, for example, Ruby-on-Rails framework recommends using Passenger in flavor of other options (`http://rubyonrails.org/deploy`).

When run under a web server the Passenger creates at least two processes—itself and an application. This can be a problem if it is used on cheap OpenVZ powered VPS hosting where memory amount used by an application is very critical. This is where FastCGI helps: when run with FastCGI Redmine occupies at least one process (application).

In case you still don't feel sure about which option to choose, let's summarize:

- If you plan to use Redmine for a heavy-loaded forge site you should think about using Nginx with Unicorn/Thin and possibly HAProxy.
- For all other cases or if you are just unsure go with Apache or Nginx and the Passenger module.

While choosing you should also consider your other requirements and services you plan to run on the same server. For example, you will definitely need Apache if you plan to use `Redmine.pm` for authenticating Subversion/Git users against Redmine.

Redmine or ChiliProject?

In the open source world, a good project can't just die or become worse because such projects always have a community ready to support it or take it over. If something goes wrong with a project its community can always make a fork. But the reason for making a fork can be just a wish to make the project better. Usually the appearance of a fork also divides the community, however, this does not make the fork or the project worse. In fact with the fork the original project gets a solid competitor—itself. And competition is what makes project developers strive for the best.

The history of open source knows many examples of forking and rewriting software what ends with the appearance of a new, better, or just different project. We do not need to search for such examples: Joomla was forked from Mambo, Gforge from SourceForge, X.Org from XFree86, Apache from NCSA, LibreOffice from OpenOffice.org, and many more.

You perhaps noticed that every page of Redmine contains a line **Powered by Redmine © 2006-2012 Jean-Philippe Lang** at the bottom. Jean-Philippe is the author of Redmine and its project manager but there were more people involved in this great project and one of them was Eric Davis. In 2011, due to project management concerns and community patches inclusion policy Eric Davis with some other Redmine core developers (most of whom are finnlabs (`www.finn.de`) employees) forked Redmine into the ChiliProject. This is how forking is explained on the ChiliProject site (`https://www.chiliproject.org/projects/chiliproject/wiki/Why_Fork`):

> *However, in the view of some of Redmine's leading developers, the maintenance and evolution of Redmine has not been as predictable and responsive as its developer community is capable of. Integration of community-created patches were too sporadic, lacked a clear methodology, and was interfering with the effectiveness of the Redmine project for its users. Over the past two years, several members of Redmine's community worked to resolve management bottlenecks through clear suggestions and contributions. They also attempted to broaden and open up the development process to more contributors. But efforts via public and private forums to discuss the goals and future direction with the project manager of Redmine failed, as the current project manager did not share these priorities.*

> *A group of developers from the Redmine community has therefore concluded that the only way to ensure continued, sustained and stable development of our favorite project management solution is to fork it. We, long-standing community members and contributors, pledge to uphold the ideals of Free and Open Source Software ethics, governance and development practices in order to produce a reliable project management system released under the name of ChiliProject in February 2011.*

Luckily at the moment Redmine and ChiliProject do not differ much so almost everything written in this book applies to ChiliProject as well.

So which one to choose? Let's discuss the difference now:

- Of course, Redmine is older. It has been proven to live, to survive and be successful, its developers were active over five years and continue to be (besides Jean-Philippe there are Toshi Maruyama, Etienne Massip and others), it's stable.

- Redmine has a bigger community than ChiliProject. But this does not mean that ChiliProject is worse though, most users have not moved to ChiliProject because they see no reason. Such a big community is mainly due to age. However, this means that most likely you will get support for Redmine faster.

- Redmine comes in Bitnami, Turnkey, it is available in official repositories of Debian and Ubuntu, it is available for hosting at Plan.io, HostedRedmine and more. But again it's mainly due to its age.

- Redmine does not get changed much, it feels like a well supported software with major changes coming rarely (except 2.0.x which moved to Rails 3 but it was a developers' headache, not a users'). By changes, here I meant functionality and UI changes, which required users to update their third-party tools or get used to.

- ChiliProject, on the contrary, introduces major changes with each major release. It feels like ChiliProject developers finally have a possibility to implement things they've wanted for a long time. However, these changes add much work for developers of third-party tools and many things should be learned by users.

- ChiliProject promotes openness of development process and readiness for contribution. If you or your organization plan to modify the core or you just feel you or your organization can do this and you are ready to share your modifications, you should consider using ChiliProject. To some extent ChiliProject is for enthusiasts and advanced users.

- ChiliProject lacks a good plugins registry which is available for Redmine, it has only a plugins compatibility list. However, Redmine plugins registry is far from being perfect (for example, it's incomplete and lacks some search capabilities).

- The situation with themes is even worse: Redmine has many themes but they are not compatible with ChiliProject anymore since Version 3.x of the latter. ChiliProject 3.x does not seem to have any third-party themes available (ChiliProject prior to 3.0 worked fine with Redmine themes).

Having mentioned theme changes in ChiliProject 3, let's see what its new default theme looks like:

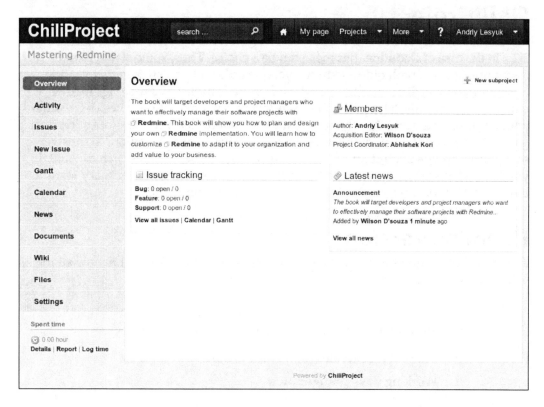

Some up-to-date information about differences in Redmine and ChiliProject is also available on the website of the latter: `https://www.chiliproject.org/projects/ chiliproject/wiki/Differences_Between_Chiliproject_and_Redmine`.

You might expect features comparison in this topic. But theoretically features of Redmine and ChiliProject can be merged relatively easily into each other. So any features comparison here can become outdated when this book comes into your hands. So instead I decided to review different approaches these projects are taking. I hope this information is enough for you to decide.

Overall, ChiliProject seems to be in "transitional" period when its features, look and feel, design, and so on are changed and at the end of this period ChiliProject will turn into a completely different project management solution. Maybe it worth waiting for this period to finish but maybe it's worth helping the ChiliProject guys to move.

On the other hand, Redmine is a proven, stable solution, well-known, and well-documented.

Recent versions of Redmine and ChiliProject

In most cases everyone uses the most recent version of an application, which is 2.2.x in the case of Redmine. But there can be a choice. Thus, some stable Linux distributions come with older Redmine versions. Should you stick to that version or should you install the recent one which is more complex and assumes further manual checks for updates and doing multiple manual migrations? Besides, what if your organization uses a hardly modified copy of Redmine and therefore sticks to a particular version? Should you allocate resources for a hard migration? To answer such questions you should know a few things about those versions such as what do you lose, what will you get and so on. In this topic, we will review primary features introduced by some recent versions of Redmine and ChiliProject.

Redmine versions

At the time of writing this topic the recent version was 2.2.x. We will review all major versions down to 1.4.x.

- **2.2.x**

  This version comes with the following noticeable features:

    - Support for private comments in issues
    - Working days configuration

- **2.1.x**

  This version upgrades Redmine to Rails 3.2.x, which switches from Prototype to jQuery. This also requires developers to update their third-party tools. Besides, the version comes with the following features:

    - Ability to require issue fields or make issue fields read-only per status, tracker, and role
    - Support for subforums
    - Ability to close (freeze) projects

- **2.0.x**

  The Version 2.0.x is the upgrade of Redmine to Rails 3.1.x. It was released along with Version 1.4.x that is we got two stable versions at the same time (nothing like this ever happened before)! This version was released mainly for developers so they could upgrade their third-party tools.

- **1.4.x**

  This version includes the following new noticeable features:
    ◦ Support for multiple repositories per project
    ◦ Support for multiple values for "List", "User", and "Version" custom field types
    ◦ Ability to add non members to the watcher list of an issue

Basically, due to migration to Rails 3 and, therefore, huge changes in API at the time of writing this book, not all Redmine plugins have been ported to Redmine 2.x.x yet.

ChiliProject versions

The most recent version of ChiliProject at the time of writing this topic is 3.x.x. Unlike previous versions, this version ships with some new interesting features. Earlier there were versions 1.x.x and 2.x.x but only the latter was bringing a really new project.

- **3.x.x**

  ChiliProject 3.x.x was released with the following noticeable changes:
    ◦ Comes with new design (not compatible with Redmine themes any more)
    ◦ Introduces Liquid template language (conditions, loops, and more in Wiki)
    ◦ Support for issue tags
    ◦ Comes with jQuery

- **2.x.x**

  ChiliProject 2.x.x is compatible with Redmine 1.1.x and comes with many internal changes.

Helping Redmine

What would be Redmine without many people contributing to it? Most likely it would not exist at all. Any contribution is very important for a free open source project, an active and passionate community is what makes such projects good.

Hearing about contributing to a free open source project most people assume some development but there are manu more areas where you can help. For example, this book helps Redmine by spreading information about it, teaching how to use it and demonstrating its abilities. You help Redmine by purchasing this book not only because you become a potential fan of this project but also because Packt Publishing, the company which publishes this book, will pay a royalty to Redmine.

Let's discuss how else can you can help Redmine:

- As it has been already mentioned let's start with development: If you are a developer you can help by contributing code or patches to Redmine. To do this you should know Ruby and Ruby-on-Rails but if you know Perl you can still help by improving `Redmine.pm`. You can help even more if you know HTML and/or JavaScript because these technologies are intensively used by Redmine and may need improving. If you know neither of the above technologies you can still help by for example, developing a REST API client library for Redmine using technologies you know.

  Some links regarding development for Redmine:

  - General information: `http://www.redmine.org/projects/redmine/wiki/Contribute`
  - Subversion repository: `http://redmine.rubyforge.org/svn/`
  - Git repository: `https://github.com/redmine/redmine`

- If you are a designer you can make new themes for Redmine. This is an extremely important area as a good theme attracts more users.
  - See also: `http://www.redmine.org/projects/redmine/wiki/HowTo_create_a_custom_Redmine_theme`

- You can write articles, blog posts, tutorials, improve source code documentation (which uses RDoc), and more. You can do this in English or any other language.

- Regarding other languages: You can also translate Redmine, its official or unofficial tutorials and so on, into other languages.
  - See also: `http://www.redmine.org/projects/redmine/wiki/HowTo_translate_Redmine_in_your_own_language`

- If you are just a user or are going to become a user, do not neglect to report bugs or to suggest new features. If you are not sure that something is a bug still open a discussion on the Redmine forum and ask the community. Many bugs are hard to find and not many people report them.

- And last: You can show your support for Redmine by making a donation.

    ◦ See: `http://www.redmine.org/projects/redmine/wiki/Donors`

In a similar way you can help not only Redmine but also its fork ChiliProject and many free open source plugins for Redmine.

Summary

The goal of this chapter was to familiarize you with Redmine and get you ready to dig deeper into this web application. Therefore we have reviewed not only advantages and the interface of Redmine but also have checked its installation components. We have also discussed ChiliProject as it's a community fork of Redmine and it's important to know about it if you become (or have become) a member of the Redmine community.

I tried to share as much knowledge about Redmine, its fork and its installation components as possible so you could understand them better, learn what options you have and would be able to choose the right option. Still remember that usually the best option is the one which is used by most users so if you choose an uncommon option you should be sure about the reasons for doing this.

The knowledge you have gained reading this chapter will help you in the next chapter as you will need to decide what components you will use for installation. However, the next chapter covers only common options. Anyway if you chose other options it's still worth reading the next chapter to see how the installation is done.

2
Installing Redmine

Now, when we know what Redmine is and what it looks like, we can proceed to the next step of our relations with it that is to get Redmine up and running. Thus, generally, this chapter is about setting it up and maintaining it and is intended mostly for administrators.

We will discuss installing and maintaining Redmine but we won't review the upgrading process. The first reason for not doing this is that it can change and the second reason is that it's not actually required in order to learn or to use Redmine. Instead we will discuss what we need to do and consider before upgrading.

In this chapter, we will cover the following topics:

- Preface
- Installing Redmine from the package
- Installing Redmine from sources
- Using TurnKey Redmine appliance
- Using BitNami Redmine stack
- Maintaining Redmine

Preface

I have always believed that installation is not just a matter of making an application run, it's much more, as it involves making important decisions which can be hard to change in the future such as:

- What components and/or platform should be chosen for running an application (which is covered in the previous chapter)?
- What version (or fork) should be used?
- What source should be used to install an application from?

Of course, the answers to these questions depend on the goals of using Redmine, which in turn, raises other questions such as:

- Will this be the production?
- Is this temporary or for development?
- Is there someone who will maintain the installation?
- Should it be easy to maintain or should it be scalable and platform independent?

Most people will just go with the officially recommended installation procedure which is, in fact, just the most common. The official procedure does not actually consider platform peculiarities just because it would be too many cases to document. Following this procedure one gets a completely separate subsystem not connected to the host system and to its package management tools. So such subsystem will require manual maintenance, can easily get broken with changes in the host system, can have obscure conflicts, and so on. This often ends up with the subsystem being, in fact, unmaintained and with some fear of touching it. In addition, the official installation procedure is the most complex one.

Therefore under this topic, we will review not only the officially recommended procedure, which is actually a good choice in some cases, but will also check some other common procedures. All these procedures differ in the source they get Redmine from. By source type these procedures can be divided into three categories:

- Prepackaged Redmine
- Official SVN/Git repository or tarball
- Appliance containing all you need to run/install Redmine

The first category assumes that a Redmine package is available. By package I mean a specially prepared software archive containing not only Redmine itself but also tools for installing Redmine into the system. The best known package formats are RPM (for Red Hat based Linux distributions) and DEB (for Debian based Linux distribution). Actually it's not a big deal to create such a package but another requirement is that such package should be maintained and actively supported! Otherwise using it has no sense.

With a Redmine package, you need to answer just a couple of questions to install Redmine but this is not the only thing which makes packages so attractive. Packages are processed by system package manager, which also resolves conflicts and installs dependencies. Usually a package comes from a repository along with its dependencies and other system packages. And this means that system package manager will be able to update Redmine flawlessly when a new version of its package is released. If no new version is available the package manager won't allow dependencies to be updated if this will break Redmine! This makes maintenance of Redmine much easier.

The problem is that Redmine is not yet available as a package in many Linux distributions. At the time of writing this topic Redmine package is available (and well-supported) in Debian-based Linux distributions such as Debian, Ubuntu, and Mint. Some Redmine package are also available in Mandriva based Linux distributions such as Mandriva and Mageia. As Mandriva uses RPM this package can potentially work for Red-Hat-based distributions such as CentOS and Fedora but I personally, have never tested it.

It may be that by the time you read this topic there will be Redmine packages for other Linux distributions. At least you should really try to find them as this will make maintenance easier! When looking for a package check if it is actively supported, is it well-tested, is it in official repository, check feedback about the repository it is in (if it's not the official one), check feedback on the package itself and so on.

As you might guess I recommend using the Redmine package if possible mainly due to easy maintenance. However, you should note that usually a packaged software has an older version than the recent one. Thus at the moment of writing these words the recent Redmine version is 2.2.x and the recent version of the packaged Redmine in Ubuntu is 1.4.x, in Debian stable it is even older, that is 1.0.x. So if you want to be up-to-date (just up-to-date, not secure as Ubuntu/Debian guys follow security news and make updates if vulnerabilities appear) you can go with the recent official version. However, be sure to allocate resources for maintaining your Redmine installation and to document your changes to the system (do mention that you installed Redmine without using system package manager).

But do not hurry to leave this text and move to the appropriate topic: there is an even easier way. The third category is about appliances. An appliance contains all you need to run an application. In the case of Redmine the appliance should contain a web server (for example, Apache plus Passenger), a database server (for example, MySQL), Ruby, Rails, and so on. There are two well-known appliances for Redmine, which are TurnKey Linux appliance and BitNami Stack.

As it comes from the name TurnKey Linux Redmine appliance contains a ready-to-use Linux installation which can be run under VirtualBox or VMWare, deployed to VPS (OpenVZ, Xen, or OpenStack based) or Amazon EC2 cloud. It is also available as a Live CD ISO image, which means you can first try it and then install it. The TurnKey Linux is based on Ubuntu so after deploying or installing it you, in fact, get Ubuntu and thus can update and install additional software or security fixes from Ubuntu repositories.

While the idea of the TurnKey Linux appliance is to ease the deployment of a new server the idea of the BitNami stack is to ease the deployment of an application. A BitNami stack contains just software required to run an application (no OS) and, unlike the TurnKey, the BitNami stack also supports Windows and Mac. In addition, you can download an Ubuntu based virtual machine with the BitNami Redmine stack or deploy it to Amazon EC2 cloud.

The problem with BitNami is that it is separate from the rest of the system and so you get all the maintaining issues mentioned earlier. Despite what you could expect updating the BitNami stack is not an easy task (they recommend just to reinstall it). But the good thing is that you can also deploy other BitNami stacks to the same server, for example, you can deploy WordPress along with Redmine.

Taking the above paragraphs into account I conclude that the BitNami Redmine stack is good for development and testing and should not be chosen for production. Another thing which is good for development is that it always comes with the most recent version of Redmine. Of course, it's my opinion and you should come to yours considering everything I have written here. Now let's get Redmine installed in four different ways.

Migrating to Redmine

The official Redmine documentation includes instructions for migrating from Trac and Mantis. Community also provides migration tools for JIRA, BugZilla, and more. Check this page for recent instructions: http://www.redmine.org/projects/redmine/wiki/RedmineMigrate

For all the procedures we will be using Apache, Passenger, MySQL, and so on—the most common components—unless others are enforced by package dependencies or ship with an appliance. If, however, having read *Chapter 1, Getting Familiar with Redmine*, you have chosen different components, not covered under this topic, then you have decided to go with more advanced options and need to find tutorials elsewhere, for example on www.redmine.org. Unfortunately this book just can't cover all the options.

Installing Redmine from the package

For installing Redmine from a package we will use Ubuntu Server 12.04 LTS. Why Ubuntu? Because it's one of the most popular Linux distributions nowadays and Ubuntu is widely used along with Redmine (for example, the TurnKey Linux is also based on Ubuntu).

 This guide can also be used to install Redmine on Debian. Ubuntu and Debian are very much alike so the installation procedure should not differ much. Still some things may differ.

Assuming you have already installed Ubuntu Server 12.04 LTS (or a more recent version). If not, please do it! Assuming also that this is a *clean* installation, so we will need to install, Apache, MySQL, and so on, all software needed to run Redmine. If some software is already installed it's not a problem as it is still safe to execute the commands given. The Ubuntu (and Debian) package manager is smart enough to skip already installed software.

Installing Redmine and MySQL server

Now let's execute the following command in the console:

```
$ sudo apt-get install redmine redmine-mysql mysql-server
```

Instead of redmine-mysql and mysql-server, you can use redmine-pgsql and postgresql or redmine-sqlite and sqlite3 here. However, remember that neither PostgreSQL nor SQLite3 is reviewed in this topic.

This command will install Redmine and MySQL as well as many dependency packages including Ruby and Rails. Before doing this, the Apt-Get package manager will ask you to confirm:

```
0 upgraded, 73 newly installed, 0 to remove and 49 not upgraded.
Need to get 68.5 MB of archives.
After this operation, 221 MB of additional disk space will be used.
Do you want to continue [Y/n]? y
```

On the screen, type y and press *Enter*.

Configuring MySQL server package

After this it will download all the packages and start the installation process. Soon you will get the screen:

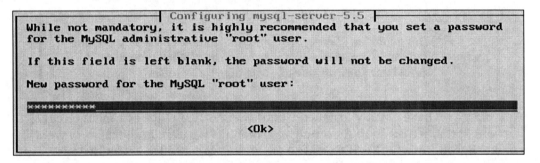

This screen asks you to enter a new password for the MySQL superuser. The same password will be used later to set up the Redmine database. After entering the password press *Tab* to switch to the **Ok** button and then press *Enter*.

You will be redirected to the password confirmation screen. Enter the same password again, press *Tab* (to move to the **Ok** button) and then press *Enter*.

After that it will take some time to install packages. In particular, it will install MySQL server and, when ready, initiate Redmine configuration.

Configuring Redmine package

The Debian/Ubuntu Redmine package supports many instances of Redmine. Several instances, for example, can be used to run Redmine in "production" and "development" modes at the same time (two instances for example, at different ports). The configurator of the package, however, will ask you to configure only one "default" instance.

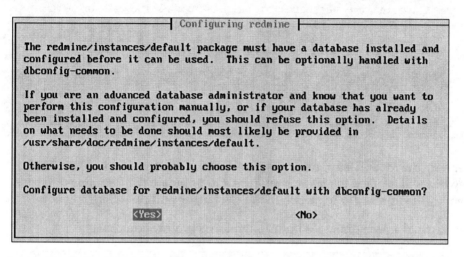

On this screen the configurator suggests its assistance in creating and configuring the database for Redmine. Unless you are willing to configure the database by yourself just press *Enter* here.

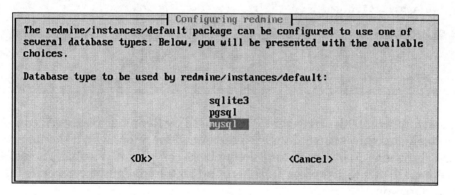

The next screen, which appears immediately, asks you to select the database backend. It has nothing to do with database servers. This screen configures the Redmine database client. As we selected MySQL at command line just press *Enter*.

And here comes the screen, which has already been mentioned:

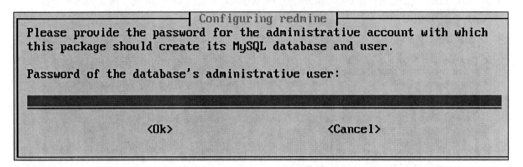

Enter here the MySQL superuser password which you specified before. This password will be used to create, configure and populate the Redmine database. When finished press *Tab* to switch to the **Ok** button and press *Enter*.

Now the final screen of the Redmine database configuration comes:

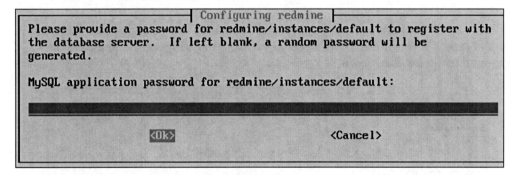

The password, what this screen asks, will be used by Redmine to access its database. It is unlikely that this password will be used elsewhere, moreover, it should not be used elsewhere! So this password should be as complex as possible. Therefore it is, perhaps, better to just press *Enter* here and let the configurator generate the password for you.

 You may also need to specify this password in Apache configuration files for advanced SCM integration.

After this screen the Redmine package configurator will perform some finalizing work and return to the shell prompt.

That's it! Redmine has been installed and configured and is ready to run. But the system is not yet ready to run Redmine. We need a web server to do this. As a web server we will use Apache. Besides Apache, as you should remember from *Chapter 1*, *Getting Familiar with Redmine*, we need something to run a Ruby application and this is going to be the Passenger module for Apache.

Installing Apache and Passenger

So let's now install Apache and Passenger:

```
$ sudo apt-get install apache2 libapache2-mod-passenger
```

As before you will be asked to press *Enter*. After this the package manager will download the specified packages and their dependencies, will install them and start Apache:

```
Enabling module reqtimeout.
Setting up apache2-mpm-worker (2.2.22-1ubuntu1) ...
 * Starting web server apache2
apache2: Could not reliably determine the server's fully qualified domain name,
using 127.0.1.1 for ServerName
                                                                        [ OK ]
Setting up apache2 (2.2.22-1ubuntu1) ...
Setting up libapache2-mod-passenger (2.2.11debian-2) ...
 * Reloading web server config apache2
apache2: Could not reliably determine the server's fully qualified domain name,
using 127.0.1.1 for ServerName
                                                                        [ OK ]
Setting up ssl-cert (1.0.28ubuntu0.1) ...
Processing triggers for libc-bin ...
ldconfig deferred processing now taking place
s-andy@ubuntu:~$ ~
```

If everything has gone well, you should see **[OK]** to the right from **Starting ...** and **Reloading ...** messages, as seen on the screenshot. You may also get the warning you see on the screenshot, but do not worry, it just means you need to set Apache's **ServerName** property to a proper value.

Now, if you load the newly installed website using an URL for example, `http://127.0.1.1`, you should get:

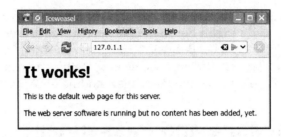

This is the default webpage of Apache web server.

Connecting Redmine and Apache

But, wait, where is Redmine? Right now Redmine is not connected to Apache. Unfortunately, despite the power of Debian package management software this part should be configured manually. Luckily it's not so complex: the Debian Redmine package contains sample configuration files for Redmine under `/usr/share/doc/redmine/examples` directory. In this directory you will find sample configurations for Apache and FastCGI or Passenger, Lighttpd, Nginx and Thin. In this directory we have two sample files for Apache2 and Passenger: **apache2-passenger-alias.conf** and **apache2-passenger-host.conf**. The former should be used if you want to run Redmine under some URL path for example, `www.yourdomain.com/redmine`. The latter should be used if you want to run Redmine under subdomain or as the primary application on your domain.

Assuming that you have installed a clean Ubuntu (as I did) especially for Redmine, that is, that you want to use the server only for Redmine or for Redmine as the primary application. Let's copy **apache2-passenger-host.conf** to `/etc/apache2/sites-available/` (the path for site configurations on Debian/Ubuntu).

```
$ sudo cp /usr/share/doc/redmine/examples/apache2-passenger-host.conf /
etc/apache2/sites-available/
```

Actually this file contains configurations for two Redmine instances, "default" and "instance2", and on two different ports, 3000 and 3030. Let's clean it up to get a configuration for the "default" instance only and for the default port. We should get something like:

```
# These modules must be enabled : passenger
<VirtualHost *:80>
        # ServerName my.domain.name
        # this is the passenger config
        RailsEnv production
        # create a link in /var/lib/redmine/default/passenger to
          /usr/share/redmine
        PassengerAppRoot /var/lib/redmine/default/passenger
        SetEnv X_DEBIAN_SITEID "default"
        Alias "/plugin_assets/" /var/cache/redmine/default/
        plugin_assets/
        DocumentRoot /usr/share/redmine/public
        <Directory "/usr/share/redmine/public">
                Order allow,deny
                Allow from all
        </Directory>
</VirtualHost>
```

 I changed `localhost:3000` to ***:80**, removed port numbers and the second **<VirtualHost>** configuration.

Before we proceed we need to do what is advised in the configuration file. To create symbolic link **passenger** in **/var/lib/redmine/default** pointing to **/usr/share/redmine** (the directory Redmine was installed into).

```
$ sudo ln -sf /usr/share/redmine /var/lib/redmine/default/passenger
```

Now we need to "apply" our new site. Remember we have copied **apache2-passenger-host.conf** to `/etc/apache2/sites-available/`? This directory stores available sites' configurations, as it comes from the name, and enabled sites configurations are stored in `/etc/apache2/sites-enabled/`. So we need to "move" our new configuration file into the latter directory. Let's do it in the correct Debian/Ubuntu way:

```
$ sudo a2ensite apache2-passenger-host.conf
```

The **e2ensite** script creates symbolic links in `/etc/apache2/sites-enabled/` pointing to sites configuration files in `/etc/apache2/sites-available/`. The similar script `e2dissite` can be used to disable sites. So let's now disable the default site which comes with Apache in Debian/Ubuntu (the one displaying **It works!**):

```
$ sudo a2dissite default
```

Let's now reload Apache to activate the new configuration:

```
$ sudo service apache2 reload
```

Now when we load the site we get:

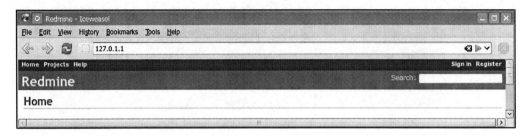

Congratulations! We have successfully installed Redmine. But still there are things we need to do before making a break for coffee and moving ahead.

Verifying and completing installation

Click on the **Sign in** link in the top-right corner to log in to our Redmine. Use `admin` as a login and as a password.

After you have signed in, click on the new item **Administration** on the top dark blue menu bar. Administration sections will appear on the right sidebar. Select the **Information** section.

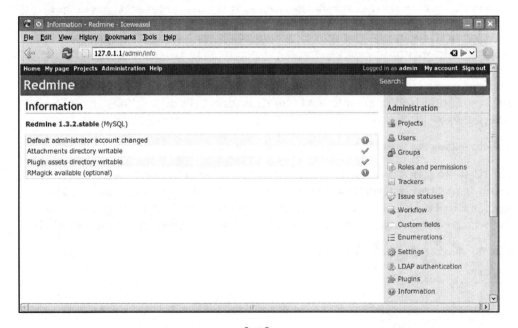

The above screenshot shows the screen one should always check after installing Redmine! As you see it contains the checklist that should be used to verify the installation. Changing administrator account is a common procedure for any type of installation while installing RMagick is specific, that's why we came to this screen.

 RMagick is Ruby interface for the ImageMagick image processing library. This library is used by Redmine for Gantt chart export. It can also be used by some third-party plugins.

So to install RMagick execute the following command:

```
$ sudo apt-get install ruby-rmagick
```

Now reload Apache again to apply:

```
$ sudo service apache2 reload
```

After Apache reloads, we get the green checkmark to the right from RMagick.

The only procedure left is changing the administrator account. To do this click on the **Users** link on the administration sidebar, open profile of the *admin* user (the only user available) and change login and password to some other values.

Conclusion

As you see this type of Redmine installation is quite easy and involves a few commands. Besides easiness, I believe, it has the following benefits:

- The installed Redmine conforms to **FHS (Filesystem Hierarchy Standard)**, that is, configuration files are located in /etc/redmine, Redmine itself in /usr/share/redmine, cache in /var/cache/redmine, logs in /var/log/redmine, and so on. That is, any administrator, who is aware of FHS (even if he/she is not aware of Redmine), will be able to understand the Redmine file structure, and system tools, such as log analyzers, will be able to pick up and process Redmine files.

- As Redmine was installed as a part of the Linux distribution, the system will be able to maintain it. Thus Redmine can be updated with the rest of the system and other system updates are unlikely to break Redmine.

Installing Redmine from sources

This is the most complicated but the officially recommended installation method. It is also the best documented one. Unlike using Debian/Ubuntu packages, TurnKey appliance or BitNami stack these instructions may differ for other versions of Redmine. Therefore you should treat this topic as an example of installation, you should also be aware that these instructions can become outdated and, thus, you should simultaneously consult the official installation tutorial which can be checked using the URL: http://www.redmine.org/projects/redmine/ wiki/RedmineInstall.

Like in the previous tutorial we will use the "clean" Ubuntu Server 12.04 LTS.

Downloading and installing Redmine

To start we need to select the location for Redmine. Let's select /opt/redmine (fine for FHS):

```
$ sudo mkdir -p /opt/redmine
```

This command will create the /opt/redmine directory. Now let's move into it:

```
$ cd /opt/redmine
```

Next we need to get the latest Redmine version in tar.gz archive from URL: http://rubyforge.org/frs/?group_id=1850. At the time of writing this topic the latest Redmine version was 2.2.0. In other words, this instruction was written for this version.

So get the archive:

```
$ sudo wget http://rubyforge.org/frs/download.php/76627/redmine-
2.2.0.tar.gz
```

Now unpack the archive into the current directory (which should be /opt/redmine):

```
$ sudo tar xvf redmine-2.2.0.tar.gz
```

This command will unpack everything into the redmine-2.2.0 subdirectory. Move there:

```
$ cd redmine-2.2.0
```

Installing RubyGems and Bundler

Redmine comes with Bundler support. Bundler is a Ruby Gem dependency manager which is in some way similar to the Debian/Ubuntu package manager used in the previous topic. In other words, Bundler simplifies the deployment process by checking and ensuring that all dependencies are installed.

The problem is that the Bundler is not available in our "clean" system. Moreover neither gem nor ruby is available. So we need to install them first:

```
$ sudo apt-get install rubygems
```

This command will install the gem tool and all its dependencies. When you are asked for confirmation, just press *Enter*.

Now we can install the Bundler. To do this we will use the gem tool:

```
$ sudo gem install bundler
```

```
s-andy@ubuntu:/opt/redmine/redmine-2.2.0$ sudo gem install bundler
Fetching: bundler-1.2.3.gem (100%)
Successfully installed bundler-1.2.3
1 gem installed
Installing ri documentation for bundler-1.2.3...
Installing RDoc documentation for bundler-1.2.3...
s-andy@ubuntu:/opt/redmine/redmine-2.2.0$
```

Resolving Bundler errors

When you run the Bundler, it fetches gems from www.RubyGems.org and tries to install them failing only in case of missing system libraries (not gems, the Bundler can resolve only gem dependencies). This way, by such errors, you can determine what system libraries are missing.

Let's review a sample of such failure:

```
Installing mysql (2.8.1) with native extensions
Gem::Installer::ExtensionBuildError: ERROR: Failed to build gem native extension
.
        /usr/bin/ruby1.8 extconf.rb
checking for mysql_query() in -lmysqlclient... no
checking for main() in -lm... yes
checking for mysql_query() in -lmysqlclient... no
checking for main() in -lz... no
checking for mysql_query() in -lmysqlclient... no
checking for main() in -lsocket... no
checking for mysql_query() in -lmysqlclient... no
checking for main() in -lnsl... yes
checking for mysql_query() in -lmysqlclient... no
checking for main() in -lmygcc... no
checking for mysql_query() in -lmysqlclient... no
*** extconf.rb failed ***
Could not create Makefile due to some reason, probably lack of
necessary libraries and/or headers.  Check the mkmf.log file for more
details.  You may need configuration options.
```

As seen on the screen the Bundler failed to install the mysql gem. Thus, the line:

```
checking for mysql_query() in -lmysqlclient... no
```

Tells that it failed to find the `mysql_query()` function in the `mysqlclient` library. The most common reason for such error is that the library is actually missing and this assumption is right as we run it on the "clean" system and we have not installed MySQL client yet. Also note that Bundler needs not just libraries but also their development files.

Searching for a file in non-installed packages under Debian/Ubuntu

Sometimes the Bundler gives the filename which it cannot find. For such cases you can use the `apt-file` tool. To install `apt-file` and initialize its database do:

```
$ sudo apt-get install apt-file
$ apt-file update
```

After this you can search for a missing file, for example, to find `Magick-config` file run:

```
$ apt-file search Magick-config
```

Installing MySQL client and ImageMagick

We reviewed this sample to demonstrate how errors given by the Bundler can be resolved. Now let's install all the system library dependencies including but not limited to the MySQL:

```
$ sudo apt-get install libmysqlclient-dev libmagickcore-dev
libmagickwand-dev
```

This command will install development files for MySQL and ImageMagick libraries as well as the libraries themselves.

Installing dependencies using Bundler

Now let the Bundler install all the Gem dependencies:

```
$ sudo bundle install --without development test postgresql sqlite
```

Here we skip PostgreSQL and SQLite dependencies as we are going to use MySQL. Also we skip dependencies used for development and testing.

You can also skip **RMagick** by adding rmagick keyword to the—without option. In this case you can skip installation of libmagickcore-dev and libmagickwand-dev as well.

If the dependencies installation was successful you should get:

```
Your bundle is complete! Use `bundle show [gemname]` to see where a bundled gem
is installed.
```

Installing MySQL server, Apache, and Passenger

As we plan to use the MySQL server we need to install it as well. Besides we need to install Apache and its Passenger module. The procedure of their installation is identical to the one we used in the previous topic.

```
$ sudo apt-get install mysql-server mysql-client apache2 libapache2-mod-
passenger
```

Here we will skip all the details related to installing MySQL, Apache and Passenger as they were reviewed before. For more information, see the *Configuring MySQL server package* and *Installing Apache and Passenger* sections.

Setting up the database

Now when we are ready to go further let's create the database for Redmine. Run MySQL client:

```
$ mysql -u root -p
```

It will ask the password of the MySQL server's superuser which you should have specified during installation of the MySQL server.

Execute the following SQL queries in MySQL client:

```
CREATE DATABASE redmine CHARACTER SET UTF8;
CREATE USER 'redmine'@'localhost' IDENTIFIED BY 'your_password_here';
GRANT ALL PRIVILEGES ON redmine.* TO 'redmine'@'localhost';
```

Don't forget to replace your_password_here with your password.

Now we should specify the database details in Redmine configuration files. Example of the database configuration can be found in the `config/database.yml.example` file. Let's rename it into `database.yml`:

```
$ mv config/database.yml.example  config/database.yml
```

Now open the `config/database.yml` file in your favorite editor and modify it so it will look like:

```
production:
  adapter: mysql
  database: redmine
  host: localhost
  username: redmine
  password: your_password_here
  encoding: utf8
```

Replace `your_password_here` with the password you specified in the SQL query.

Finalizing Redmine installation

Now we need to initialize Redmine state files:

```
$ rake generate_secret_token
```

After that initialize the Redmine database with the commands:

```
$ RAILS_ENV=production rake db:migrate
```
```
$ RAILS_ENV=production rake redmine:load_default_data
```

The first command initializes the database structure and the second command inserts initial data (such as trackers, administrator account, and so on) to the database. The second command will also ask you the language of the initial data.

Redmine distribution does not include the directory for plugins' static files so it needs to be created:

```
$ mkdir public/plugin_assets
```

Configuring Apache

At this moment Redmine has been already installed and configured but we need to configure Apache to run it. So let's move to the Apache configuration directory:

```
$ cd /etc/apache2
```

Now append the following lines into the `apache2.conf` file (do this under root):

```
<VirtualHost *:80>
        RailsEnv production
        PassengerAppRoot /opt/redmine/redmine-2.2.0
        DocumentRoot /opt/redmine/redmine-2.2.0/public
        <Directory "/opt/redmine/redmine-2.2.0/public">
                Order allow,deny
                Allow from all
        </Directory>
</VirtualHost>
```

This is the configuration of the virtual host which will run Redmine.

In Debian/Ubuntu virtual hosts are defined in files located in the `sites-enabled` subdirectory. Apache in these Linux distributions comes with the default site which needs to be disabled to let Redmine work. This can be done by the command:

```
$ sudo a2dissite default
```

Now reload Apache with the command:

```
$ sudo service apache2 reload
```

After this if you open the browser and point it to the IP or hostname of your server you should get:

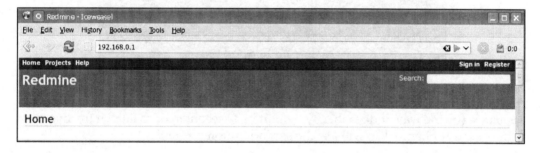

You can now log in into your new Redmine installation using login `admin` and password `admin`. As these are the default login and password you should change them as soon as you log in.

Using TurnKey Redmine appliance

First, we need to fetch the Redmine appliance from the following URL:
`http://www.turnkeylinux.org/redmine`. For this book I will be using the
ISO image as it's, perhaps, the most common option and can be installed on a
new server. You can also download the virtual machine image or images ready
for deployment to VPS.

 Be aware that at the time of writing this topic TurnKey Linux
Redmine appliance was outdated as it was running Redmine 1.4.x.

After inserting CD into CD-ROM and rebooting or turning on the computer we get:

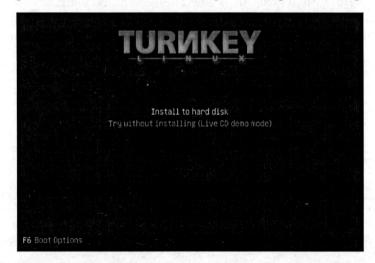

As you see this splash screen allows us to choose either to immediately install the
appliance (by the way, it does this by default in 30 seconds) or to launch the live
demo of the appliance. We will use the second option for now.

Shortly after pressing the *down-arrow* key and *Enter*, TurnKey asks for the
root password.

This will be the main system password so be sure to make it as strong as possible. After specifying this password and pressing *Enter* you will also need to specify the confirmation. After doing this you will be asked to enter another password:

This will be the password for MySQL superuser. Like the system root password this one should be strong enough. Specify the password and press *Enter*, then specify the confirmation and press *Enter* again.

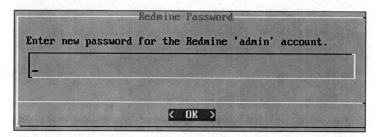

This password is for the Redmine administrator. This is replacement of the default one, which is "admin". This way the TurnKey ensures you won't be using Redmine with the default well-known password. The username of the administrator account, however, remains the same that is **admin**.

Specify the password and confirmation. After that you will get:

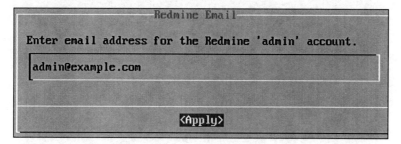

This time the TurnKey Linux asks for the email of the administrator account this way ensuring you won't forget to update it. Specify your email and press *Enter*.

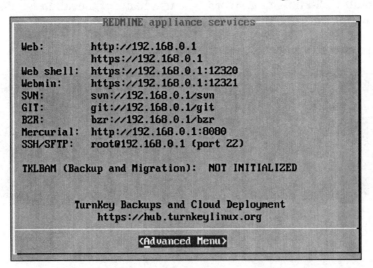

In addition to making the Redmine installation easier the TurnKey Linux offers Amazon based backup and cloud hosting services. This screen is the promotion of these services. If you registered for these services you can specify your API key here. If not press *Tab* twice to make the **Skip** button active and then press *Enter*.

That was all. The next screen contains details of the running system:

```
┌───────────────REDMINE appliance services───────────────┐
│                                                         │
│  Web:          http://192.168.0.1                       │
│                https://192.168.0.1                      │
│  Web shell:    https://192.168.0.1:12320                │
│  Webmin:       https://192.168.0.1:12321                │
│  SVN:          svn://192.168.0.1/svn                    │
│  GIT:          git://192.168.0.1/git                    │
│  BZR:          bzr://192.168.0.1/bzr                    │
│  Mercurial:    http://192.168.0.1:8080                  │
│  SSH/SFTP:     root@192.168.0.1 (port 22)               │
│                                                         │
│  TKLBAM (Backup and Migration):  NOT INITIALIZED        │
│                                                         │
│          TurnKey Backups and Cloud Deployment           │
│             https://hub.turnkeylinux.org                │
│                                                         │
│                   <Advanced Menu>                       │
└─────────────────────────────────────────────────────────┘
```

That's actually the screen of the running TurnKey Linux system. The same screen you get when you install the system on disk (this is the screen you get each time you boot the server).

As shown on the screen TurnKey Redmine comes with Subversion, Git, Bazaar, and Mercurial servers, which are already configured and integrated with Redmine. Besides the system is also running SSH server, Webmin, and web shell, so you could connect to the system remotely.

Now you can play with Redmine by opening the browser and pointing it to http://192.168.0.1 (use the URL which is shown on your screen):

As seen from the screenshot, TurnKey Redmine is missing RMagick but you can install it using the following command in the shell:

```
$ sudo apt-get install ruby-rmagick
```

If you like the system you can press *Enter* on the **Advanced Menu** button in the TurnKey system screen and then select the **Install** menu item:

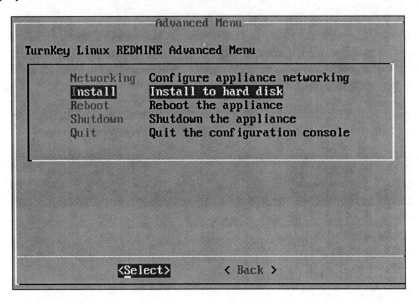

The further installation procedure won't be reviewed here as it is actually the Ubuntu/ Debian installation procedure and is quite simple. After rebooting you will be asked the same questions you were asked to run the live demo (root password, MySQL password and so on). In the end you will get the same TurnKey Linux screen with the **Advanced Menu** button but which, this time, won't have the **Install** menu item.

Using BitNami Redmine stack

In order to install the BitNami Redmine stack we need to download the installer first. You can do this by going to the URL at `http://bitnami.org/stack/redmine`.

The BitNami Redmine installer comes with everything you need to run Redmine, thus, it includes Apache, MySQL, Rails, Ruby, Passenger for Linux and Mac, and Thin for Windows. If you check the above URL you will also notice the "module" installer. This installer should be used if you have already installed another BitNami stack (not the Redmine one). In this case, the installer will add Redmine to the existing installation.

Under this topic, we will review how to install the BitNami Redmine stack on Microsoft Windows. We will use the stack, not the module, assuming that you have not installed any other BitNami stacks before. The installation procedure is very much the same for all OSs due to the cross-platform BitRock installer which is used by BitNami.

So let's now run the installer which is `bitnami-redmine-2.2.0-0-windows-installer.exe` in my case. The first question it asks is the language of installation:

Here we choose English, which is default, and press the **OK** button. The next screen is the welcome screen of the BitRock installer:

Click on the **Next** button here after which you will be asked to choose installation components:

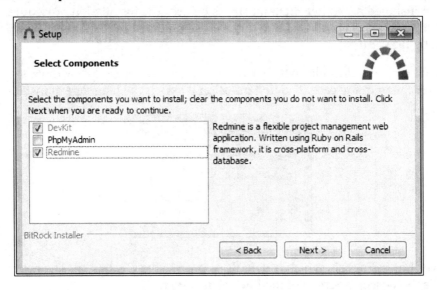

As you see in addition to the **Redmine** component the BitNami Redmine stack also includes **DevKit,** which is needed to run Redmine 2.1.x and higher under Windows, and **PhpMyAdmin,** which can be very useful if you plan to use Redmine for development. As I don't plan to use it this way I uncheck **PhpMyAdmin** here and click the **Next** button.

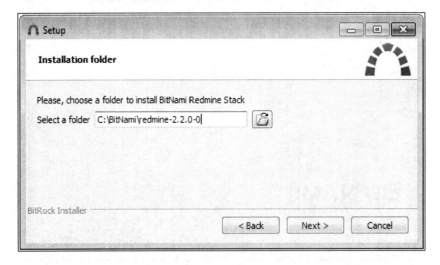

The default installation folder is fine so we just click on the **Next** button here and get to the window:

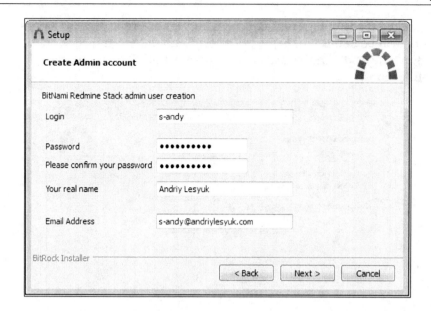

With this dialog window the BitNami Redmine stack is configuring the administrator account of Redmine, the one default login and password of which are "admin". It's really great that BitNami included this dialog in the installation!

Just enter your data into this dialog, as I have done, and click on the **Next** button:

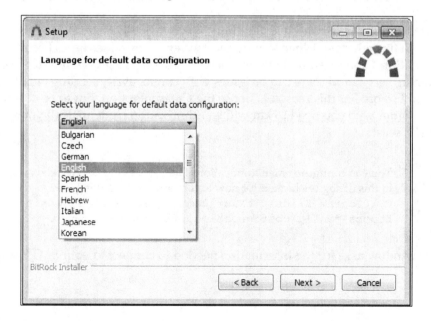

Here we choose the language of Redmine. Thus, for example, tracker names in Redmine will be in this language. We select **English** here and click on the **Next** button. The next window asks whether we would like to configure email notifications:

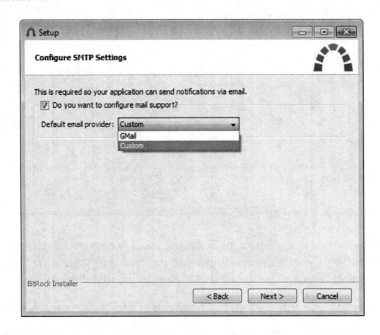

Email notifications are essential for Redmine so you should really check the checkbox in this window. When you do this two email provider types become available: **GMail** and **Custom**. I would not recommend using **GMail** as it is an external mail server and there can be issues with connectivity, sending emails may be slow and so on. For this reason I choose the **Custom** option. But to be able to use the **Custom** type you need to know the authorization credentials of your local SMTP server.

You can configure email notifications later by leaving the checkbox in this dialog unchecked for now and manually modifying the
`C:\Program Files\BitNami Redmine Stack\apps\redmine\`
`htdocs\config\configuration.yml` file after installation.

The next window asks for the information needed to connect to your SMTP server:

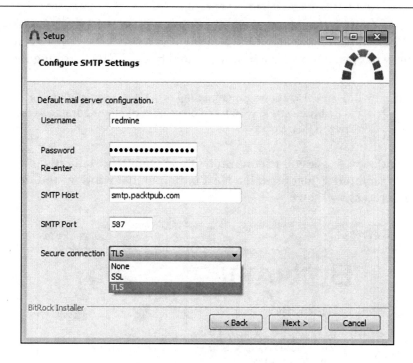

Enter here the authorization credentials of your SMTP server and click on the
Next button.

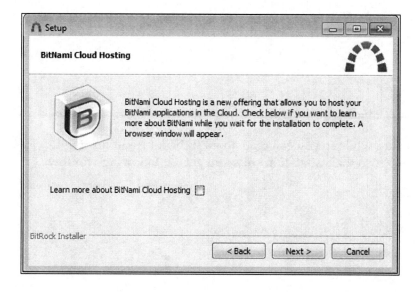

Like TurnKey Linux BitNami offers cloud hosting services which are also based on Amazon. You can read more about the offering if you check the checkbox in this dialog. This will open a browser window pointed to the URL describing the services.

 BitNami also allows downloading of AMI images, containing the Redmine stack, which can be used to deploy Redmine to the Amazon EC2 cloud.

The next window will ask you to confirm that you want to install BitNami Redmine stack on your computer. Just press the **Next** button in that window and the installation process will start:

This will take a while so you can read about BitNami cloud hosting services meanwhile. When the installation ends you get the following window:

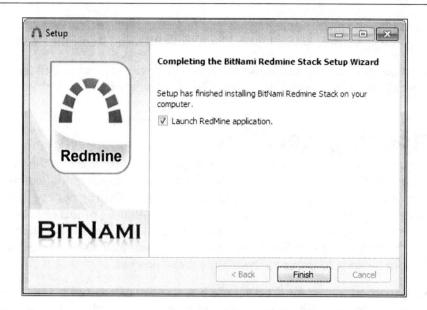

Congratulations! Redmine has been installed on your computer! You can check the **Launch RedMine application** checkbox, this will open a new browser window pointing to the page:

This is your BitNami stack home page. If you have installed several BitNami modules you will see here several links like **Access BitNami Redmine Stack**.

Clicking on the **Access BitNami Redmine Stack** link will redirect you to the `redmine` location under which the just installed Redmine will be available.

Maintaining Redmine

In my opinion the proper maintenance of an application installation is the third by importance after the proper installation and the proper configuration. Leaving an installation unmaintained you risk having many issues including but not limited to security and upgrade ones. For this reason at the beginning of this chapter I recommended to use the outdated Redmine from Debian/Ubuntu repositories as opposed to the manually installed recent Redmine. Therefore also we will review here what can be done to improve the maintenance process.

The most important reason for the upgrade is discovery of a security issue. In other words, you need to track new versions of Redmine to be sure that you upgrade as soon as the fix is available for such issue. But if you use the Redmine package from the Debian/Ubuntu repository you do not need to track Redmine separately as the Debian/Ubuntu security team does this for you, but you still need to track new updates of the Linux distribution (*which should be done anyway even if you manually installed Redmine*).

You, perhaps, wonder how the outdated version can be fixed if the fix comes with the new version? The Debian/Ubuntu security teams port the fix to the older version or provide their own.

So how do you know when new Redmine is released? You can subscribe to Redmine news using the ATOM feed: `http://www.redmine.org/projects/redmine/news.atom`. The appropriate news should mention the reason for the release—was it a security release, bug fixes or new features release.

To read ATOM feeds you can use Google Reader, Mozilla Thunderbird etc.

However it's not only the matter of upgrading Redmine if you use plugins. And, most likely, you do.

If you use any plugins for Redmine do not hurry to upgrade when new version of Redmine comes as this may break your Redmine installation! First you need to check if plugins, which you use, support the new version.

Thus, you can check a plugin page which can be found using the Redmine plugins registry: http://www.redmine.org/plugins.

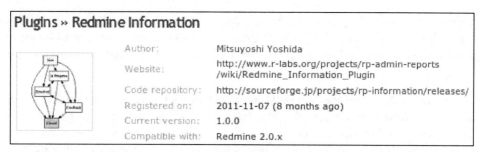

Plugins » Redmine Information	
Author:	Mitsuyoshi Yoshida
Website:	http://www.r-labs.org/projects/rp-admin-reports /wiki/Redmine_Information_Plugin
Code repository:	http://sourceforge.jp/projects/rp-information/releases/
Registered on:	2011-11-07 (8 months ago)
Current version:	1.0.0
Compatible with:	Redmine 2.0.x

Unfortunately not all plugins are listed on this resource and not all information for plugins is up-to-date there so you may need to check each plugin separately. Try checking the home page which could be specified in the installed plugin (**Administration – Plugins**). See also *Chapter 10, Plugins and Themes*.

Luckily not all new releases of Redmine break the work of plugins. Thus, only minor releases of Redmine are known to do this. By minor I mean the second number in the version string, for example, in 2.2.0 the major version number is 2, the minor version number is 2 and 0 is the tiny version number. The tiny releases are unlikely to break the work of plugins.

However, to be sure your Redmine won't become unusable it's recommended to test the upgrade process on a separate installation, a copy of the production environment, first.

Summary

Different users have different goals, some users aim to have the stable installation without the need to pay much attention to it, some users prefer to be up-to-date with recent features, other users just want to give it a try and so on. That's why we reviewed all the above options of Redmine installation. Thus, there is no need to spend much time for setting up Redmine from sources, if you just want to play with it. So having read this chapter you now have an idea, which option is the best for you, and should be able to install Redmine quickly and easily.

Most probably you end up reading this chapter with the running Redmine. If it's so you can take time out to play with Redmine for a while. Doing this would be good because when you get back to the book you will understand what is written in the next chapters better.

However, remember, that the just installed Redmine is too raw. Before using it you should spend some time configuring it. That's what we are going to speak about in the next chapter. But don't expect to see only basic configuration there. We have only one chapter for configuring Redmine, so we will also review the advanced configuration. That's perhaps why the next chapter should be interesting not only for the ones, who will be configuring Redmine, but also for everyone else, as they will see, what powerful things can be done in Redmine.

3
Configuring Redmine

In this chapter, we will speak about configuring Redmine. You might expect to see explanations for all the administration settings here. But we will review only a few of them as I'm sure that most of the options do not need explanation or can be easily essayed. So instead we will focus on hard-to-understand options and those ones which need more configuration or have some obscurities. You will also learn how to ask for help and what information you should provide to make your issue clear for others.

So why should you read this chapter if you are not an administrator? Many features are available only if they have been configured. Thus reading this chapter you will learn what extra features exist and get an idea of how to enable them.

In this chapter, we will cover the following topics:

- The first thing to fix
- Administration settings
- Troubleshooting

The first thing to fix

A fresh Redmine installation has only one user account, which has administrator privileges.

Information	
Login *	admin
First name *	Redmin
Last name *	Admin
Email *	admin@example.net
Language	English
Administrator	☑

In other words this account is exactly the same for *all* Redmine installations. That's why it is extremely important to change the credentials of this account immediately after completing the installation process especially for Redmine installations which can be accessed publicly.

The administrator credentials should be changed in **Administration | Users**, in the *admin* user.

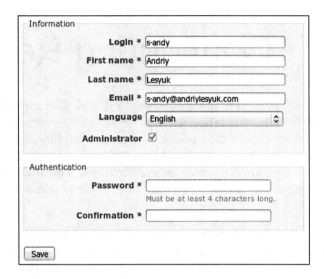

It's recommended to change both **Login** and **Password** (and **Confirmation**).

Administration settings

Whatever is possible to configure at the global level (the opposite is the project level) can be found under the **Administration** link in the left-top menu. This link, of course, is available only for administrators.

When you click on the link you get the list of available administration sections. Most of the sections are for managing different Redmine objects such as projects, trackers, and so on. Such sections won't be reviewed under this topic for three reasons: first, most of them are intelligible and need a little explanation; second, many of them will be reviewed in the next chapters, and third, in this chapter we discuss only general, system-wide configuration. Such configuration is bottled in the **Settings** section, as shown in the following screenshot:

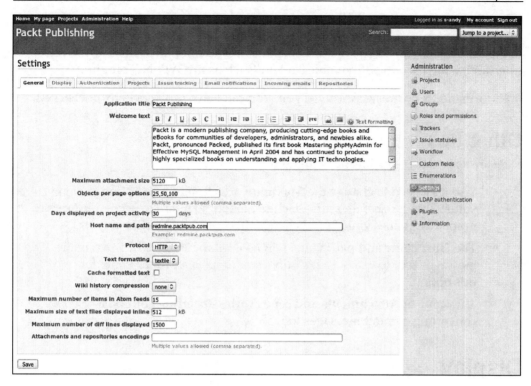

Of course, all such settings can't fit into a single page so Redmine uses tabs to organize them.

The **Projects** and **Issue tracking** tabs will be reviewed in the next two chapters.

General

So let's start with the **General** tab, which can be seen in the previous screenshot.

Cache formatted text

As mentioned in *Chapter 1, Getting Familiar with Redmine*, Redmine supports text formatting using Textile. While converting text from Textile into HTML is performed quite fast, in some circumstances, you may want to cache resulting HTML. If so, this checkbox is what you need.

When this option is checked all Textile content, which is larger than 2 KB, will be cached. The cached HTML is going to be refreshed only when any changes are made to the Textile content. So you should take this into account, if you use any Wiki extension, which produces dynamic content (such as my WikiNG plugin).

If performance is not very critical for you, you can leave this checkbox unchecked.

Other tips

Here are some other tips for the **General** tab:

- You may need to change the **Maximun attachment size** option to some large value. Thus project files are attachments too, so if you expect your users to upload large files you should change this option to a better value.

- The **Host name and path** value will be used to render URLs in e-mail messages sent to users, so it's important to have a proper value for this option.

- The value of **Attachments and repositories encodings** option is used for converting commit messages to UTF-8.

Display

The name of the next tab is **Display** and, as it comes from the name, this tab contains settings related to the look and feel:

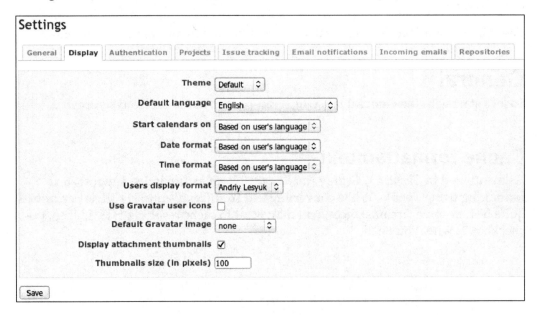

Default language

I'm fairly sure that you know what this option means but there is a thing related to this option, you should be aware of: Despite the value of this option if some string in the core Redmine or in a plugin has no translation it will use English.

Using Gravatar user icons

Once I used a WordPress form to leave a comment on someone's blog. This form asked me to specify the first name, the last name, my e-mail, and the text. After submitting it, I was surprised to see my photo near the comment. That's what Gravatar does.

Gravatar stands for **Globally Recognized Avatar** and it uses the user's e-mail to show an avatar associated with it. It's quite secure as it does not transfer a plain e-mail address but uses its hash instead. Of course, in order to have an avatar image displayed in Redmine a user needs to submit it to Gravatar first (this will be reviewed in *Chapter 9, Personalization*).

Anyway having this option checked is a good idea (*unless you don't have Internet connection*).

Default Gravatar image

But what happens if Gravatar is not available for a user? This is what the **Default Gravatar image** option is for. The following table shows the five modes available:

Modes	Icons	Description
Wavatars		Generated faces with differing features and backgrounds
Identicons		A geometric pattern
Monster ids		A generated "monster" with different colors, faces etc.
Retro		A generated 8-bit arcade-style pixelated face.
Mystery man		A simple, cartoon-style silhouetted outline of a person.

All modes, besides **Mystery man**, generate unique avatars based on the user's e-mail hash.

Redmine Local Avatar plugin

Consider installing Redmine Local Avatar plugin if you prefer users to upload their avatars directly onto Redmine: `https://github.com/ thorin/redmine_local_avatars`

Display attachment thumbnails

If this option is checked all image attachments, whatever object (for example, Wiki or issue) they are attached to, will also be displayed as clickable thumbnails under the attachment list. If the user clicks on the thumbnail, the full-size image will be opened.

In order for this option to work you must have ImageMagick installed.

Authentication

The next tab in administration settings is **Authentication**. The following screenshot shows the various options available in the **Authentication** tab:

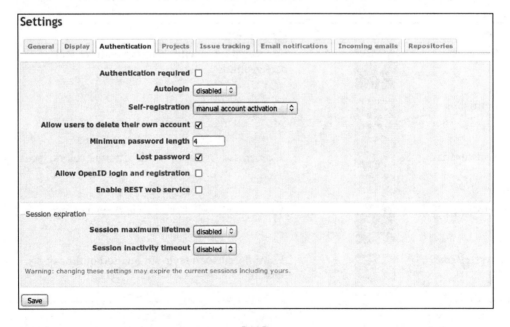

Allow OpenID login and registration

If you have a public site with open registration you, perhaps, know (or you will know, if you want your Redmine installation to be public and open for user registration) that users do not like registering on each site. It's fair enough as they do not want to have another password to remember or share their passwords on a new, and therefore yet untrusted, site. And it's also a matter of remembering another login ID and sharing their e-mail address.

That's where OpenID is useful. **OpenID** is an open standard of the authentication protocol in which authentication (*password verification*) is performed by an OpenID provider. This protocol is quite popular and is supported by companies such as Google, Yahoo!, PayPal, AOL, LiveJournal, MySpace, IBM, VeriSign, and WordPress. In other words, their websites can act as OpenID providers and therefore users can log into Redmine using accounts on these sites.

If your Redmine installation is public it's, perhaps, a good idea to enable this option.

Redmine OpenID is broken

Due to the bug in the Redmine core users can't authenticate using Google OpenID. To support Google, you need to install the OpenID Fix plugin from `http://projects.andriylesyuk.com/projects/openid-fix`.

However, to log in using OpenID, users will need to specify **OpenID URL**, in addition to **Login** and **Password**:

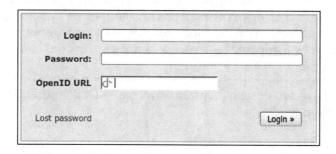

OpenID URL is a URL of an OpenID provider. Thus for Google this URL is `https://www.google.com/accounts/o8/id`.

OpenID Selector

Instead of asking the users to remember their OpenID URLs, you can use Jorge Barata's OpenID Selector plugin for Redmine. Download it from `http://projects.jorgebg.com/projects/redmine-openid-selector`.

If the **Allow OpenID login and registration** checkbox is disabled, this means, that you don't have the `ruby-openid` library installed.

To install it under Debian/Ubuntu run:
```
$ sudo apt-get install ruby-openid
```
Under other OSes do:
```
# gem install ruby-openid
```

LDAP authentication

Yes, I know that there is no LDAP under the **Authentication** tab. Here we will discuss the **LDAP authentication** section under the **Administration** menu as this section is related to the authentication.

Just as OpenID is good for public sites to authenticate external users without registration, LDAP is good for private sites to authenticate internal corporate users. Besides Redmine many other applications support authentication against LDAP server, for example, MediaWiki, Apache, JIRA, Samba, SugarCRM, and many more. As far as LDAP is an open protocol it is also supported by some directory servers such as Microsoft Active Directory and Apple Open Directory. Therefore LDAP is often used by companies as a centralized users directory and an authentication server.

You can add a LDAP server using **Administration | LDAP authentication | New authentication mode**:

New authentication mode (LDAP)

Name *	Packt Publishing LDAP
Host *	ldap.packtpub.com
Port *	636 ☑ LDAPS
Account	cn=ldapadmin,dc=ldap,dc=packtpub,dc=
Password	••••••••
Base DN *	ou=users,dc=ldap,dc=packtpub,dc=com
LDAP filter	
On-the-fly user creation	☑

Attributes

Login *	uid
First name	givenName
Last name	sN
Email	mail

Create

Note the **On-the-fly user creation** option, if this option is checked users' accounts will be automatically created when they log in to Redmine the first time. If this option is not checked users will need to be added manually. If the **On-the-fly user creation** option is checked, you will also need to specify **Attributes**, as they will be used to fetch users' details from LDAP.

> Describing what all the options mean and what values they should have is out-of-scope for this book. You should consult LDAP server administrator for their values.

In addition, LDAP authentication in Redmine can be done against multiple LDAP servers. Redmine allows selecting an authentication source (*mode*) for each user (it's also possible to select between LDAP and internal Redmine authentication).

Enable REST web service

For third-party tools integration Redmine provides REST API which can be turned on by this checkbox. For example, Redmine REST API is used by the Redmine Mylyn Connector and the RedmineApp for iPhone. If you do not use or do not plan to use any external Redmine tools it is safe to uncheck this option.

E-mail integration

Redmine e-mail integration can be divided into two parts namely e-mail sending (notifications) and e-mail receiving. Both parts can be **partially** configured in **Administration | Settings** under **Email notifications** and **Incoming emails** tabs.

Sending e-mails

Most likely if you open the **Email notifications** tab on a just installed Redmine, you will get the following screen:

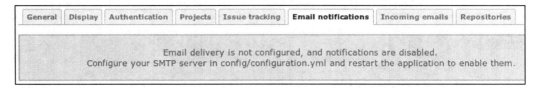

As you might guess, this means that you can't fix this using the web interface. In other words, in order to configure **Email notifications** we will need to modify the system file of Redmine and then configure them through the administration web interface.

Configuring e-mail notifications using configuration.yml

Actually the e-mail delivery is the only thing which should be configured using the `config/configuration.yml` file. You could ask: Why not configure this using web interface? I guess, the answer would be: Because it's not a job of the Redmine administrator but of the system administrator as only the system administrator knows what delivery methods are available.

In the `config` subdirectory of the Redmine root directory (which is `/usr/share/redmine` on Debian/Ubuntu), you should find the file `configuration.yml.example`. Copy (or rename) this file to `configuration.yml`:

```
$ cp configuration.yml.example configuration.yml
```

In this file, you will find sample configurations, one of which you should select for your Redmine installation. The file contains the default e-mail configuration, which is also an example but enabled, so you will need to modify it! Find this configuration under the `default` section (line starts with `default:`):

```
# Outgoing emails configuration (see examples above)
email_delivery:
  delivery_method: :smtp
  smtp_settings:
    address: smtp.example.net
```

```
port: 25
domain: example.net
authentication: :login
user_name: "redmine@example.net"
password: "redmine"
```

Redmine can be run in production or development environments. The default section contains configuration options for all environments. So to specify separate configurations for other environments just specify the options under the appropriate section.

The delivery_method option accepts the following values: :sendmail, :smtp, :async_sendmail, and :async_smtp. The :async_sendmail and :async_smtp methods deliver e-mails in separate threads thus not making users wait for the delivery to complete. So asynchronous delivery methods should be used on installations involving sending many e-mails, when a SMTP server is slow or hardly accessible or if you experience slow loading of pages which send e-mails (for example, on issue changes, wiki page additions, changes, and so on).

From the above delivery methods I, personally, would recommend to use :sendmail or :async_sendmail as these methods will use the sendmail system tool. The sendmail tool is a part of **Mail Transfer Agent (MTA)** (MTA is a software that performs mail sending), that is, it ships with MTA and uses it to send e-mails. In other words, if you use sendmail you use the default delivery configuration of the operating system. So if the system administrator changes the system e-mail delivery configuration Redmine will automatically use it without any reconfiguration. Such configuration is also easier to maintain as you don't have to remember Redmine e-mail settings.

```
email_delivery:
  delivery_method: :sendmail
```

But you can also select a local or remote SMTP server instead by specifying :smtp or :async_smtp delivery method. In this case you will also need to specify smtp_settings to let Redmine know how to connect to this server.

Avoid using external SMTP servers as, in case of Internet connection loss, email messages won't get sent. This will also slow down Redmine performance.

Let's review options that can be specified inside `smtp_settings`:

- The `address` option should contain IP or hostname of the SMTP server. If you put `localhost` here think about using `:sendmail` instead

- The `port` option should contain the TCP port number of the SMTP server. Normally it is `25` or `587` if TLS is used (for example, Gmail).

- The `domain` option contains the value for the `HELO SMTP` command. Normally it's the domain part of the e-mail address. For Gmail (but not Google Apps) you should specify `smtp.gmail.com` here.

- The `authentication` option accepts values such as `:plain`, `:login`, or `:cram_md5`. You need to consult your system administrator on which authentication method should be used. For Gmail this should be `:login`.

- The values of `username` and `password` options will be used to authenticate against the SMTP server.

- The sample configuration misses the `enable_starttls_auto` option which should be set to `true` if TLS is used to connect to the SMTP server (normally it should be used if the port number is `587`). Set it to `true` for Gmail.

> Don't use a personal account in `smtp_settings` as the SMTP server (for example, Gmail) may overwrite the from address with the account's address (normally the e-mail specified in the **Emission email address** option should be used). Thus, visually, all notifications may come from this personal address. Better create a special account for this purpose.

Configuring e-mail notifications using web interface

So now, when we have configured e-mail delivery, let's apply our configuration by restarting Redmine and check the **Email notifications** tab again:

| General | Display | Authentication | Projects | Issue tracking | **Email notifications** | Incoming emails | Repositories |

Emission email address redmine@example.net

Blind carbon copy recipients (bcc) ☑

Plain text mail (no HTML) ☐

Default notification option Only for things I watch or I'm involved in ⌄

Select actions for which email notifications should be sent.

☑ Issue added
☑ Issue updated
　☐ Note added
　☐ Status updated
　☐ Priority updated
☐ News added
☐ Comment added to a news
☐ Document added
☐ File added
☐ Message added
☐ Wiki page added
☐ Wiki page updated

Check all | Uncheck all

Emails header

Emails footer

You have received this notification because you have either subscribed to it, or are involved in it.
To change your notification preferences, please click here: http://hostname/my/account

Save

Send a test email

As e-mail notifications settings effect users and many e-mails from a single source used to be treated as spam these settings are very important. It's important to configure them so they won't bother your users!

The value of the **Emission email address** option will be used as the from e-mail address in the e-mails sent from your Redmine. It definitely should be changed! Normally they set this address to something like `no-reply@yourdomain.com` but I would recommend setting it to some real e-mail address instead, for example, to the support staff's e-mail ID.

If you uncheck the **Blind carbon copy recipients (bcc)** option, each user who receives a notification e-mail will be able to see which other users have received it as well. So it's normally a good idea to leave this option checked.

The most important option is, perhaps, the **Default notification option**. This option specifies which notification "mode" will be set for each new user. Let's review the supported modes in detail (see also *Chapter 9, Personalization*):

- **For any event on all my projects**: This mode should never be set by anyone else besides the users themselves as in this mode users will be notified about all events in projects they are members of. From my experience I can tell that such users, especially if they do not know Redmine, more likely will configure their e-mail clients to move such e-mails to a separate folder and will never read them rather than change this option to another value. That's why I believe that the users themselves should select this mode. But if you still want this mode to be default be sure to check as few actions (under **Select actions for which email notifications should be sent** section) as possible.

- **Only for things I watch or I'm involved in**: This mode is selected by default. In this mode users will be notified about events in issues they own (they are authors of) or are/were assigned to.

- **Only for things I am assigned to**: In this mode, users will be notified about events in issues they are or were assigned to.

- **Only for things I am the owner of**: In this mode, users will be notified about events in issues they are authors of.

- **No events**: This mode disables e-mail notifications for a user.

 All modes, except **No events**, will still send notifications to a user if this user is watching the object (for example, issue).

The **Select actions for which email notifications should be sent** block contains the list of events Redmine will notify on. Only administrators (and only on this tab) can control which events will generate notifications. In other words, if you uncheck for example **Issue updated** event users will never be notified about any changes in issues! Therefore I, personally, would recommend to check all available actions here. Otherwise users may subscribe to notifications assuming they will get notified on particular events and then get frustrated with the absence of such notifications. Let's leave this for users to control what they get.

The next two blocks are intelligible. They contain texts which will be inserted into e-mail before and after the notification text. Be sure, however, to change `http://hostname/my/account` to the actual URL.

Now, when we have finished configuring e-mail notifications, you can click on the **Send a test email** link to check if and how e-mail delivery works. This will send a test message to the email you specified in your Redmine account.

Configuring reminding e-mails

Redmine issues have optional due date attribute. Would it not be cool to be notified about the issue due date in advance? So let's do it?

Redmine ships with a special rake task which can be used to generate notifications about upcoming issues due dates. The name of this task is `redmine:send_reminders`. It accepts the following options:

- `days` (defaults to 7): The number of days before a due date
- `tracker` (all trackers are used if not specified): The numerical (internal) tracker ID
- `project` (all projects are used if not specified): The identifier (which is used in URL) of the project
- `users` (all users are notified if not specified): The numerical IDs of users to notify separated by comma

The syntax of the command to run the `redmine:send_reminders` task is:

```
$ rake redmine:send_reminders days=7 tracker=1 project= mastering-redmine
users=1,5 RAILS_ENV=production
```

Let's configure our Redmine to remind all users about issues due dates a day before they are due but not on weekends. Let's use `cron` for this.

- We will need to put into `cron` the following command for Mondays, Tuesdays, Wednesdays, and Thursdays:

  ```
  rake redmine:send_reminders days=1 RAILS_ENV=production
  ```

- And the following command for Fridays:

  ```
  rake redmine:send_reminders days=3 RAILS_ENV=production
  ```

- Now open crontab using the following command:

  ```
  $ crontab -e
  ```

You may need to specify a different user using -u option:

```
$ sudo crontab -u www-data -e
```

If you are not sure whether your current user account can be used just try running the rake task manually first.

- This command will open an editor. Now add the following two lines:

```
0 10 * * 1-4 /usr/bin/rake -f /usr/share/redmine/Rakefile
redmine:send_reminders days=1 RAILS_ENV=production
```

```
0 10 * * 5 /usr/bin/rake -f /usr/share/redmine/Rakefile
redmine:send_reminders days=3 RAILS_ENV=production
```

- Use which rake to determine the path to the rake tool.
- Save changes and exit the editor.

The first command will be run at 10:00 on Mondays, Tuesdays, Wednesdays, and Thursdays and the second command will run at 10:00 on Fridays.

Selecting days before due date

This task will generate reminder e-mails for all issues, due dates of which are due in the next number of days, that is, if you specify 7 days, users will get notifications about issues due in 6 days and in 1 day. Running such a task (with days=7) everyday can really bother your users so that's why we select 1 day. In other words, you should execute the task once in the same number of days (for example, if you use days=7 execute the task only on Mondays).

Receiving e-mails

While the e-mail invention predates the Internet invention e-mail is still one of the primary electronic ways to communicate. Thus, having a public issue tracker for my projects I still keep getting e-mails from users describing issues. That's why, perhaps, email integration is one of the essential features of modern issue trackers. And Redmine does have it.

If you had a look at the Redmine directory structure you might notice the extra directory containing different scripts and a sample plugin. Despite of what you could think these files are not, in fact, *extra* tools but one of the most important features of Redmine (well, except the sample plugin). We will review all these tools in this chapter. Right now we start with the rdm-mailhandler.rb. Probably you already guessed from its name that this is the tool that implements e-mail receiving for Redmine.

In addition to the `rdm-mailhandler.rb`, Redmine comes with two rake tasks which also can be used for receiving emails namely `redmine:email:receive_imap` and `redmine:email:receive_pop3`.

The difference between these two primary solutions is in the method by which these tools are invoked. The `rdm-mailhandler.rb` was designed to be launched on a mail server by for example, Postfix, while rake tasks were designed to fetch e-mails from a mail server remotely. Of course, the tool launched by a mail server on receiving an e-mail is better for several reasons: first, it gets executed only when an email comes, that is, it does not work for nothing and, second, Redmine gets an e-mail immediately after it comes to a mail server, that is, without any delay. But the tool which fetches e-mail from a remote mail server also find its consumer especially if a remote mail server is for example, Gmail, and therefore there is no way to install the former tool there.

For the above reasons, we will review both tools here. But let's start with discussing what exactly Redmine can fetch using e-mail.

Format of incoming emails

In addition to new issues Redmine is able to recognize issue comments and board messages. That is, for example, if you are getting notifications about new issues you can just reply to a received notification and the message you will type will be added as a note to the issue. The same way you can answer someone's note or changes if you watch an issue and receive notifications about changes in it. A similar scenario is also supported for messages in forums.

> If you want to receive replies through email you should change the
> **Emission email address** to the e-mail address you plan to receive e-mails
> on. So the notifications come from the same address and users just need to
> click on **Reply** in their e-mail clients.

Of course, for a new issue to be created Redmine needs some attributes. They are, at least, tracker, subject, status, and priority (these attributes are required). Good news is that they can be specified in the tools which will be used for fetching e-mails. But what if your Redmine requires some custom fields? Besides, if you have hardcoded values of attributes would it not be too limited?

Luckily Redmine supports specifying attributes in the message body and supports many more attributes that just required ones. Let's check a sample e-mail body:

```
Hi!

I have an issue...
```

```
These are attributes:
Assigned to: Andriy Lesyuk
Tracker: Support
Status: New
Priority: Urgent
Category: Email queries
Target version: 1.0.0
Start: 2012-07-01
Due date: 2012-07-18
Estimated time: 20
Done ratio: 50
Custom field: Value
```

As you see even values for custom fields can be specified.

Besides new issue e-mails the attributes can be specified in replies to existing issues as well. Of course whether changes will be applied to the issue, as well as whether a new issue will be created with the specified attributes values, depends on permissions of the user who sends the e-mail (the user gets identified by the from e-mail address).

To allow specifying project, tracker, status, priority, and category in the e-mail body you need to specify all these attributes in the `allow_override` or `allow-override` option at the command line for the appropriate tool (see below).

You probably thought that having all those attributes in the issue description or in the note text is not good. For this reason Redmine allows configuring, after which lines the description should be truncated. Go to **Administration | Settings | Incoming emails** tab, as you see in the following screenshot there can be many lines specified:

So for the preceding sample e-mail, we can specify "These are attributes:" here to remove attributes from issue description or note text. Of course, the delimiters should be negotiated with customers.

 I believe the two hyphens line is essential to have here as it is often used to delimit message body from signature.

If one specifies other e-mail addresses in **To** or **CC** field and if these e-mails are registered in Redmine (there are accounts with these e-mails) the corresponding users will be added to issue watchers. However, watchers are not added from replies.

If the e-mail has attachments these attachments will be added to an issue or to a forum message. Of course, the size limit specified in **General** tab at **Administration | Settings** is applied to such attachments as well.

Fetching e-mails through web service

Having read the title you, perhaps, asked yourself: What web service? Yes, we need the web service to receive e-mail messages which are sent by the `rdm-mailhandler.rb` tool. This web service needs to be enabled before we proceed. To do this go to the **Administration** area using the link in the top-left menu, then open the **Settings** section and click on the **Incoming emails** tab:

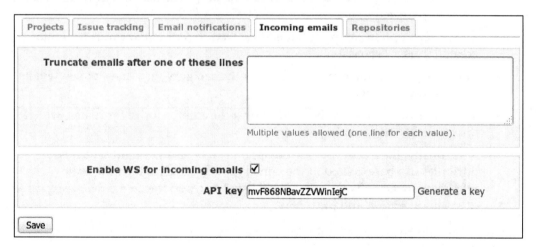

Check the **Enable WS for incoming emails** option and then click on the **Generate a key** link. After that Redmine will generate a web service key for you. Click on **Save**.

Now copy the `rdm-mailhandler.rb` tool to your mail server and place it into `/usr/local/sbin`. Please note that you may need to install Ruby on the mail server to be able to run this tool.

Let's now discuss arguments for this tool which should be used on the mail server. The mandatory arguments are `url` and `key`:

- The `url` argument should be set to Redmine's home page URL, for example, `http://redmine.packtpub.com`.

- The `key` argument should be set to the key we have generated above.

Also the following optional arguments are available:

- The `unknown-user` option accepts values such as, `ignore` (the default), `accept`, and `create`. With the default `ignore` value, all e-mail messages which come from an e-mail that is not listed in Redmine (if it is not specified as an e-mail in any account) will be ignored. If the `accept` value is set, issues created from such e-mail messages will be authored by *Anonymous* user. And, finally, if the `create` value was specified new user accounts will be created.

- The `project` option can be set to the identifier of the project in which issues will be created. If this option is not set, the project identifier should be explicitly set in the e-mail message body.

- The `tracker` option can be set to the name of the tracker, which will be used for newly created issues.

- The `status` option can be specified to set a different initial status for issues created from received e-mails.

- The `category` option can be used to set the category for issues, which will be created from e-mails.

- The `priority` option can be used to set a different priority for issues, which are created from incoming e-mails.

- And, finally, the `allow-override` option can be used to limit which issue attributes can be specified in the e-mail message body. Here, the issue attributes are actually the previously listed five options: `project`, `tracker`, `status`, `category`, and `priority`.

So the tool should be executed in the following way:

```
/usr/local/sbin/rdm-mailhandler.rb --unknown-user create --project
mastering-redmine --url http://redmine.packtpub.com --key
mvF868NBavZZVWinIejC
```

The rest depends on what mail server you are using. As we just can't review all the available mail servers in this book let's assume you use Postfix and it is configured to use a plain text file for aliases, for example /etc/aliases. If you don't use it, please consult your system administrator on how to do this for your configuration (we need to forward messages intended for a particular email to the standard input of the rdm-mailhandler.rb).

Open the /etc/aliases file and add the following line:

```
issues: "|/usr/local/sbin/rdm-mailhandler.rb --unknown-user
create --allow-override=project,tracker,status,category,priority
--project mastering-redmine --url http://redmine.packtpub.com --key
mvF868NBavZZVWinIejC"
```

Here issues is the username part of the e-mail address (full address can be for example, issues@packtpub.com).

> **Getting project from e-mail address**
>
> Thomas Guyot-Sionnest developed a *frontend* for rdm-mailhandler.rb which supports subaddresses such as issues+mastering-redmine-@ packtpub.com. This way a project can be specified in the e-mail address, then this project is passed to rdm-mailhandler.rb with the project option.
>
> http://www.redmine.org/projects/redmine/wiki/ MailhandlerSubAddress

Now you should be able to receive issues and forum messages by e-mail.

Fetching e-mails using IMAP/POP3

In some cases you may be unable to register the rdm-mailhandler.rb tool on your mail server, for example, if you use Google Apps. In these cases you can still fetch issues and forum messages from e-mails using special rake tasks. Such tasks are available for IMAP and for POP3. Which one to use depends on your mail server's capabilities but, generally, IMAP protocol is more powerful than POP3, so the IMAP rake task allows more than the POP3 one as well. Gmail supports both.

The command for fetching e-mails from IMAP looks like:

```
$ rake redmine:email:receive_imap host=imap.gmail.com port=993
ssl=1 username=issues@packtpub.com password=LIIWLmedev6M9yAJ
RAILS_ENV=production
```

Let's review options available for the IMAP and POP3 rake tasks:

- The `unknown_user` option like the `unknown-user` option for `rdm-mailhandler.rb` supports values such as `ignore`, `accept`, and `create`. Meanings of these values are the same as for `rdm-mailhandler.rb`.

- Options `project`, `status`, `tracker`, `category`, `priority`, and `allow_override` also accept the same values and have the same meanings as the corresponding options of `rdm-mailhandler.rb`.

- The `host` option should hold IP or hostname of the mail server. Default value is `localhost`.

- The `port` option should contain the port number of the mail server. For IMAP the default value is `143` and for POP3 it is `110`.

- The `ssl` option is available only for IMAP and should be set to `1` if the IMAP server supports SSL.

- The `username` and `password` options define credentials which should be used for connecting to IMAP or POP3 server.

- The `folder` option, which can be specified for IMAP, holds the name of the folder to process. The default name is `INBOX`.

- The `apop` option can be used to select APOP authentication for the POP3 server.

The IMAP protocol allows moving e-mail messages between server folders. Therefore these two additional options are available for IMAP:

- The `move_on_success` option specifies the name of the folder where the successfully processed e-mails should be moved.

- The `move_on_failure` option specifies the name of the folder where the ignored e-mail messages should be moved.

Now, when we know what options we can use, let's put the rake task into the `cron` to check the IMAP server once in an hour (do this under the user, which runs Redmine, or specify the username for `crontab` with -u option):

```
$ crontab -e
```

This command will open the editor. Add the following line there:

```
45 * * * * /usr/bin/rake -f /usr/share/redmine/Rakefile --silent
redmine:email:receive_imap host=imap.gmail.com port=993 ssl=1
username=issues@packtpub.com password= LIIWLmedev6M9yAJ unknown_
user=create allow_override=project,tracker,status,category,priority
RAILS_ENV=production
```

This tells `cron` to run the rake task on 45th minute of every hour. `/usr/bin/rake` is the full path to the `rake` tool which can be obtained using `which rake`. `/usr/share/redmine` which is the root directory of Redmine installation.

Repositories integration

Repository integration is an awesome feature of Redmine. I just can't imagine this tool without it! So, I believe, you will like Redmine for having it. But as soon as you know how deep this integration can be, I'm sure, you will love Redmine even more!

We will start with configuring repositories and ensuring that the basic integration works. Then we will discuss how to turn Redmine into a repository manager.

Configuring repositories

So here we came to the last tab of the administration settings that is the **Repositories** tab:

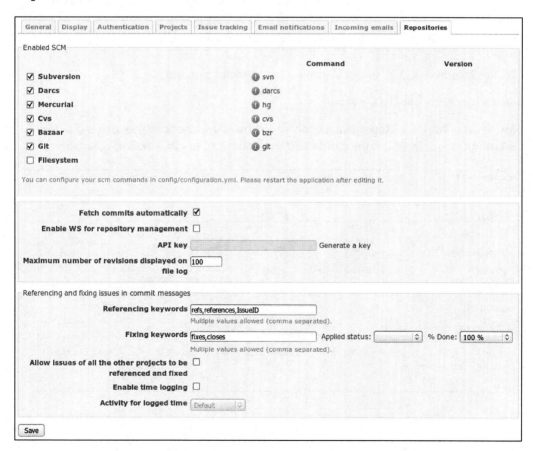

There were days when Redmine did not show those exclamation marks thus was not hinting about issues with SCMs. Luckily nowadays to check if a SCM is properly installed we just need to go to this tab.

The hint below the checklist advises that you may need to specify paths to the SCM commands in **config/configuration.yml**. Actually you need to do this in rare cases, for example, when you installed SCMs from sources. In other cases, you just need to install SCMs.

You probably do not want to install all SCMs. But, still, let's shortly review how to install each of them on Ubuntu/Debian.

SCMs	Command
Subversion	`$ sudo apt-get install subversion`
Darcs	`$ sudo apt-get install darcs`
Mercurial	`$ sudo apt-get install mercurial`
CVS	`$ sudo apt-get install cvs`
Bazaar	`$ sudo apt-get install bzr`
Git	`$ sudo apt-get install git`

Having installed SCMs restart Redmine using the command:

```
$ sudo service apache2 reload
```

Now if you check the **Repositories** tab you should see check marks instead of exclamation marks near commands and version numbers in **Version** column:

Enabled SCM	Command	Version
☑ **Subversion**	✔ svn	1.6.17
☑ **Darcs**	✔ darcs	2.7.99.1
☑ **Mercurial**	✔ hg	2.0.2
☑ **Cvs**	✔ cvs	1.12.13
☑ **Bazaar**	✔ bzr	2.5.0
☑ **Git**	✔ git	1.7.9.5
☐ **Filesystem**		

You can configure your scm commands in /etc/redmine/<instance>/configuration.yml. Please restart the application after editing it.

Be sure to disable SCMs which have not been installed or which have any issues (shown as exclamation marks).

> **Security warning**
>
> Don't ever enable the **Filesystem** SCM! With this SCM enabled users having **Manage repository** permission will be able to read the filesystem of the server as Redmine does not restrict the path which can be used for this SCM.

Updating repository change sets

The main feature provided by the SCM integration is the ability to see repository change sets under the **Repository** tab. Here is what I refer to:

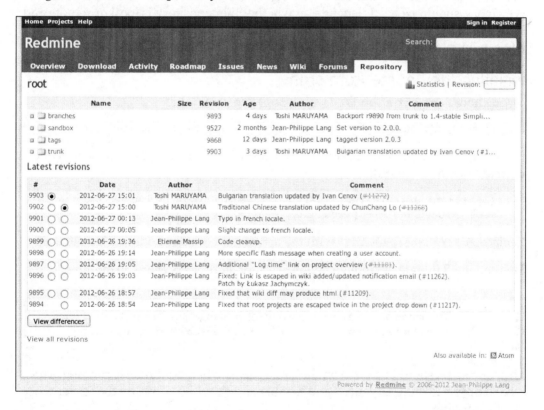

The **Repository** tab lets view or download files, browse directories and revisions, compare revisions, check changes, and more. To be able do this Redmine needs to fetch changesets from the repository. Normally it does this each time a user accesses anything under the `projects/<project>/repository` URL (under the **Repository** tab).

In other words, when you click on the **Repository** tab it fetches change sets, when you click on for example, the **trunk** subdirectory it fetches change sets, then when you click on a file it fetches change sets! If Redmine does not need to serve many users and the repository is local, this should not be a big problem. But what if the Redmine installation serves many users and fetches change sets from a remote repository?

This behavior can be controlled by the **Fetch commits automatically** option, which is present in **Administration | Settings | Repositories**. To disable fetching change sets each time a user visits the **Repository** tab, just uncheck this option. But, wait, how will Redmine update change sets in this case? Without recent change sets the **Repository** view will quickly become outdated.

Redmine comes with several out-of-the-box solutions for resolving this problem. Which one should be used depends on whether the repository is local or remote and from where the update will be initiated. In other words, there are two places where you can initiate the change sets fetching—from cron or from SCM hook.

Initiating the update from cron

If you choose cron, you should use the following command:

```
$ ruby script/runner "Repository.fetch_changesets" -e production
```

Just put this line into crontab (under the user, which runs Redmine, or specify the username with -u option):

```
*/30 * * * /usr/bin/ruby /usr/share/redmine/script/runner "Repository.
fetch_changesets" -e production
```

Replace /usr/share/redmine/ with the actual path of your Redmine installation.

This code will initiate fetching of change sets for *all* projects every 30 minutes.

 This command can also be used to fetch change sets for a just added huge repository as it can take too much time for a web interface to do this.

This, of course, should be done on the same server where Redmine is running. The second option is more advanced and flexible and should be done on the server where SCM is running.

Initiating the update from SCM hook

All SCMs, at least ones I used to work with, support "hooks". **Hooks** are just scripts located in a special subdirectory or listed in a configuration file of the repository.

Thus, for Subversion this directory is `hooks`, for Mercurial hooks are specified under the `[hooks]` section in `.hg/hgrc`, for CVS hooks are specified in `commitinfo` file, for Bazaar hooks can be put either to `.bzr/hooks` directory or listed in `bazaar.conf` file, for Git hooks should be put into `.git/hooks` directory, and so on. These scripts get triggered when an event occurs, for example, when a user commits a change set to a repository. Yes, this is exactly where we should initiate fetching change sets for Redmine!

To do this we will use the web service provided by Redmine and accessible under URL `sys/fetch_changesets` but first we need to enable this web service by going to **Administration | Settings | Repositories** tab:

Fetch commits automatically	☐
Enable WS for repository management	☑
API key	db4ejsoF7EaeYtISyvMJ Generate a key
Maximum number of revisions displayed on file log	100

Check the **Enable WS for repository management** option and click on the **Generate a key** link.

Now create a hook script for your SCM (check SCM's documentation for format, name of script, and location) and put the following command there:

```
curl -O /dev/null "https://redmine.packtpub.com/sys/fetch_changesets?k
ey=db4ejsoF7aeYtISyvMJ"> /dev/null 2>&1
```

Replace `https://redmine.packtpub.com` with the actual URL of your Redmine installation and `db4ejsoF7aeYtISyvMJ` with the key which was generated for you.

 Use HTTPS protocol in the URL to encrypt the key, when it is sent over the Internet.

Of course, different projects usually use different repositories, which may be on different servers and even use different SCMs. Therefore this web service supports an additional query argument `id` which should be set to a project identifier, for example:

```
https://redmine.packtpub.com/sys/fetch_changesets?key=db4ejsoF7aeYtISy
vMJ&id=mastering-redmine
```

The drawback of this option is that we need to configure each repository separately. Anyway it is recommended to specify the id, especially if your Redmine installation hosts many projects. Otherwise Redmine will update all repositories in all projects.

> **Fetching change sets from Github**
>
> Git SCM supports only local repositories in Redmine but it's possible to make a clone from Github and then keep the local copy up-to-date using Jakob Skjerning's Github Hook plugin:
>
> `https://github.com/koppen/redmine_github_hook`

Automatic repositories creation

We discussed in the earlier section how to make Redmine work as a repository browser, that is a known Redmine's feature and which, in fact, works out of the box (if a SCM is installed, of course). Now let's speak about Redmine as a repository manager.

In the default Redmine installation the repository URL, which we specify in the repository form (that can be found in project: **Settings | Repositories | New repository**), should already exist on the server.

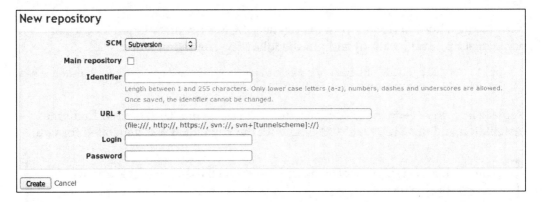

If this is a new project, this means, you need to ask your system administrator to create a repository for you first. On practice many organizations utilize SCM management software such as SVNManager to ease this process. For example, you create a repository in SVNManager and then add it to Redmine's project.

Not everyone knows that Redmine actually has a special tool for automatic creation of repositories. Its name is `reposman.rb` and it's located in the `extra/svn` subdirectory of your Redmine installation. How does it work? This tool should be launched periodically by `cron` on the SCM server. When run it connects to Redmine, fetches a projects list, checks if repositories are defined for all projects and creates repositories for projects which do not have repositories yet. Let's utilize it?

First, we need to know where repositories should be located. If the SCM server has already been configured, figure out what is the path for repositories and which SCMs are available.

If no SCM server exists let's just create a path for repositories for now and later, in the next topic, we'll add the SCM server. Assuming we are going to use Subversion. To conform to the FHS let's select `/var/lib/svn` as a path for Subversion repositories:

```
$ sudo mkdir /var/lib/svn
```

If you have not enabled the web service for repository management, as it was described in the previous topic, do it now as the `reposman.rb` tool uses this web service to create repositories.

Now it's time to create a repository.

If you have not created any project yet, do it now. This can either be a test project or a real project. Click on the **Projects** item in the top-left menu and then click on the **New project** link. The following form will be opened:

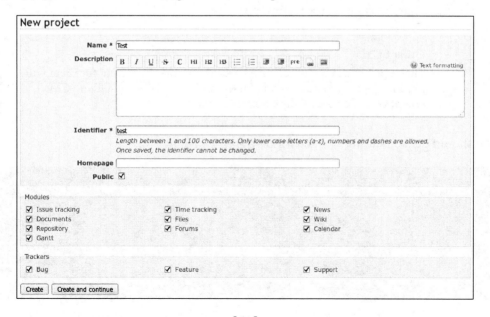

Fill in the **Name** and **Identifier** textboxes. I put **Test** and **test** in these fields as I will use this project only for testing. Click on the **Create** button.

Now, when we have a project which does not have a repository yet, let's get back to the console and test the `reposman.rb` tool. Run it in the following way:

```
$ sudo /usr/share/redmine/extra/svn/reposman.rb --owner=www-data --svn-
dir=/var/lib/svn --url=file:///var/lib/svn --redmine-host=localhost
--key=db4ejsoF7aeYtISyvMJ --verbose
```

If the SCM server is located on a different physical server you will need to copy `reposman.rb` there. So the path to the `reposman.rb` may differ.

Let's see the various attributes present in the earlier mentioned command:

- The `owner` option specifies username of the user who will own repository files on the SCM server
- The `svn-dir` option points to the path where repositories will be located
- The `url` option specifies the external path to the repositories (it may look like `http://redmine.packtpub.com/svn`). Redmine will use this `url` to fetch change sets from repository
- The `redmine-host` option holds the IP or hostname, which will be used by the `reposman.rb` tool for connecting to Redmine
- The `key` option specifies the key Redmine generated for the web service.
- The `verbose` is given for testing purposes

Other SCMs

The `reposman.rb` tool can also be used for other SCMs but for them you need to specify the `scm` option, for example, `--scm=Git`. Other SCMs, except Git, also require the `command` option.

You should get something like the following screenshot:

```
s-andy@ubuntu:~$ sudo /usr/share/redmine/extra/svn/reposman.rb --owner=www-data
--svn-dir=/var/lib/svn --url=file:///var/lib/svn --redmine-host=localhost --key=
db4ejsoF7aeYtISyvMJ --verbose
querying Redmine for projects...
retrieved 1 projects
treating project Test
        repository /var/lib/svn/test registered in Redmine with url file:///var/
lib/svn/test
        repository /var/lib/svn/test created
s-andy@ubuntu:~$
```

Now if you open the **Settings** tab of the **Test** project and open the **Repositories** tab there you should see:

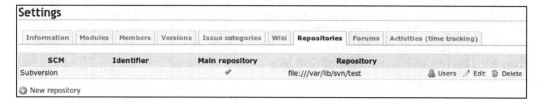

After we have checked how `reposman.rb` works, we should add it to `cron` so it will run periodically and create repositories if some new projects get registered. Execute the following command:

```
$ sudo crontab -e
```

And append the following line:

```
15 * * * * /usr/share/redmine/extra/svn/reposman.rb --owner=www-
data --svn-dir=/var/lib/svn --url=file:///var/lib/svn --redmine-
host=localhost --key=db4ejsoF7aeYtISyvMJ
```

This tells `cron` to run `reposman.rb` on the 15th minute of every hour.

Exit the editor after saving changes. From now on *all* your projects will have repositories automatically created for them.

SCM Creator

For easy repository creation you can also use the SCM Creator plugin which currently works with Subversion, Git, Mercurial, and Bazaar. However, the SCM Creator plugin can only create local repositories (located at the same server where Redmine is).

`http://projects.andriylesyuk.com/projects/scm-creator`

Advanced repositories integration

If you checked the **Roles and permissions** section of the **Administration** area you might have noticed the **Commit access** permission. This permission has nothing to do with Redmine as a web application as no commit access is possible within Redmine. This permission is for what they name "advanced integration" and it involves an extra tool `Redmine.pm` which is located in the `extra/svn` directory.

Normally, a Subversion server is set up using the Apache web server with the WebDAV module. Same configuration can be used for Git server, Mercurial server and, if I'm not mistaken, for Bazaar server. But Redmine core developers, however, seem to prefer Subversion, maybe that's why the `Redmine.pm` tool was initially written for this SCM (at the moment it also has support for Git smart protocol). This tool handles authorization and is actually a Perl module for Apache, which uses ModPerl to access Apache module API.

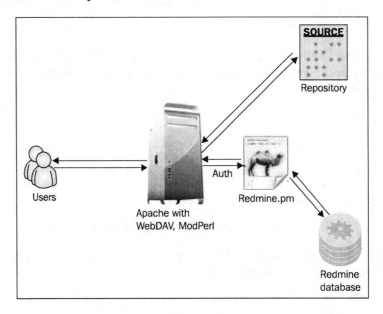

So what does it do? When a user requests access to a repository, Apache "asks" `Redmine.pm` if it should authorize or forbid a user. To give the answer `Redmine.pm` consults the Redmine database by directly connecting to it and inspecting its records. The access to a repository is granted or denied based on the answer of `Redmine.pm`.

In other words, Redmine controls who has access to the repository. The access is given depending on a user's role and its permissions. Thus, if a user's role in a project has the **Commit access** permission this user can commit changes to a project's repository and so on.

 If you need to allow read-only access for anonymous users make the project public and grant the **Browse repository** permission to the **Anonymous** role.

So let's see now how to configure the advanced integration for Subversion.

We'll start with installing and configuring Subversion server. Assuming you use Debian/Ubuntu to run the SCM server and have already installed Apache. Execute the following command:

```
$ sudo apt-get install libapache2-svn libapache2-mod-perl2 libapache-dbi-perl
```

This command will install WebDAV, ModPerl, and Perl DBI.

On Debian/Ubuntu, if you installed Redmine from the official package, `Redmine.pm` should be in `/usr/share/redmine/extra/svn/` (in `extra/svn` subdirectory of your Redmine installation). Copy it into `/usr/lib/perl5/Apache`:

```
$ sudo mkdir /usr/lib/perl5/Apache/Authn
```

```
$ sudo cp /usr/share/redmine/extra/svn/Redmine.pm /usr/lib/perl5/Apache/Authn/
```

 You can still copy `Redmine.pm` to the same location on a different server if you are going to use a separate server for Subversion.

Now we need to know where repositories will be located. If you have chosen the path earlier, when reading the previous topic, use that path. Otherwise let's select `/var/lib/svn`:

```
$ sudo mkdir /var/lib/svn
```

At the moment, we have all we need to start configuring Apache and Subversion. Now you can add Subversion repositories configuration to the Apache configuration files either into the existing `<VirtualHost>` directive (if you want Subversion to be accessible under some location for example under `/svn`) or into new `<VirtualHost>` directive (if you want to use Subversion under subdomain for example, under `svn.packtpub.com`). Here we will try the first option, for the second option you need to create a new virtual host first.

We will use the `apache2-passenger-host.conf` file, which we have added when installing Redmine on Ubuntu using the official Ubuntu `redmine` package. Open this file and add the following lines there before the closing `</VirtualHost>` directive:

```
PerlLoadModule Apache::Authn::Redmine
<Location /svn>
        DAV svn
        SVNParentPath /var/lib/svn
```

```
        Order deny,allow
        Deny from all
        Satisfy any

        AuthType Basic
        AuthName "Packt Publishing Subversion Server"
        PerlAccessHandler Apache::Authn::Redmine::access_handler
        PerlAuthenHandler Apache::Authn::Redmine::authen_handler

        RedmineDSN "DBI:mysql:dbname=redmine_default;host=localhost"
        RedmineDbUser redmine
        RedmineDbPass HJJQHGppgx0hYvijITVbEQiLTzoQpVv1

        <Limit GET PROPFIND OPTIONS REPORT>
            Require valid-user
            Satisfy any
        </Limit>
        <LimitExcept GET PROPFIND OPTIONS REPORT>
            Require valid-user
        </LimitExcept>
    </Location>
```

Instead of the sample credentials (database name, username, password, and so on) use your real ones. If you are not sure about them take them from `/etc/redmine/ default/database.yml`, if you installed Redmine from package, or from `config/ database.yml` otherwise.

 Also replace `localhost` with IP or hostname of your Redmine server if you use a separate server for Subversion. You might also need to modify the `bind-address` of MySQL server on the Redmine server in this case.

When ready, restart Apache:

```
$ sudo service apache2 reload
```

Try accessing some of your projects' repositories now. I will use the previously created repository for the Test project:

```
$ svn ls http://localhost/svn/test
```

It gives nothing to me as my test repository is empty and my `Test` project is public. But when I uncheck the **Public** option in the project settings I get a warning as shown in the following screenshot:

```
s-andy@ubuntu:~$ svn ls http://localhost/svn/test
Authentication realm: <http://localhost:80> Packt Publishing Subversion Server
Password for 's-andy':

-----------------------------------------------------------------------

ATTENTION!  Your password for authentication realm:

   <http://localhost:80> Packt Publishing Subversion Server

can only be stored to disk unencrypted!  You are advised to configure
your system so that Subversion can store passwords encrypted, if
possible.  See the documentation for details.

You can avoid future appearances of this warning by setting the value
of the 'store-plaintext-passwords' option to either 'yes' or 'no' in
'/home/s-andy/.subversion/servers'.
-----------------------------------------------------------------------
Store password unencrypted (yes/no)? no
s-andy@ubuntu:~$
```

Congratulations now! You are ready to go with the advanced Subversion integration.

Advanced Git integration can be configured in the very same way but with some Git specific modifications. The same could be also done for Mercurial and Bazaar so it would be unfair to review only Git here and it would be too much to review all of them. Other SCMs' modifications may also differ for other Redmine versions so instead you should, probably, check the official tutorials for advanced integration of other SCMs:

`http://www.redmine.org/projects/redmine/wiki/HowTos`

Troubleshooting

No one is lucky enough to never have an issue with an application. So it's essential for a user to know where to ask for assistance, how to do this and what information should be provided to make the issue as clear as possible. That's what we'll discuss now.

Before asking a question it's always worth ensuring that no one has asked this question before and that the answer has not been given yet. Besides, of course, Google, you can search for similar issues on www.redmine.org using the search form http://www.redmine.org/search:

Search

[_____] ☑ All words ☐ Search titles only

☑ Issues ☐ News ☐ Documents ☐ Changesets ☑ Wiki pages ☑ Messages ☐ Projects ☐ Redmine plugins

[Submit]

In most cases the answer, if it exists, gets found in **Issues** or **Messages**, the answer to a frequently asked question can be also found in **Wiki pages**.

If you can't find the answer using this search form the first thing to check is whether the issue is really related to Redmine. It just can be related to one of the plugins you are using. The easiest way to check this is to try disabling all plugins (or one-by-one to determine which one causes the issue). This can be done just by renaming plugins' init.rb files, for example:

```
$ mv redmine_scm/init.rb  redmine_scm/init.rb.bck
```

Caution

But please be careful when doing this as Redmine ships with some core plugins which you should not disable! For Redmine 1.4.x and below and ChiliProject 2.x and below these core plugins are in the same directory as third-party plugins. Check **Administration | Plugins** for the list of third-party plugins you have in your Redmine.

This command should be executed in the plugins' directory which is plugins in Redmine 2.x.x, vendor/chiliproject_plugins in ChiliProject 3.x or vendor/plugins in older versions of the both. After executing such command you need to restart Redmine:

```
$ sudo service apache2 reload
```

If this appeared to be an issue in a third-party plugin, you need to contact the author of this plugin or its community. Check the **Plugins** section in **Administration** for installed plugins' home pages (but note that not all plugins specify home pages).

If this is a Redmine issue it's the time to prepare details. You can start with getting details about your environment under which you run Redmine. To get them you can execute the following command:

```
$ RAILS_ENV=production ruby script/about
```

This command gives the following output for my test:

```
Environment:
    Redmine version                       2.2.0.stable
    Ruby version                          1.8.7 (i486-linux)
    Rails version                         3.2.9
    Environment                           production
    Database adapter                      MySQL
Redmine plugins:
    no plugin installed
```

This information should be provided along with the issue.

Before asking Redmine developers or community a question about some issue you should also check log files first! In many cases log files can give you a hint about the source of the problem or, at least, become useful in resolving it. Error messages from log files, if any present, should be also provided to ones who you ask your question.

Redmine usually stores its log files in `log` subdirectory of its root directory. However, if you used the Redmine package from the Debian/Ubuntu repository to install Redmine, log files are stored in the `redmine` subdirectory of the `/var/log` directory. This subdirectory should contain the directory for each instance of Redmine, named after the instance. Log files are in the instance's directory. The name of the log file is `production.log` for the `production` environment and `development.log` for the `development` environment.

Normally a log file consists of blocks like:

```
Processing AdminController#plugins (for 127.0.0.1 at 2012-07-08
19:35:25) [GET]
    Parameters: {"controller"=>"admin", "action"=>"plugins"}
Rendering template within layouts/admin
Rendering admin/plugins
Completed in 42ms (View: 29, DB: 4) | 200 OK [http://127.0.0.1/admin/
plugins]
```

This is the block without any errors.

An erroneous block looks like:

```
Processing UsersController#show (for 127.0.0.1 at 2012-07-01 21:16:07)
[GET]
  Parameters: {"controller"=>"users", "action"=>"show", "id"=>"1"}
Rendering template within layouts/base
Rendering users/show

ActionView::TemplateError (undefined local variable or method
`fielname' for #<ActionView::Base:0x9ff47a0>) on line #14 of app/
views/users/show.html.erb:
11:   <% end %>
12:   <% @user.visible_custom_field_values.each do |custom_value| %>
13:   <% if !custom_value.value.blank? %>
14:     <li><%=h custom_value.custom_field.name%>: <%=h show_
value(custom_value) %></li>
15:   <% end %>
16:   <% end %>
17:     <li><%=l(:label_registered_on)%>: <%= format_date(@user.
created_on) %></li>

    vendor/plugins/extended_fields/app/helpers/extended_fields_helper.
rb:8:in `find_custom_field_template'
    app/views/users/show.html.erb:14:in `block in _run_erb_
app47views47users47show46html46erb'
    app/views/users/show.html.erb:12:in `each'
    app/views/users/show.html.erb:12
...
Rendering /usr/share/redmine/public/500.html (500 Internal Server
Error)
```

If you are getting something like this, it's definitely an error in the code.

Usually such error is accompanied with the following screen in the browser:

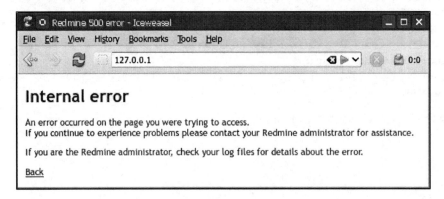

Or with the following screen, if you use Passenger:

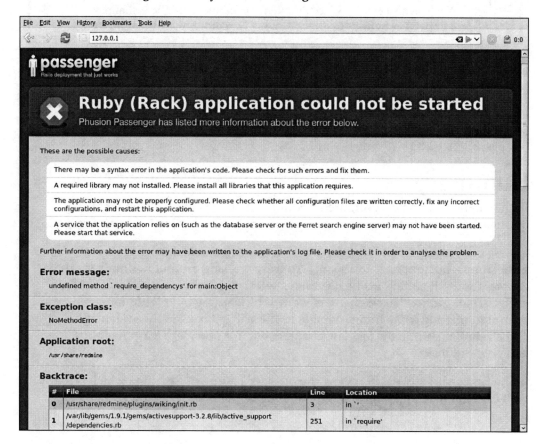

If you get something like the previous screenshots look for erroneous logs!

By the way, the earlier error in logs shows an error in a plugin, not in the core. Note the line:

```
vendor/plugins/extended_fields/app/helpers/extended_fields_helper.
rb:8:in `find_custom_field_template'
```

It contains the plugins path (vendor/plugins) that means you should contact the author of the plugin for this issue. The name of the plugin which causes the issue is extended_fields (*and I am its author so do not worry this issue has been fixed*).

Before reporting the issue to www.redmine.org, you can try asking the Redmine community about it by joining the official #redmine channel on the FreeNode IRC network. To do this you will need an IRC client.

You can also use the Web IRC client to join the #redmine channel: http://webchat.freenode.net/?channels=redmine&uio=d4

Otherwise register on www.redmine.org and create a new issue or post a message to forums.

If you found a possible security vulnerability report it to e-mail security@redmine.org and not to issues.

Summary

In this chapter, we have configured Redmine. Also we have learned what information is needed by people to be able to help you resolve a Redmine issue.

I guess you have got a little bit tired with all those general details, reviews, installations, integrations, and so on. We were walking around Redmine for three chapters and not getting inside it (besides settings, of course). But this is the last such chapter for now! Next chapters we will be learning only Redmine so you can even start missing some things outside it. We will get back to the system, files and all similar stuff in the last few chapters but, for now, let's learn Redmine and only Redmine.

In the next chapter, we will review the primary feature of Redmine which is really well implemented and which made Redmine so popular, issue tracking.

4
Issue Tracking

It's almost impossible to conclude that Redmine is more a project management application or an issue tracker but its issue tracking feature is definitely what has made it so popular. Issue tracking is not possible without having a project, while project management is still possible without issues, but we spend most of our time dealing with Redmine as an issue tracker. In other words, issue tracking is an essential component of Redmine which, however, depends on many other Redmine components but which you must learn to use Redmine effectively. For these reasons, we start reviewing Redmine functionality from its issue tracking capabilities.

As it was just mentioned the issue tracking module is too deeply tied into other Redmine modules to be reviewed separately. However, the opposite is also true, other modules use issues too intensively to skip issue tracking and start from reviewing other modules. So here we will try concentrating on issue tracking but also mentioning other modules if they are applicable. Do not worry if you don't know the mentioned modules yet, I will give you the directions to where you will be able to check them quickly.

In this chapter, we will cover the following topics:

- Creating an issue
- Issue page
- Issue list
- Updating issue
- Getting updates on issues
- Issue related settings

Creating an issue

In order to be able to create an issue, you need to have a project so create one if you have not done this yet (use **Projects | New project**). You can also jump to the *Creating a project* section in *Chapter 5, Managing Projects*, where project creation is described, and then come back here.

If you already have a project, or when you have created it, navigate to the **New issue** tab of the project menu:

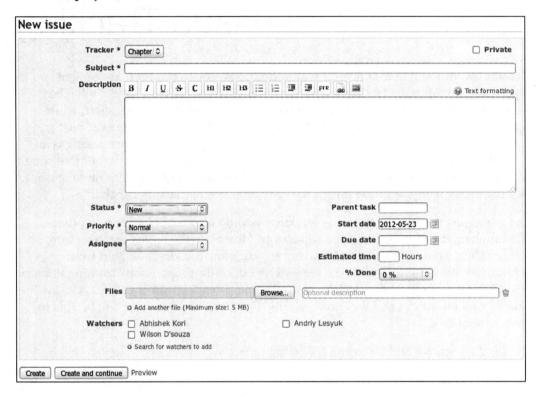

The preceding screenshot shows the form that Redmine users use to create issues.

 Issues can be also created from e-mails, if you have configured e-mail receiving, or with third-party tools, if you have enabled REST API.

Let's discuss each element of the issue creation form:

- In Redmine, the **Tracker** name is used to describe the type of the issue, thus, the appropriate item in JIRA (a popular commercial alternative to Redmine) is named literally "Issue type". By default, Redmine adds the following trackers:

    ○ **Bug**

    ○ **Feature**

    ○ **Support**

    You can delete, modify or add trackers by going to Administration | Trackers, which we will review in *Chapter 8, Access Control and Workflow*. In my demo project, I have added new tracker **Chapter** which you see selected in the previous screenshot.

- The **Private** checkbox can be used to make the issue visible only to you and other members of the groups that you are a member of. However, if a project is private too, such users should also be members of the project.

- The **Subject** field, like the e-mail subject, should briefly describe the issue. In most cases, the tracker and the subject of an issue (besides the unique numerical identifier) are visible to users on Redmine pages containing links to the issue page. Therefore, the content of this field is very important.

> The subject should give the basic idea about the issue, should not be ambiguous or too long.

- I believe that the **Description** field does not need an explanation, but the thing that is worth mentioning here is that you can use rich text formatting within it (click on the **Text formatting** link to get an idea of its capabilities). We will also review the Wiki syntax, which enables text formatting, *Chapter 7, Text Formatting*. From this moment, in further text of the book, I will refer to the Redmine rich text formatting as the Wiki formatting.

> Remember that using rich formatting helps draw the eye to the key messages and highlight specific data such as code blocks in your issue description, which improves overall readability of your issue.

- The **Status** field defines the status of the issue such as whether it is active, does anyone work on it, is it resolved, and so on. In the previous screenshot, the **New** status is selected as this is a new issue and, therefore, this status is selected by default. The default issue status as well as available statuses and their order can be configured by going to **Administration | Issue statuses**.

- The **Priority** field reflects how urgent or critical the issue is. Values for this field and their order can be customized in **Administration | Enumeration**. There you can also select the default value.

- The **Assignee** field holds the name of the user who will be responsible for resolving the issue. Only members of the project can be selected here, that is, if you want to assign an issue to someone you must first add that person to project members (this can be done under the **Members** tab in project settings).

- The **Parent** task field can hold the numerical identifier of another issue to which the new issue will be added as a subtask.

- The **Start date** and **Due date** fields can hold the period during which the issue is to be worked on. These fields, if both are specified, are used to display the issue on the Gantt chart. Each of these fields are also used to display the issue in the calendar. The **Due date** field can be used for sending reminder e-mail messages, if the latter was configured.

- The **Estimated time** field can be used to specify how many hours will be required to resolve the issue. This field is especially useful if you use the time tracking module because, in this case, it allows you to control the time spent for an issue.

 Normally, you should not set the estimated time for an issue unless it is assigned to you or you are a manager for the person the issue is assigned to.

- The **Done** field, also known as done ratio, stores the percentage of completion for an issue. Thus, ideally by the start date, if it is specified, it should be **0%** and by the due date, if it is specified, it should be **100%**. This field is also used for the roadmap to show the overall progress for a version.

- Redmine supports any number of attachments for an issue. Each file can have a description. The size of each file is limited by the **Maximum attachment size** option which is present in **Administration | Settings | General** (in my case this option is set to 5 MB).

Be sure to always describe the file you attach to an issue. Even if it's a single attachment, you should describe it in the optional description textbox as some other users may add other files later.

- Each issue can be *watched*. If you "watch" an issue you will:
    - Be able to see the list of watched issues on **My page** (if you enabled the **Watched issues** block there, this page will be reviewed in *Chapter 9, Personalization*).
    - Be notified about any changes in the issue by e-mail (if e-mail notifications were enabled and configured; refer *Chapter 3, Configuring Redmine*, on how to configure e-mails).

Issue watchers can be added when an issue is created but only check boxes for project members are explicitly available. To add non-members to **Watchers**, you need to click on the **Search for watchers to add** link.

The previous screenshot shows the **Add watchers** window and the list of all users that are available for adding. You can type a part of the first name or last name to filter the list. When you click on the **Add** button the selected users will appear with checkboxes in the main form.

- When ready with editing the issue, you can click on the **Create** button to save it and move to the issue page, or you can click on the **Create and continue** button to save it and navigate back to the new issue form for adding another issue.

- The **Preview** link can be used to preview the issue description, in particular, to see how Wiki formatting is going to be rendered.

However, the form we have just reviewed is incomplete. This is, actually, the form you get on a just installed Redmine and it should contain more elements if you have configured the project. We will speak about configuring projects in the next chapter. Now let's talk only about things which add new elements to the new issue form.

To configure properties such as, which issue form fields should be required or read-only per issue status, member role, and tracker, go to **Administration | Workflow | Fields permissions**. This will also be reviewed in *Chapter 8, Access Control and Workflow*.

Custom fields

Redmine supports custom fields which can be added to issues as well. If added, issue custom fields will also appear on the issue form. We will review custom fields in the *Chapter 11, Customizing Redmine*.

Issue categories

In many cases having just tracker (issue type) is not enough for describing an issue. Let's take the **Feature** tracker. Is it a UI feature? Is it a new functionality of the project? Is it, maybe, an API feature? As you see on some complex projects you may need an additional field to make an issue more exact. Redmine provides such field. Why is it missing? You need to add at least one value for it to appear on the new issue form.

Go to the project settings (select the **Settings** tab on a project page) and select the **Issue categories** tab as shown in the following screenshot:

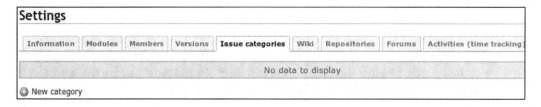

Now click the **New category** link to add a category as shown in the following screenshot:

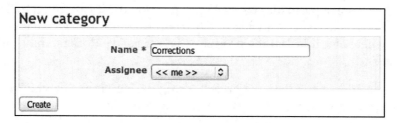

The **Assignee** field can be set to a user to whom issues of this category will be automatically assigned (unless, of course, the assignee was explicitly specified). Thus, if you have different employees responsible for different parts of your project, you can create categories named by these parts and specify corresponding employees here as assignees for these categories. This way, reporters only need to select part of the project and issues will automatically get assigned to corresponding responsible employees.

But wait, how do reporters select the category? If you check the new issue form now, you will see an additional field:

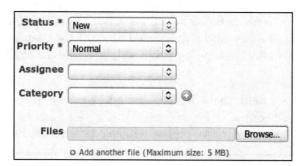

The icon at the right-hand side of the field appears only for users having the **Manage issue categories** permission. Such users may add issue categories right from the new issue form.

> Some examples of issue categories are **API**, **Reporting**, **Frontend**, **Backend**, and **UI**.

Issues and project versions

If you are planning to have several future versions of your project, in which version do you plan to resolve particular issues? This question draws attention to the need to be able to assign an issue to a version. The form we have reviewed earlier does not have any fields for this. But the project—that we used—does not have any version either.

As soon as you add a version to the project, using the **Versions** tab which can be found in the project's settings, the new field appears on the form:

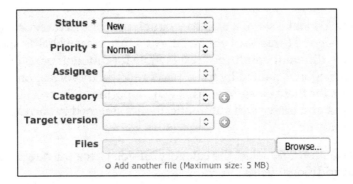

The **Target version** field holds the name of the version in which the issue is to be resolved. The value of this field will be used to show the issue on the project roadmap and in the version change log (both will be reviewed in the *Chapter 5, Managing Projects*).

Similar to the **Category** field, the ⊙ icon allows adding versions directly from the new issue form. Of course, to be able to do this a user must have the **Manage versions** permission. Version management will also be reviewed in details in the next chapter.

Issue page

When we add an issue and click on the **Create** button, we get redirected to the issue page (shown in the screenshot):

The goal of this page is not only to show you the information about the issue but also to give you all instruments, which you need to work with this issue.

All the content of the issue is located inside the big yellow block. There you will also find the **Previous** and the **Next** links allowing you to move through the issue list.

 Note that parameters of the issue list are preserved.

Below the yellow block you will find **History** that contains the list of changes made to the issue and includes information on what was changed, when it was changed, and by whom.

The sidebar on the issue page contains contextual links—most of which we will review in *Chapter 5, Managing Projects*—and the **Watcher** section, which can be used to add watchers to the issue.

Subtasks

When reviewing the issue page, I specially skipped the **Add** link to the right from the **Subtasks** label as I believed it was worth reviewing it separately. This link redirects you to the new issue form with the prefilled **Parent task** field, in other words, it is the shortcut for adding subtasks.

But what are subtasks? Let's study the following screenshot to know more about it:

Subtasks				Add
~~Topic #13~~: Creating issue	Closed	Andriy Lesyuk		
▸ ~~Topic #14~~: Issue categories	Closed	Andriy Lesyuk		
▸ ~~Topic #15~~: Issues and project versions	Closed	Andriy Lesyuk		
Topic #16: Issue page	In Progress	Andriy Lesyuk		
▸ Topic #17: Subtasks	In Progress	Andriy Lesyuk		
▸ Topic #18: Related issues	New			

In the earlier screenshot, you see the subtasks that I have added to my demo project. Besides just being shown in the hierarchical view these tasks also share the priority (the highest priority of all children is used for the parent task), the start date (the earliest date is used), the due date (the latest date is used), the done ratio (calculated using children done ratios), and the estimated time (the sum is used). Redmine does not allow setting values for these attributes explicitly for parent tasks.

Hierarchical view issue

Redmine has problems showing the hierarchical view of tasks as it considers the current sort order. On the earlier screenshot, the hierarchy is preserved because issues are sorted by numbers and they are sequential. So, to achieve the hierarchical view you need either to keep the sequential numbers of issues by creating them in the correct order or to use the Smart Issues Sort plugin of Vitaly Klimov, which resolves this issue: http://www.redmine.org/plugins/redmine_smart_issues_sort.

Related issues

Another form element that I purposefully skipped is the **Add** link which is placed to the right from the **Related issues** label. Like with Subtasks this feature was too important to review it with others so I wanted to speak about it in a separate topic.

If you click on the **Add** link the following form will appear just under the **Related issues** label:

The **Related issues** form can be used to list issues related to the current one. For each related issue you can also specify the type of relation. The following screenshot shows the types of relation available:

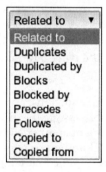

These types are mostly used not just to indicate the relation but they also provide implicit functionality. The types of relation are explained as follows:

- **Related to**: This is one of the relation types that does not affect anything. This is the type you should use if you just want to mark that issues are related.

- **Duplicates**: This type tells Redmine that the current issue should be closed too when the related issue gets closed.

- **Duplicated by**: This type forces the related issue to be closed too when the current one gets closed.

- **Blocks**: This type does not allow the related issue to be closed until the current issue is open.

- **Blocked by**: This type tells Redmine to forbid the closing of the current issue until the related issue is open.

- **Precedes**: This type forces the related issue to start after the due date (plus optional delay in days) of the current issue.
- **Follows**: This type forces the current issue to start after the due date (and optional delay in days) of the related issue.
- **Copied to**: This type marks the related issue as a copy of the current one and is automatically set by Redmine on issue copy.
- **Copied from**: This type marks the current issue as a copy of the related one and is automatically set by Redmine on issue copy.

Also, types **Precedes** and **Follows** use an additional value called delay. For this reason these types add an additional field **Delay** to the form (see following screenshot for reference):

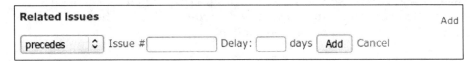

Using the **Delay** field, you can specify number of days that should pass between the due date of the previous issue and the start date of the next issue.

> The mentioned implicit functionality can become a source of confusion. Thus, if duplicate issues are assigned to different employees closing one of them will lead to closure of another and this can come as a surprise to the assignee of the latter. Adding preceding issues with empty start and due dates can lead to clearing the following issue dates. Therefore you should be especially careful when adding issue relations.

When added, related issues are shown under the **Related issues** label as shown in the following screenshot:

Related Issues				Add
precedes Chapter #5: Managing projects	New	07/19/2012	08/05/2012	
follows ~~Chapter #3~~: Configuring Redmine	Closed	06/13/2012	06/30/2012	

Issue list

Having checked the issue creation and issue view pages, let's now move to the **Issues** tab in projects menu where all the issues get listed. Just like the issues view page, the issues list has UI elements intended to assist in manipulating issues and the list. The following screenshot shows how the **Issues** page looks:

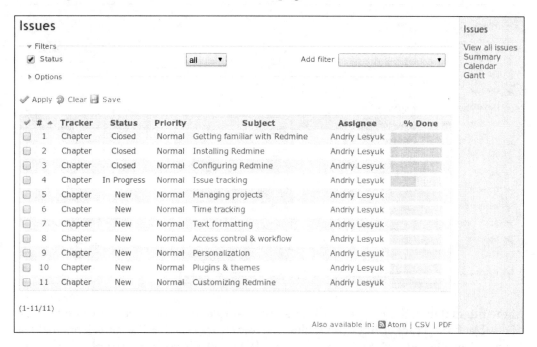

The sidebar content is generally the same as you have seen on the issues page. The **View all issues** link opens the listing with all view parameters reset to default values. The form under the **Issues** title and above the list is the one you can actually use to customize the list parameters. Let's discuss it in detail.

By default issues are filtered by their status and only open issues are listed. But you can add other filters as well. Thus, you can filter issues listing also by **Tracker, Priority, Author, Assignee, Category, Target version, Subject, Start date, Due date, Completion, Relation**, and much more. The following screenshot shows some filters that are available:

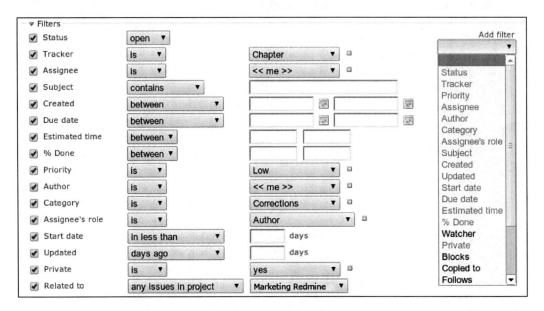

Many filters define their own conditions: for example, issues can be filtered by a part of a subject; the **Tracker** filter can include several trackers (the little plus icon enables the multiselect mode); date filters support relative conditions for example, **less than days ago, this week, in more than (days)**; and so on. The best way to learn the filters is, perhaps, to play with them. Do it now if you have enough issues, and if you don't, you can play with them on www.redmine.org.

You must have noticed the **Options** label. After clicking on it the following options (shown in the following screenshot) appear:

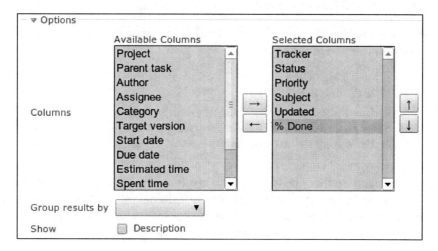

In the **Options** tab, we can choose which columns to show in the issue list. Thus, for adding a column we select it in the **Available Columns** box, click on the right arrow button and then click on the **Apply** button. You can optionally use the top arrow button to move the columns to get your desired column alignment.

The **Group result by** option is even more powerful. To show you what it does let me select the **Status** value.

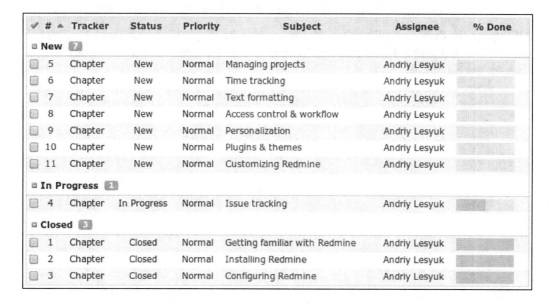

In the previous screenshot, as you see, the listing gets divided into groups, each group label includes the count of issues in the group and each group can be collapsed or expanded (using the gray plus/minus icon).

The **Show** option, if **Description** is enabled, adds the issue description to the list as a separate row below the main issue row.

Global issue list

Redmine also has a global issue list, which can be accessed using the **View all issues** link on the project list page (click on the **Projects** link on the top-left menu to get there).

Every time you click on the **Apply** button to apply your listing parameters they also get saved into your browser's cookies. This way, whenever you load the list again, you get the same customized view. To clear the cookies, you need to use the **Clear** link or the **View all issues** link that is available on the sidebar.

Custom queries

All new users, who have come to your Redmine site, despite their roles will see the same issue list. It's fine, unless you want them to be able to get the list of issues that they are interested in with just one click. Thus, having defined the parameters for the issue list you can: show issues which should be tested to your testers; show features in future versions to public users; show features to developers; and so on.

All this can be done with the same dialog we just used. Choose your issue list parameters that you want to share with others or want to save for later use and click on the **Save** link.

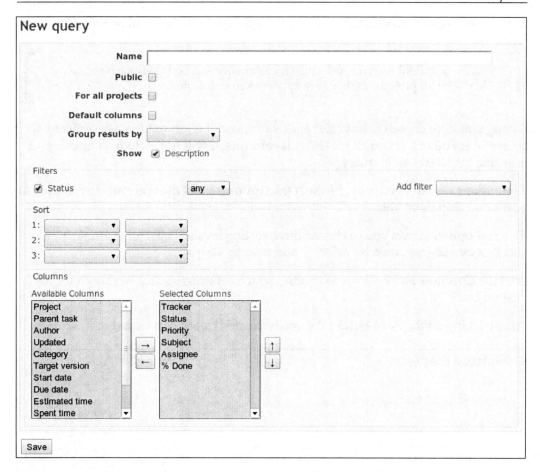

The preceding screenshot shows the page that lets you save issue list parameters and create a custom query.

The **Public** checkbox will make this query available for everyone, including anonymous users.

The **For all projects** checkbox will make this query available for all projects.

 Be careful when creating public custom queries, especially such queries for all projects, as they may appear to be unsolicited.

Saying you have chosen columns, that fit your needs better, but they are unlikely to be useful for others. If you check **Default columns**, it will not include your columns selection into the custom query.

The options **Group results by**, **Show (Description)**, and **Filters** are already known to you so we skip them here.

The **Sort** option allows you to choose three sorting levels. Thus, for example, you can sort first by assignee, then by priority, and then by status.

And the **Columns** block allows to choose, which columns should be shown for the custom issue list.

After clicking on the **Save** button the newly created query gets added to the sidebar:

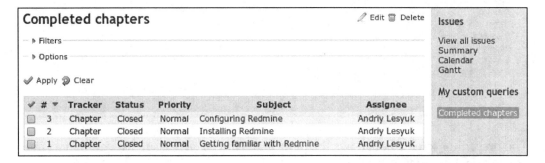

When you are viewing the query (and the current query is saved into the browsers cookies just like the list parameters) it is highlighted on the sidebar and its name appears as a title instead of just "Issues". Also, the **Edit** and **Delete** links appear in the top-right corner of the main content area. You can use these links to modify or delete the query.

Updating issue

Now it's time to check how to update issues. To open the update form you need to click on the **Update** link, which is located in the top-right corner of the issue page (in the contextual menu). The **Update** form gets opened below the last history entry and looks like this:

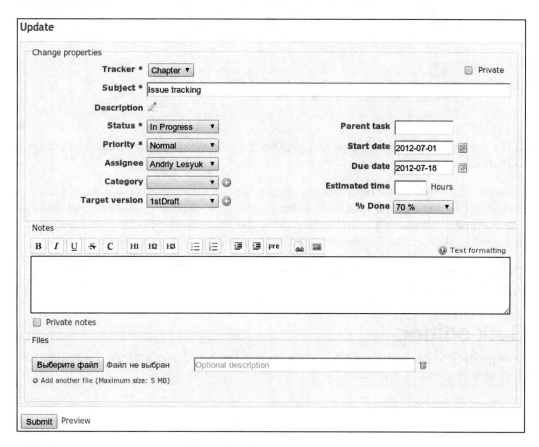

Almost all fields of the update form are already known to you. The missing **Description** field is actually hidden by default to save space and can be revealed by clicking on the pen icon.

The only new fields are **Notes** (which, like the **Description** field, supports Wiki formatting), and **Private notes**, (which, if set, make the notes visible only to project members having the **View private notes** permission). These fields can be used to add comments to the issue. After adding notes they appear in the history as shown in the following screenshot:

In the preceding screenshot, you can see that the private comments have a red strip to their left.

Note the two icons in the bottom-right corner. The pen icon allows you to edit the comment (if you have the **Edit own notes** permission, of course) and another one lets you quote the comment. By the way, quoting the issue description is also easy, you just need to click on the **Quote** link for this (to do so, go to the top of the issue page).

You might think that we are done with issue editing. But it's not so, Redmine also supports "bulk editing".

Bulk editing

Let's go back to the issue list. Right-click on any issue and you will see the contextual drop-down menu, as shown in the following screenshot:

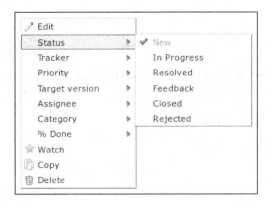

This menu provides you with a quick way of setting one value at a time for several issues.

It's not, however, recommended that you make one change at a time, unless it's just going to be a single change, as such changes will be added as separate history entries and e-mail notifications will be sent for each change separately.

If you plan to make several changes at a time to many issues, you will find the **Edit** contextual menu item more suitable. This menu item activates the bulk edit form:

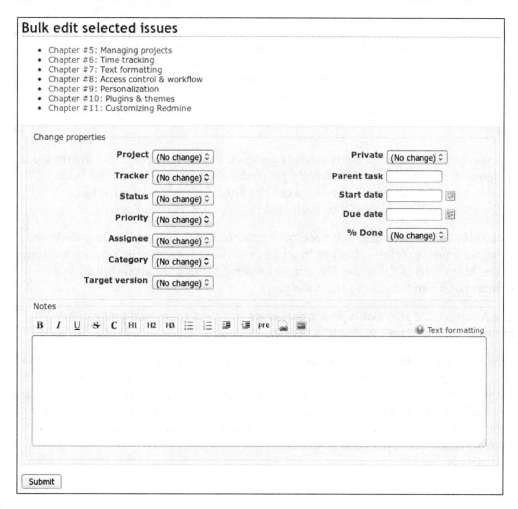

This form is similar to the issue edit form but changes made here apply to several issues.

Getting updates on issues

It's very important to know when the issue you are working on gets updated especially if it gets updated by a customer. So in this topic, we will review how to make sure that you will receive notifications about updates.

Redmine comes with e-mail notifications support, which can be enabled by users on a per-user and per-object basis using the "watching" mechanism. Thus, to be notified about changes made in an issue you need to open the issue page and click on the **Watch** link in the issue contextual menu which can be found at the top- and bottom-right corners.

> For watching to work, e-mail notifications should be configured (see *Chapter 3, Configuring Redmine*) and enabled for issue updates (and everything inside it) in **Administration | Settings | Email notifications**.
>
> Also, the **No events** notification type in the user's profile should not be selected. This option, in fact, disables all e-mail notifications.

If it was you who created the issue, it is assigned to you or if you were the previous assignee of the issue, you will already get updates about changes in this issue (in this case whether you will receive notifications depends on your settings in the user profile, which will be reviewed in *Chapter 9, Personalization*).

To be able to watch issues, you need to register in Redmine first. Luckily Redmine provides a way to follow changes in an issue without watching it. You can subscribe to the Atom feed of the issue. The corresponding **Atom** link can be found at the bottom-right hand corner of the issue page.

The Atom feed is also available for the issues list. Using this feed you can get information about new issues in a project.

While you can't "watch" new issues, you can still configure e-mail notifications about new issues to be sent to you. To do this, go to your profile using the **My account** link in the top-right menu. Under the **Email notifications**, select the **For any event on the selected projects only** option and select the projects you want to get notifications about the new issues for. But note that in this case you will be notified about any changes made to projects and not only new issues.

Issue related settings

Perhaps, settings we will review in this topic should have been reviewed at the beginning of the chapter and not at the end. But, this time, I wanted you to check the functionality first and then to learn how to configure and enable it.

Enabling or disabling issue tracking

Everything you have read in this chapter until now can actually be disabled for a project with just one click. I'm not sure, however, who and why may need to do this. Anyway just in case you got Redmine with issue tracking disabled by someone else or by default, here is how to enable (or disable) the issue tracking for a project.

Open the project's settings by clicking on the **Settings** tab in the project's menu and then click on the **Modules** tab in the **Settings** menu. Make sure the **Issue tracking** module is checked as shown in the following screenshot:

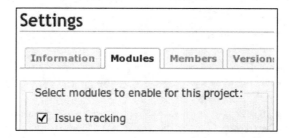

Unchecking the **Issues tracking** checkbox disables issue tracking for that project.

 The issue tracking module can be also disabled for projects by default in **Administration | Settings | Projects**.

Configuring issue tracking globally

In the previous chapter, we skipped two tabs in **Administration | Settings**, there I promised to explain them in the next two chapters. So it's the time to learn the **Issue tracking** tab. The following screenshot shows the various options available under the **Issue tracking** tab:

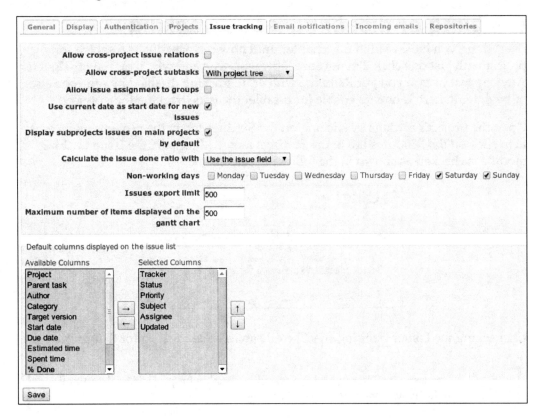

Let's go through the available options:

By default, you can add a related issue to an issue, but only if both are in the same project. If projects hosted on Redmine are related, it can be useful to be able to add related issues from different projects. To make this possible, check the **Allow cross-project issue relations** checkbox.

By default, you can't assign an issue to more than one user. By checking the **Allow issue assignment to groups** checkbox, you make it possible to assign an issue to a group. Groups can be created and edited in **Administration | Groups**.

Note, that assigning an issue to a group may end up with nobody taking responsibility for the issue, especially if the issue is boring.

I discovered that in most cases the first thing I do after creating a new issue is to clear the current date from the **Start date** field. So I'm quite happy that the **Use current date as start date for new issues** option exists. Unless you are sure all users will be creating issues on the day these issues should start, or you need any value in the **Start date** field, uncheck this option.

The **Display subprojects issues on main projects by default** option is unfortunately an option that can lead to confusion. If all of your subprojects are related deeply to parent projects you may want to enable this option to have subprojects issues listed along with issues in parent projects. However, having forgot or not having noticed this feature, users may eventually navigate to a subproject and then wonder where the other issues disappear to, or may wonder why certain settings (for example, issue categories, custom fields) configured for the parent project (and not for subprojects) do not work for some issues.

Despite what it may sound like, the **Calculate the issue done ratio with** option actually allows you to choose between the manually done ratio and the automatically done ration calculation.

If this option is set to **Use the issue status**, the **Done** issue field will disappear from the issue edit form and there will be no way to set the done ratio explicitly. For the automatic done ratio to work, you must configure done ratios for your issue statuses in **Administration | Issue statuses**. Otherwise issue done ratio will always be zero percent:

Issue statuses

New status   Update issue done ratios

Status	% Done	Default value	Issue closed	Sort		
New		✔		⇧ △ ▽ ⇩	🗑	Delete
In Progress	20			⇧ △ ▽ ⇩	🗑	Delete
Resolved	80			⇧ △ ▽ ⇩	🗑	Delete
Feedback	90			⇧ △ ▽ ⇩	🗑	Delete
Closed	100		✔	⇧ △ ▽ ⇩	🗑	Delete
Rejected			✔	⇧ △ ▽ ⇩	🗑	Delete

After switching to the automatic done ratio calculation you can click on the **Update issue done ratios** link to recalculate all done ratios.

> The **% Done** field for issue statuses is only available when the **Calculate the issue done ratio with** option is set to **Use the issue status**.

If the **Calculate the issue done ratio with** option is set to **Use the issue field**, users should specify the issue done ratio by themselves. But unfortunately in practice they often don't. For this reason, perhaps, the **Use the issue status** value, described earlier, was added and you should consider using it if the done ratio value is important for you.

The last option I would like to mention is the **Default columns displayed on the issue list**. Instead of making users select columns they want to see in the issue list, you should determine (in some way which is out of scope here) which columns are most common and select them on this page.

Issues and repository integration

In case you are already bored with the repository integration topics, let's see a really interesting way of integration.

We'll speak about settings available in **Administration | Settings | Repositories**:

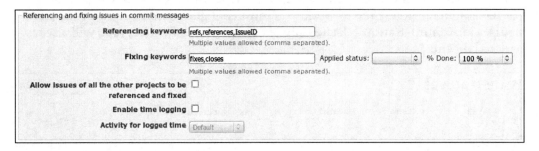

The **Referencing keywords** option specifies the words which, if found in commit messages before an issue number (# plus a number), produce issue references. You can specify several words separated by commas for this field. In commit messages, there can also be several issues listed after the words separated by commas (as well as by spaces or ampersands (&)). In practise, most likely you will want to put an asterisk (*) here which means that no special word is required for a reference to be created.

But what is a reference? Let's check the issue shown in the following screenshot:

Defect #11085

Wiki start page can't be changed

Added by Stanislav German-Evtushenko about 1 month ago. Updated about 1 month ago.

Status:	Closed	**Start date:**	
Priority:	Normal	**Due date:**	
Assignee:	-	**% Done:**	0%
Category:	Project settings		
Target version:	2.0.2		
Affected version:	2.0.1	**Resolution:**	Fixed

Description

- Redmine version: 2.0.1 (stable)
- Project settings -> Wiki -> Start page
    - Default value is: Wiki - **can't be changed**

History	Associated revisions
Updated by Jean-Philippe Lang about 1 month ago #1	Revision 9768
	Added by Jean-Philippe Lang about 1 month ago
• **Status** changed from *New* to *Confirmed*	
• **Target version** set to *2.0.2*	Fixed that wiki start page can't be changed (#11085).

Updated by Jean-Philippe Lang about 1 month ago   #2

- **Status** changed from *Confirmed* to *Resolved*
- **Resolution** set to *Fixed*

Fixed in r9768.

Updated by Jean-Philippe Lang about 1 month ago   #3

- **Status** changed from *Resolved* to *Closed*

Merged in 2.0-stable.

The block you see under the **Associated revisions** title is an issue reference which was created by a SVN commit command like (The **Fixing keywords** field was set to "*" (asterisk)):

```
$ svn commit -m "Fixed that wiki start page can't be changed (#11085)."
```

An issue can be referenced any number of times. The words specified in the **Fixing keywords** field can also change issue statuses and done ratios. All you need to do is choose which status and what done ratio to set. Unfortunately, you can specify only one status and one done ratio.

For example, if the **Applied status** option was set to **Closed**, the **% Done** was set to **100%**, and the **Fixing keywords** option included `closes`, the following SVN command would close the issue and set its done ratio to **100%**:

```
$ svn commit -m "Fixed that wiki start page can't be changed (closes #11085)."
```

The **Allow issues of all the other projects to be referenced and fixed** option controls whether you can reference and fix issues in other projects from the repository of another project. This is unlikely to be needed unless all your projects are deeply related.

Summary

Having learned the issue tracking module, you may consider you have learned Redmine as most of its users work mainly with issues. Other modules are not as critical to know for a usual user and, as it has been mentioned, the whole Redmine interface is quite easy to understand. But as this book is not named "Redmine: The very basics" I assume you want to learn more to be able not just to use, but also to master Redmine. And also if you want, to manage with Redmine!

The next chapter is intended mostly for project managers and site owners as it describes the capabilities of Redmine as a project management and project hosting application. But it will also be interesting for usual users as it teaches how to navigate projects, find information, and shares best practices.

5
Managing Projects

Don't confuse the title of this chapter with project management. This chapter is not about project management in software engineering but about managing projects in Redmine. Despite this, it actually targets project managers (as well as project owners, PR, and so on) as it describes what tools are available for projects and how they can be used. However, for the same reason, this chapter should not be ignored by regular users as it teaches you how to find the information that you need, where to put requests, how to subscribe to changes, and much more.

If the previous chapter described Redmine as an issue tracker, this one speaks about it as a project management and project hosting software. This is a kind of secondary role of Redmine.

In this chapter, we will cover the following topics:

- Modules
- Global configuration
- Creating project
- Basic project tabs
- Configuring project
- Closing project
- Project maintenance best practices
- Project list
- Administrating projects

Modules

In the previous chapter, I mentioned "modules" many times, especially "the issue tracking module". I think from the context you must have concluded that a "module" is a part of functionality, and that's correct. This is a part of functionality which is used for projects, therefore, modules are often called **project modules**.

Modules are like bricks, using which you can build a home page for your project. On the other side they also provide a way to disable functionality which is not needed. In fact, modules are nothing more than "virtual units" as they are not plugins, their files are not stored separately from the core, and so on.

I thought a lot before starting this chapter with modules and I decided to do this as you will have to choose which modules to enable for a project or all projects and which not. But how would you know without understanding what is provided by those modules?

Modules can be also added by plugins but here we will discuss only the core modules. However, not all of them will be reviewed. Thus, in the previous chapter, we have actually discussed the issue tracking module, but we have skipped the **Roadmap** tab which is also provided by this module, so we will review only this tab here. Also we will skip the time tracking module as it will be reviewed in the next chapter.

Issue tracking

The whole previous chapter was about what this project module does. As I have mentioned there I can't imagine the reason why one may need to disable it but, anyway, such capability is supported.

Roadmap

In addition to the **Issues** and **New issue** tabs, which have been already discussed, when enabled, this module adds the **Roadmap** tab:

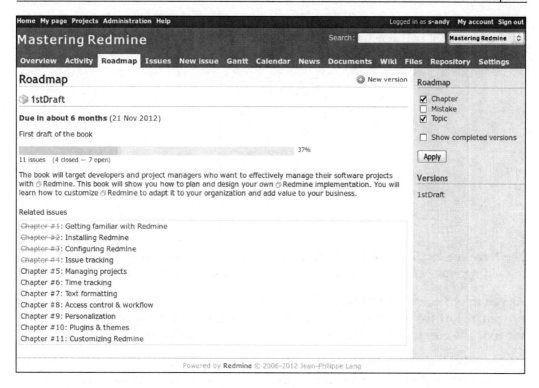

This page shows the overall progress for versions of the project and lists closed and open issues for some trackers this way producing feature lists for versions.

On the sidebar, you can select trackers which will be shown on the roadmap. By default only trackers with the **Issues displayed in roadmap** option checked (in **Administration | Trackers**) are selected here.

The roadmap shows only open versions by default but you can change this by checking the **Show completed versions** option and clicking on the **Apply** button.

If a project has subprojects there will also be **Subprojects** option allowing you to trigger showing subprojects' versions and issues on the roadmap.

Under the **Versions** label, you see the list of all available versions (my project has only one version which is named **1stDraft**). Completed versions will be available under the toggle box with the same title, for example:

Versions
1.06
1.07
2.00
▾ Completed versions
1.00
1.01
1.02
1.03
1.04
1.05

The **New version** link you see in the top-right corner of the content area is a shortcut for adding new version (we will review versions later in this chapter).

As you might guess the **1stDraft** title near the yellow box icon is the title of the version. Below the title the effective date is shown if it has been specified for the version. The effective date line also includes human readable remaining time.

The progress bar, the main element on the roadmap page, uses a simple algorithm to show done and completeness ratios (the latter uses a slightly lighter color). The done ratio (or closed issues ratio) shows how many issues from the total number are closed. The completeness ratio shows what percentage of the rest of the issues are completed. For both ratios Redmine tries to take estimated hours into account.

 You can click on issues counts below the progress bar to see the list of the referenced issues.

Below the progress bar and above the issue list, Redmine shows the content of the associated Wiki page. What this page is and how can it be specified will be reviewed later when discussing versions.

 You can also right-click on an issue in the issue list and the contextual pop-up menu, which can be used to manipulate the issue, will appear.

Version page

If you click on the version title on the roadmap page, you will be redirected to the version page:

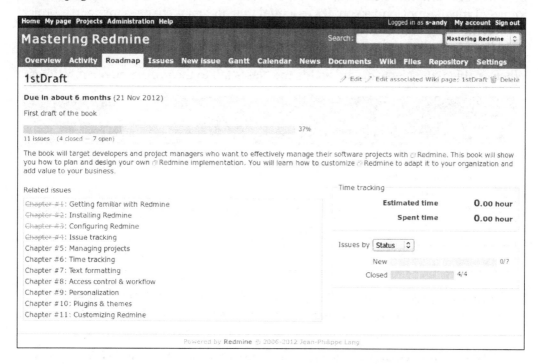

As you see the version page contains generally the same information as the roadmap but it is about one version. Also, unlike the roadmap, the version page lists all issues.

This page contains the contextual menu allowing you to modify the version (the **Edit** link), edit the associated Wiki page, or delete the version.

In addition, it has a special block which allows you to see the completeness ratios for different values of issue properties. Thus, it's possible to see the completeness progress bars for different categories, trackers, statuses, priorities, authors, and assignees. To change the view of the block, you just need to select a different issue property.

If you have enabled the time tracking module, this page also shows the total estimated time and the total spent time for issues in this version.

News

Could you imagine if there were no official news about release of your favorite project? For example, no news on the Apple website about new iOS, no official news for new Linux kernel, and so on. It's essential that all major changes made to a project are accompanied with official news from the project owners. Therefore, Redmine would not be a good project hosting solution without the **News** module.

When enabled, the **News** module adds the **News** tab to the project menu as follows:

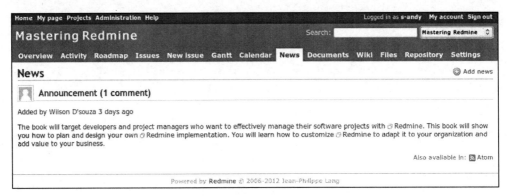

Under this tab, project news are listed with shortened content. The full content is shown when we open the news page by clicking on the news title.

 You can subscribe to the project news using the **Atom** link and your favorite RSS reader.

If you have the **Manage news** permission, you will also see the **Add news** link in the top-right corner. Clicking on this link adds the following form above the news list:

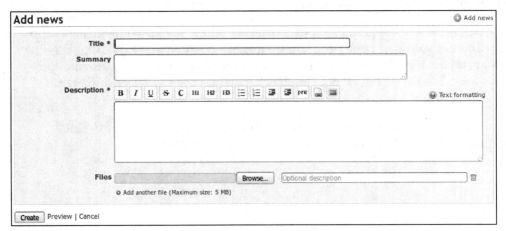

As shown the news description can use Wiki formatting. To check if the formatting is correct, you can use the **Preview** link below the form.

The **Summary** field has a special meaning and should always be specified. This field is used as a short description of the news. Don't confuse it with the shortened description shown in the news list. The summary is shorter and does not support Wiki formatting. Thus, the summary along with news title is shown on the Redmine's start page and on the project's start page.

When we click on the news title, we get redirected to the news page:

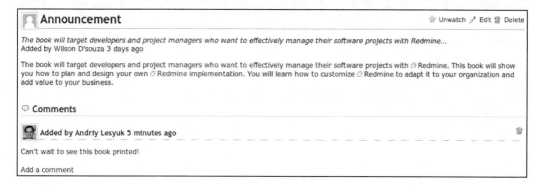

If you have the **Comment news** permission, you will see the **Add a comment** link on this page. Clicking on this link opens a form containing just one text area for comment content which also supports Wiki formatting.

If you are interested in getting notifications about new comments in the news, you can click on the **Watch** link in the contextual menu (after this the link turns into the **Unwatch** link). Other links in the contextual menu allow us to edit or delete the news.

Documents

The **Documents** module will be useful if your project has a lot of documents. So let's see what this module can do for you.

This module adds the **Documents** tab to the project menu, which is available only if a user has the **View documents** permission:

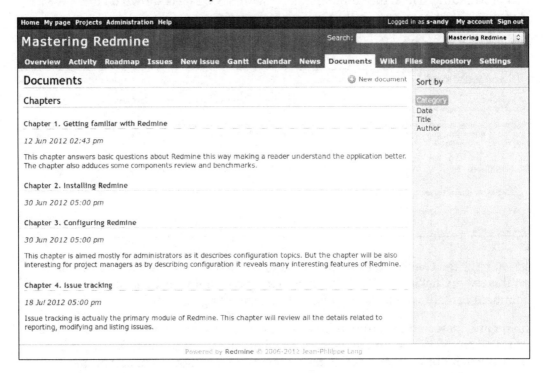

Titles *Chapter 1*, *Getting familiar with Redmine* and *Chapter 2*, *Installing Redmine*, and so on are actually document titles. Below the title, you see the date when you added the document and a short description.

In the preceding screenshot, documents are listed by categories, thus, the **Chapters** title above the document list is the value of a document category. Document categories are specified globally in **Administration | Enumerations | Document categories**.

It's also possible to list documents by date, title, and author, to do this just click on the corresponding link on the sidebar. When listed by titles instead of the whole title only the first letter is used for groups:

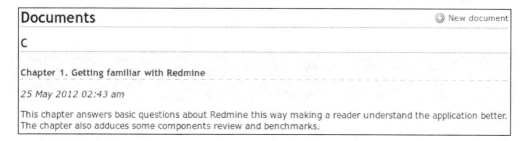

Clicking on the **New document** link opens the following form:

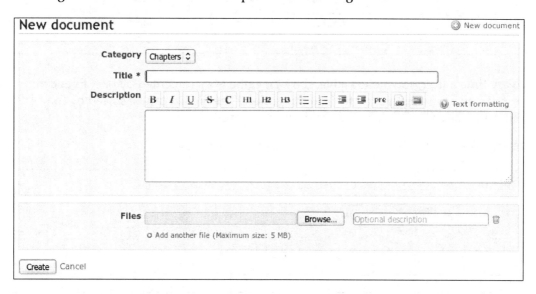

You may find it confusing that a document can actually contain many files. Just do not take it literally, in Redmine a document is a documentation unit which can include, for example, images, chapters as separate files.

To edit a document, click on its title and you will be redirected to the document page containing the **Edit** link as well as the **Delete** link.

Document Management System Features plugin

For a better document management solution you can try the DMSF plugin for Redmine from Vít Jonáš at `http://code.google.com/p/redmine-dmsf/`.

Files

You will need the **Files** module if you want users of your project to be able to download project files (for example, releases) directly from Redmine.

This module adds the **Files** tab to the project menu:

Every time a user downloads a file, the **D/L** value is incremented by one. Files can be put into a version or directly into the project. The file list can be sorted by the filename, the date, the size, and the download count.

If you click on the **New file** link you get the form as follows:

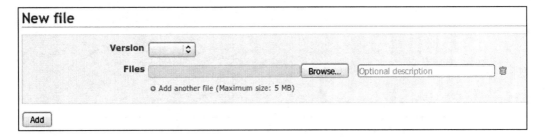

With this simple form, you can upload a file to Redmine to be placed under the **Files** tab.

What is the difference between files and documents?

Unlike documents, files can be added to a particular project version. For files, Redmine provides the MD5 hash and saves the download count. Files are available right under the **Files** tab and are sorted by the version recency. Unlike downloading files for a document attachment one needs to open the documentation unit first.

Wiki

Under this topic, we will review what is provided by the Wiki module. The Wiki syntax will be reviewed in *Chapter 7, Text Formatting*.

> Don't confuse Wiki formatting with the Wiki module, the former is a component part of Redmine and is used everywhere in it and the latter is a virtual module, which just allows you to disable the **Wiki** tab for a project. Thus, the Wiki formatting still remains available for issues, Wiki pages associated with versions, document descriptions, and so on if the Wiki module is disabled.

The **Wiki** tab plays the role of the entry point into the project Wiki system. By default there is no Wiki page in the project, that is, the entry point page just does not exist. Therefore, by clicking on the **Wiki** tab you get the Wiki page edit form (or an error, if you don't have the permission to edit the Wiki page):

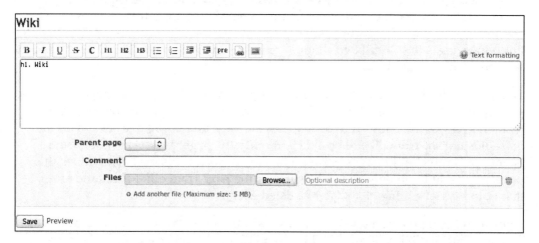

Naturally the content field supports the Wiki syntax. A short description of this syntax becomes available when you click on the **Text formatting** link. If you click on the **Preview** link, you can check how the Wiki page is going to be rendered. The preview of the page will be rendered below the form.

The form also allows you to specify the **Comment** for changes made to the Wiki page. I usually write "Created" here (a little bit later I will show you what comments are used for). Using the **Add another file** link, you can add any number of files to the Wiki page (usually these will be images, which will be shown on the page).

The **Parent page** field can be used to make a page the child of another page. This will only influence the layout and the Wiki pages index. Thus, the layout will be influenced by addition of the breadcrumbs:

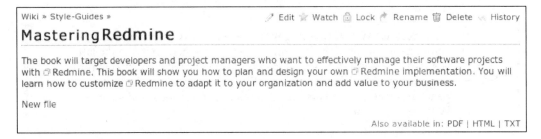

Breadcrumbs here are **Wiki** and **Style-Guides** links in the top-left corner which point to parent Wiki pages.

The preceding screenshot also shows the Wiki page layout. To the right of the breadcrumbs, you see the contextual menu. The **Edit** link from this menu redirects you to the Wiki page edit form similar to the one we have just discussed. The **Watch** link allows users to subscribe to changes made to this Wiki page. The **Delete** link can be used to remove the Wiki page.

Thus, the **Lock** link is only available to users having the **Protect wiki pages** permission. The title of the link is a little bit confusing as it may be considered that no more changes are allowed to be made to the page after you have clicked on the link—it is not so. You will still be able to modify the page, as well as other users having the **Protect wiki pages** permission. Any of such users may also unlock the page. So, this link can only be used to protect the page from other Redmine users, that is, to restrict editing of a page to trusted users.

Before discussing the **Rename** link, let's speak about how to create a Wiki page. Similar to other Wiki systems, a Wiki page in Redmine can be created in two ways:

- **By adding a page name into the URL**: For example, if URL for a project is http://redmine.packtpub.com/projects/mastering-redmine we can create Test-Page by adding its name to URL this way: http://redmine. packtpub.com/projects/mastering-redmine/wiki/Test-Page (note the additional /wiki/ path). Following this URL will invoke the previously discussed Wiki page edit form, which you can use to create new page (of course, if you have the permissions to do so).

- **By adding a link pointing to new page on any existing page**: The Wiki page you are going to create should be referenced from somewhere. Just add a link to this not-yet-existing page there. The syntax for adding a link to a page is as follows:

```
[[Test-Page|Any display text]]
```

This link will be rendered red, which means that the page it is referencing does not exist. When you click on this link, you will be redirected to the Wiki page edit form.

> The latter method is easier and should be preferable as it also sets the page you are referencing from as the parent page automatically. Don't forget to clear the **Parent page** if you did not want it though.

But what if you made a mistake in the page name? This is why the **Rename** link was added. Clicking on this link redirects to this screen:

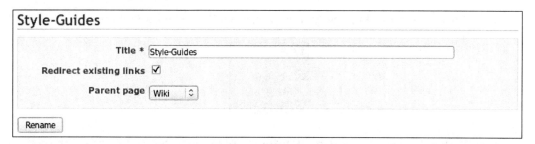

The **Title** is actually the name of the Wiki page as it is added to the URL. Therefore, another option **Redirect existing links** was added to the form. If this option is checked the page will still be accessible by the old name (and URL). On this form, you can also change the parent page.

> Always check the **Redirect existing links** option if the page was available under the old name for some time. It's recommended not only because users could save the old URL to their favorites, but also because search engine bots could have index it already.

The last link from the Wiki page contextual menu that we need to review is the **History** link. When you click on it the following screen will be loaded:

Mastering-Redmine

History

#		Updated	Author	Comment	
2	◉	28 Jul 2012 09:42 pm	Andriy Lesyuk	Added sample content	Annotate
1	◉	28 Jul 2012 08:18 pm	Andriy Lesyuk	Created	Annotate

View differences (1-2/2)

This is where the earlier mentioned comments are shown. By choosing versions (**1** and **2**) and clicking on the **View difference** button, you can check the changes that were made to the Wiki page. The **Annotate** button to the right of the version can be used to check who authored specific lines of the Wiki page.

Each Wiki page also includes links for exporting the page content into **PDF**, **HTML**, and **TXT** formats (exporting works with some limitations, of course, thus page references are not converted into rich format).

On the sidebar of each Wiki page, you will also see the navigation menu:

Wiki

Start page
Index by title
Index by date

Navigation in a Wiki system is usually implemented using the Wiki syntax (that is, through links). But if authors of Wiki pages failed to comply with it, you can always use this navigation menu to find the page you need.

Custom content on the sidebar under the Wiki tab

Redmine allows adding custom Wiki content to the sidebar of the Wiki module. To do this you just need to create a Wiki page named `Sidebar`. Its content will be shown on each Wiki page above the navigation menu. The sidebar content should start with a `h3.` title (to look similar to other sidebar titles).

The Wiki pages index is available under two links—**Index by title** and **Index by date**. The former link also displays the structure of Wiki pages:

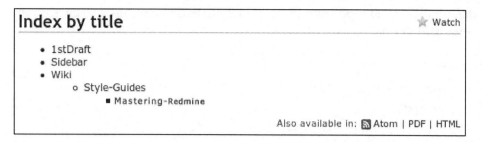

The Wiki pages index, as seen from the screenshot, can be watched. If you watch it you will be notified about every new Wiki page added to the project. In addition to watching this, you can subscribe to the list using the **Atom** link.

Redmine Wiki Extensions plugin

You might want to install the Wiki Extensions plugin by r-labs, which allows you to add tags and comments to Wiki pages, to use Wiki pages as tabs in the project menu, and much more, see at `http://www.r-labs.org/projects/r-labs/wiki/Wiki_Extensions_en`.

Repository

Redmine was designed mainly for software projects. Each software project has source code, so it's essential for Redmine to have a source code browser. Nowadays software projects often use revision control systems for collaboration, therefore Redmine also needs to support such systems. All such functionality in Redmine is provided for projects by the Repository module which adds the **Repository** tab to the project menu as well as the **Repositories** tab to the project's settings. Let's review the latter first.

Go to the **Settings** tab of the project, then select the **Repositories** tab:

By default there is no repository in the project, to add one we need to click on the **New repository** link:

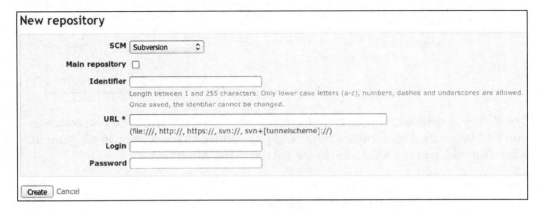

The **SCM** field in this form contains only SCMs which have been permitted by administrator in **Administration | Settings | Repositories** tab.

The **Main repository** checkbox must be set for one of project repositories (any). If it is the first repository the **Main repository** flag will be enforced on saving. If you check it for another repository this flag will be automatically unset from the previous main repository.

The **Identifier** field is required for sequential repositories as it is used to differentiate project repositories.

Values of other fields, and available fields as well, depend on SCM. To determine the correct values for these fields consult your repository administrators.

Git index is slow?

If you have commits with huge amount of modified files and directories the Git loading can become slow. Try disabling the **Report last commit for files and directories** option for Git to resolve this issue.

All SCMs require repositories to be already available. This form just registers them in Redmine, it does not create repositories. You can configure automatic repositories creation with the **reposman.rb** tool (for more information on this refer *Chapter 3, Configuring Redmine*).

> You can also use the SCM Creator plugin for Redmine which allows creating repositories directly from the discussed form, see at ~~projects~~.andriylesyuk.com/projects/scm-creator.

Afte   the repository list of
the

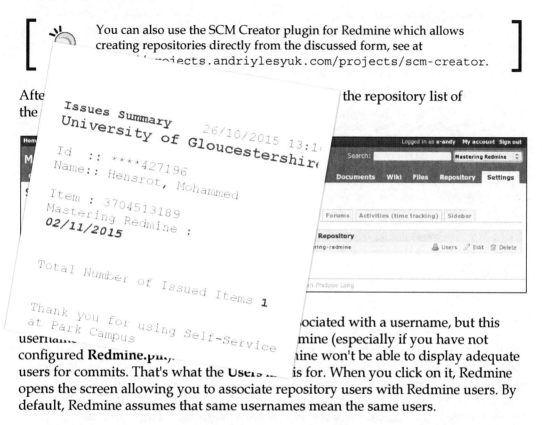

After ... ociated with a username, but this
usern...   mine (especially if you have not
configured **Redmine.p...**   ...ine won't be able to display adequate
users for commits. That's what the Users ... is for. When you click on it, Redmine
opens the screen allowing you to associate repository users with Redmine users. By
default, Redmine assumes that same usernames mean the same users.

Not sure if you have noticed but in addition to the repository, which appeared in the
repository list, the project now has a new **Repository** tab (near the **Settings** tab). This
new tab is also provided by the Repository module but appears only when at least
one repository is added to the project.

As my demo project does not have any sources, let's review the **Repository** tab on
`Redmine.org`:

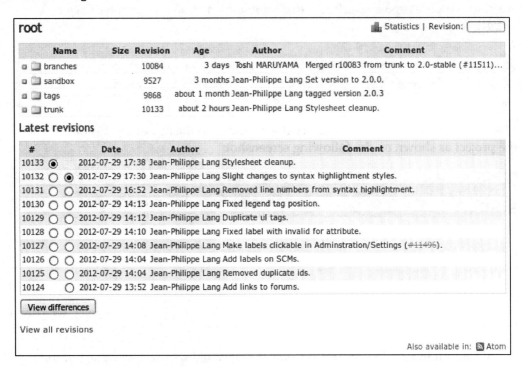

The upper part of the screen allows you to browse the source code. You can either
click on directories or use the plus icon to unfold the directory content. The lower
part contains information about the last 10 commits which were made to the
repository. To view all the commits, you can click on the **View all revisions** link.
To view some basic statistics when commits were made and who committed
changes, use the **Statistics** link in the top-right corner.

 This screen also allows subscribing to commits using the **Atom** link.

Clicking on revision numbers you can see a brief summary of changes that were made in this revision:

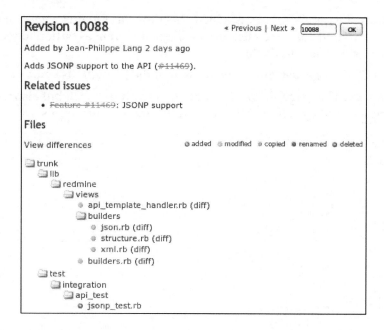

Choosing revisions and clicking on the **View differences** button on the main screen or clicking on a **diff** link on the revision page, you can check what was changed:

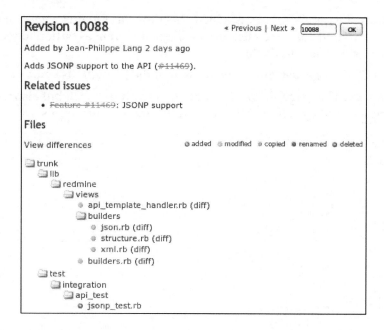

If you click on a filename, you will be redirected to the page containing all information about that file. This section will have four links:

- **History**: Lists only revisions which affect the file. On this page you can also select two revisions and click on the **View differences** button to see changes, which were made to the file.

- **View**: This page just shows the content of the file with its syntax highlighted.

- **Annotate**: This page shows the content of the file as well but also includes who authored each line of the revised file and in which revision:

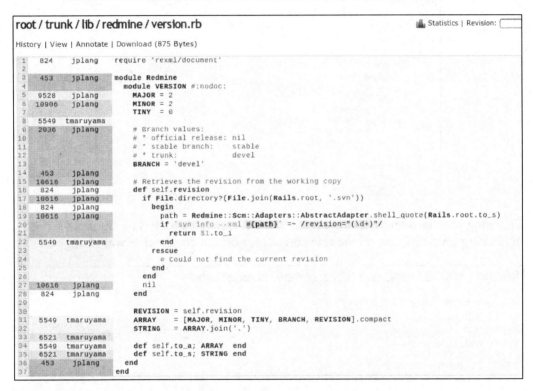

- **Download**: This link triggers the file download.

That's all I wanted to show you so far. But wait, have you wondered how the **Repository** tab looks if more than one repository is used? Absolutely the same! In the case of many repositories, the sidebar contains links allowing you to switch to different repository:

You can play with the repository browser more on your own to see all its pages and features. In my opinion, the Repository module is the most visually beautiful core module of Redmine so it's really worth playing with (if you don't have a repository to play with you can use for example, `http://www.redmine.org` or `http://projects.andriylesyuk.com` (my projects)).

Forums

The Forums module is often undeservedly ignored by Redmine users and, therefore, in practice it is underused. So what is the use of this module?

A project needs to provide some means to support users, to answer their questions, and so on. The Forums module adds discussion boards which make this possible. Each board can have a name which reflects the specific topic of discussion, for example, "Development using API". On a board, there can be an unlimited number of threads which are called **topics**, each topic can have any number of posts which are called **messages**.

But what's wrong? In practice, users rarely use forums to ask for support. Most likely they will use issues for this, especially if Redmine comes (and by default it does) with the "Support" tracker, which is intended for such usage.

You can ask: "Why not?" or "Why use forums instead?".

- First: Support issues will mix with others (bugs, features). This will make the issue list harder to read and will require users to configure filters.

- Second: When you resolve an issue you should close it! And forum threads remain open even after they have been resolved. This way with forums you will assemble the troubleshooting database while with issues you are going to get duplicates (you will need to transfer every solution to a Wiki that is good for forums as well though).

- Third: Topics can be categorized using boards. While issues also support categories, users can't subscribe to them, but they can subscribe to boards and topics. The possibility to subscribe will let volunteers help you support customers.

- Fourth: Forums and issues use different permission sets. This means that you can have a special role of community supporters and won't need to consider them when granting permissions to issues.

As you see forums are to some extent better for customer support.

 If you decide to go with forums, you may also need to remove the **Support** tracker to avoid confusion.

Before we proceed with checking the capabilities of this module, we need to configure it. Its configuration can be done in project settings under the **Forums** tab:

Click on the **New forum** link to add a new discussion board:

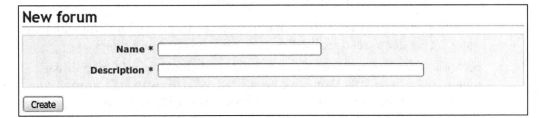

The value of the **Name** field should briefly describe the topic of the forum. The **Description** field should contain a longer description. Thus, good examples of forums are:

Name	General discussions
Description	If no other forum fits, write here
Name	Help
Description	If things do not work, ask here
Name	Development
Description	Anything about development should be written here

As soon as you create the first forum in a project, the **Forums** tab will be added to the project menu:

If you have only one forum, you will get its content once you click on the **Forums** tab, if you have more forums you will get their index first.

As you see, you can watch the forum by clicking on the **Watch** link or by subscribing to the **Atom** feed. If you have more than one forum, you will also be able to subscribe to new forums using the **Atom** link on the index page.

Now let's add a topic. When you click on the **New message** link the message edit form appears before the forum content:

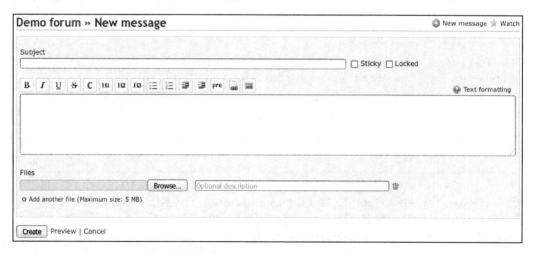

Forum messages, as you see, also support Wiki formatting and you can also preview what you have written using the **Preview** link.

New elements on this form are the **Sticky** and **Locked** options. If the **Sticky** option is set the topic will always appear on the top of the list and if the **Locked** option is set, replies will not be allowed for this topic (consider it like closing the discussion).

After saving the message you will be redirected to the topic page:

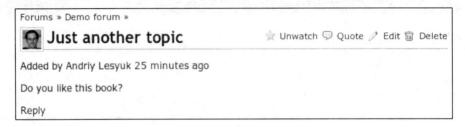

The user who creates a topic is automatically added to its watcher list (that's why we have the **Unwatch** link on the screenshot).

To reply to a message, we can use either the **Quote** link, which will insert quoted content of the original message into the reply, or the **Reply** link. In both cases, an additional form, which contains just a text area, is shown under the **Reply** link.

Now let's check back to the forum page (I added several other messages):

Here you see how sticky and locked topics are shown. The **RE: Just another topic** link is a quick shortcut to the last message in the topic. The table is sortable by the **Created, Replies**, and **Last message** columns.

Calendar

The **Calendar** module adds a tab with the same name to the project menu:

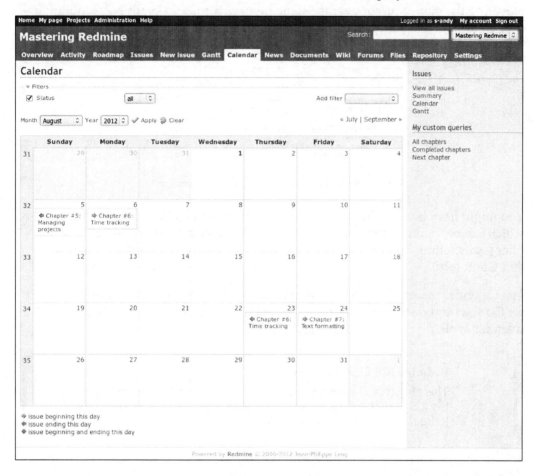

By default the calendar for the current month is shown under this tab. This calendar shows start and due dates of issues, if they are specified. Thus, the start date is shown with the green arrow pointing forward and the due date is shown with the red arrow pointing backward. If start and due date are the same the red rhombus is used instead.

If versions have the due dates, they will also get shown on the calendar:

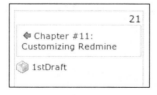

Here **1stDraft** is the name of the project version, which is also a link pointing to the version page.

Hovering the mouse cursor over the issue invokes the issue details box containing such information as assignee name, priority, status, and so on, as shown in the following screenshot:

You might have noticed that the calendar page contains a filter similar to the one which can be found on the issue list. In fact, this can be considered to be the same filter (as its settings are preserved when you move between the **Issues**, **Calendar**, and **Gantt** tabs).

The **Calendar** module is really useful if issue reporters and/or assignees always set the start and due dates. If an issue has neither it won't be displayed on the calendar at all.

Redmine ICS Export plugin

This plugin can be installed to let exporting issues and versions dates in the ICS format, which is compatible with most major calendar software: `http://code.google.com/p/redmics/`

Gantt

It seems that no project management software is complete without the Gantt chart. This type of bar chart is perfect for representing the flow of work on the project in terms of time and resources availability.

In Redmine, this chart is available under the **Gantt** tab in the project menu, of course, if the **Gantt** module has been enabled.

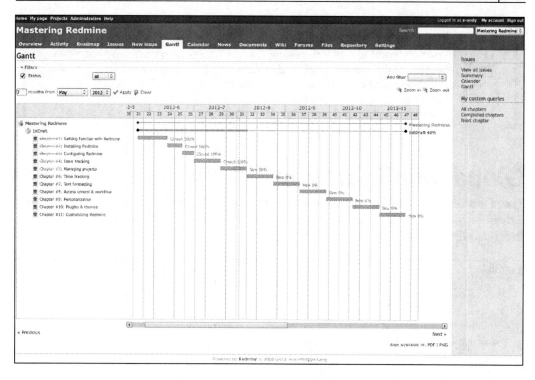

Like the calendar, the **Gantt** module uses the same issue filter which is used for issues, which means that under the **Issues** tab, you can configure what to show on the Gantt chart. The **Zoom in** and **Zoom out** links allow you to zoom the chart down to week days, or up to months respectively.

The **Previous** and **Next** links under the chart allow moving between periods. For example, if the chart shows *January – June 2012*, the **Previous** link will move to *July – December 2011* and the **Next** link will move to *July – December 2012*. The resulting chart can also be exported to PDF or PNG.

> To be able to export the Gantt chart to PNG, you need to have RMagick installed.

When you hover your mouse cursor over a bar, the issue details box, identical to the one we get by hovering the mouse cursor over issues on the calendar, is shown.

Better Gantt Chart plugin

You may want to check the Better Gantt Chart plugin originally authored by Alexey Kuleshov, which adds many interesting features to the Redmine Gantt chart including arrows, that connect related issues on the chart: `https://github.com/drewkeller/redmine_better_gantt_chart`.

Global configuration

There is still one tab in the global settings menu (which can be found in **Administration | Settings**) that we have not discussed yet. Yes, it's the **Projects** tab. Let's check it out now:

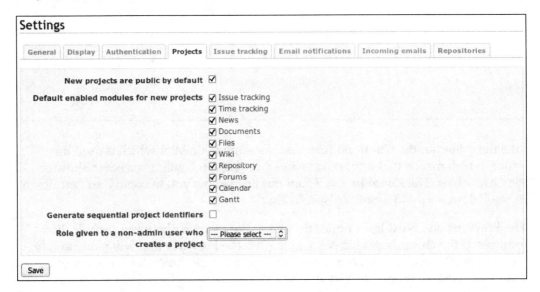

A project in Redmine can be either public or private. A public project is visible to everyone, even to unregistered users (unless you restricted access for the whole Redmine by enabling the **Authorization required** option under the **Authentication** tab). Of course, access to some of the project pages can be still restricted but even if everything is restricted the public project will still be visible! It will just appear to be empty. A private project is the opposite, it is not seen to non-members whatever you do! You can let unregistered users and non-members see everything but, still, such projects won't be visible to them.

So the **New projects are public by default** option actually specifies the default value for the **Public** checkbox of the project form. This option should be checked only if all of your projects are to be public (just to save time by not requiring users to set it). Otherwise it can happen that a project, which was to be private, can be accidentally left public. Even if you want all of your projects to be public, you may still want to uncheck this option to avoid empty projects in the project list as users may need some time to put data into them. Later, when their projects will be ready for publication, they can make them public. You should consider this especially if you position your Redmine installation as a list of active and up-to-date software, so your users won't get confused when they see no data in a project.

The next option is why we have started this chapter with modules review. Now, I believe, you can easily determine what modules you need. But remember that here we select modules which are going to be enabled by default for new projects. Users will still be able to select modules, that you have not selected here, and deselect modules, that you have selected here here.

Perhaps, it's a good idea to uncheck all modules here except the **Issue tracking** module as, in practice, users often skip modules configuration on project creation and leave them as they are. This results with empty and unused news, documents, files, Wiki, and so on.

Each project in Redmine has a unique identifier, a short string with letters, digits, dashes, and underscores in it. The main goal of this identifier is to replace the numerical ID, which is used internally by something more readable and memorable.

For this reason, I'm not sure why one may need to check the next option. Perhaps, it was added for the cases when users did not care about identifiers readability. In other words, if you just don't want users to devise project identifiers and do not care about their memorability, you can set the **Generate sequential project identifiers** option. When this option is set, Redmine generates sequential identifiers for new projects. Thus, if the identifier of the previous project was `redmine` the next suggested identifier would be `redminf` (not very smart, is it?) and if the previous identifier was `chapter-1` the next would be `chapter-2`.

For the **Role given to a non-admin user who creates a project** option, you should select a role which will be automatically assigned to the user who creates the project. This should be a role with project management permissions, of course. If you don't do this such users will get the first role from the role list (which can be seen in **Administration | Roles and permissions**), which can miss some important permissions. This way you can avoid confusion when users discover that some things are not available for them in their just created projects.

Creating a project

Now, when we have chosen default values for project fields, let's create a project. This can be done in two places, either by clicking the **New project** link on the project list (click on the **Projects** top menu item to get there) or by clicking on the link with the same name in the **Administration | Projects**. In both cases, you will get the following form:

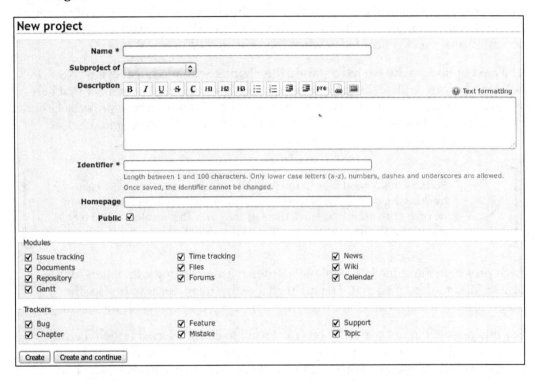

Not much to explain here, is there? However, let's speak about the best practises for filling this form. That's, perhaps, the most important form in Redmine as by using it you actually create the face for your project.

To be able to create projects, a user must have the **Create project** permission. If you want to allow any registered user to create projects you need to grant this permission to the **Non member** built-in role.

The value of the **Name** field, which is required, should be as short as possible but still descriptive. Usually you will want it to be identical to the project name. However, if your project is a part of another system you may also want to prefix it with the name of that system, for example, "Redmine SCM Creator" where "SCM Creator" is the project name and "Redmine" is the name of the system this project has been developed for.

Each project in Redmine can have any number of subprojects, each subproject can have any number of own subprojects, and so on, to any nesting level. But in what cases should subprojects be used?

Taking their implementation into account, I come to the conclusion that subprojects should be projects which are closely related to the main project but still independent. They should not be like repository branches as branches share the source code and subprojects don't (subproject can have their own repositories and do not share the parent ones). They should not be like project modules either (for example, Forums for Redmine) as the latter can't be used or distributed separately (subprojects can have their own files under the **Files** tab, so plugins for Redmine fit better than forums here). They can be related to the parent project versions (Redmine supports versions sharing with subprojects). They can share the work flow with the parent project (the roadmap of the parent project can include issues and versions from subprojects). Issues in subprojects can be related to issues in the parent project (the parent project issue list can include issues from subprojects). Different people can work on the parent project, its subprojects (members are not shared), and so on.

Of course, these are not the rules or an official recommendations (I'm not aware of any official recommendations, by the way). These are some implementation limitations and features that you should consider when adding subprojects! I just wanted to give you a general idea of what can be put into subprojects.

Redmine users often use project nesting for implementing project categories which are, unfortunately, missing in Redmine. While this helps I would recommend avoiding doing this. The side effect of such "categories" are empty projects with empty tabs and with grand total time spent for all subprojects, activity lists which include activities on subprojects, issues of all subprojects, and with some weird members (users having the **Create subprojects** permission which were added specially for creating subprojects) and so on.

Generally, the subprojects feature seems to be incomplete as often users face different limitations even when they use it the "right" way (for example, issue categories are not shared). So the decision to create a project as a subproject should be based on available features and not on the visual presentation (which is the main reason for using parent projects as categories).

But why did I write all this? All this is about the **Subproject of** option, which can be used to make one project a subproject of another one.

 You can also add subprojects using the **New subproject** link on the parent project overview page (soon we will discuss this page). Clicking on this link opens the same new project form but with the prefilled value for the **Subproject of** field.

The **Description** field should contain a short summary of the project. While this field is actually optional, it is highly recommended to specify it as it will be the first source of information about your project (it is shown on the project start page, which will be reviewed soon, and in the project list). When writing this description, remember about the target audience. Thus, for customers you should specify the main features of the project, as well as its requirements, and so on. But if Redmine is used only by developers and other employees there is no need to list its features, instead write about the location of the team, mention technologies which are used, and so on.

The meaning of the **Identifier** field was also discussed in the previous topic. Here I would like to emphasize that the value of this field should be as easy-to-remember as possible, whilst at the same time being informative and similar to the project name. It will be used in project URLs (for example, `http://redmine.packtpub.com/projects/mastering-redmine` where `mastering-redmine` is the identifier) and, therefore, will be indexed by search engine bots (for this reason it is recommended to use dashes instead of underscores in the identifier). But also it can be used by users in Wikis to create cross-project Wiki links (see *Chapter 7, Text Formatting*).

The **Homepage** field is optional and can be safely skipped. If you specify a value for it (which should start with `http://`) it will just be shown on the project start page.

The **Public** field was also discussed in the previous topic. Its value can be changed anytime so in most cases you will want to uncheck this option until the time your project is ready for going public.

Now we come to the modules again. Luckily, we already know what each module stands for so it will be easy to choose. The only thing you should take into account when choosing modules is that you should not enable them unless you plan to use them right away. Do not select modules which you are not sure you will use, it is better to enable them later, before using them. Thus, if you enable **Wiki**, be sure to add a Wiki page, if you enable **News**, be sure to write news (for example, about adding the project) and so on. Avoid users' disappointment when they come to an empty module page.

It's a little bit too early to discuss trackers and workflows as they will be reviewed later in this book. Here you see only tracker names, the associated workflows are what you actually need to consider. Also, which trackers you need, depends on the project (for example, I doubt you need the **Chapter** tracker). So the only thing, I recommend here, is to enable as few trackers as possible because high numbers of trackers may confuse your users. However, it is always a good idea to have trackers for all possible cases in your project. In this case default trackers are unlikely to be very useful and will need customizing. But all these issues will be discussed later in *Chapter 8*, *Access Control and Workflow*.

Basic project tabs

Having created a project you noticed that three tabs appeared that we have not reviewed yet. All these tabs are not provided by modules but are parts of the project itself. These are the **Overview**, **Activity** and **Settings** tabs. If all project modules are disabled, there will be only these three tabs (but the **Settings** tab will be visible only to project managers).

The **Settings** tab will be discussed in the next topic, right now let's speak about the **Overview** and **Activity** tabs.

Overview

The overview page is the project start page, therefore, it collates information that can be of interest for users. However, users who are using Redmine intensively rarely come to this page as they know where else they can find the information they need. But new project users, especially the first time users, come to this page more often. So it can be concluded that the overview page is intended mostly for new users. But, still, this page contains information which you won't find elsewhere.

So let's check the **Overview** tab:

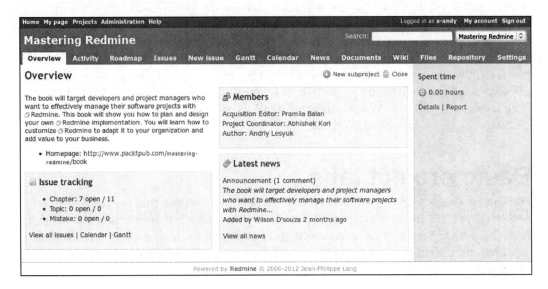

The description of the project, that you see under the **Overview** label, is what we specify in the **Description** field of the project form. Below the description, you see the value of the **Homepage** field. To the right from the **Overview** label, there is the **New subproject** link which opens the new project form with the **Subproject of** field set to this project. All these elements are already known to you.

Near the **New subproject** link, you see the **Close** link, which will be mentioned later in this chapter. On the sidebar, you see the grand total of the time spent on this project. This is related to the Time tracking module and we will discuss it in the next chapter.

And now let's speak about blocks. The content of the **Latest news** block also should be familiar to you as it contains the latest news provided by the **News** module, which was discussed before. This block also contains the **View all news** link, which actually redirects you to the **News** tab.

The next two blocks are available only on this page. The **Issue tracking** block lists the number of open and total (open plus closed) issues for each tracker in the project. Clicking on the tracker, you will be redirected to the issue list with the issue filter set to show only issues of this tracker.

The **Members** block lists all project members grouped by their roles. Project managers and administrators can see this information also in the project settings but usual users can find it only here.

Activity

At very first glance the activity page may seem to be odd as it just contains a short summary of the latest actions in the project and this information is also available elsewhere. Moreover, Redmine allows users to watch or subscribe to the actions of the objects they are interested in.

But what if you missed some notifications or there were too many notifications? In this case, you can always check the activity page and filter actions to find what you need. This is especially useful if you don't use notifications or you are interested in all events in the project (you don't have to be its manager for this).

The activity page, I'm talking about, is available under the **Activity** tab:

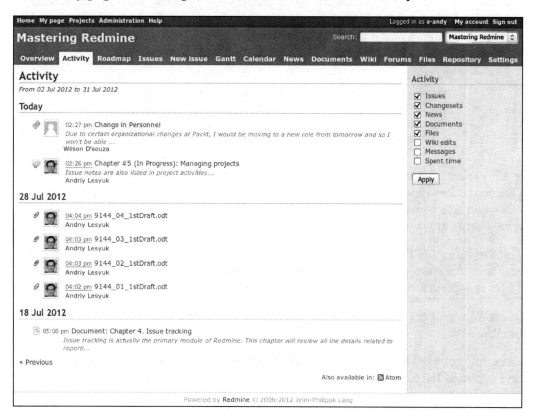

By default, the activity page shows the summary of the events in the project for the last 30 days, but the number of days can be changed using the **Days displayed on project activity** option in **Administration | Settings | General**. In the preceding screenshot, you can see the dates, for which activities are shown, under the **Activity** title. At the bottom of the activity list, you can see the **Previous** link. This link allows you to move to the previous 30 days (that is, before **02 Jul**). If you move there, to the right from the **Previous** link, the **Next** link will appear allowing you to move back. Using these links you can navigate the history of the project events.

The sidebar of the activity page contains the already mentioned filter that allows you to define what kind of events you want to see. Most of the event types, available in this filter, do not need any explanation so let's review only the ones which are less obvious. Thus, if the **Issues** checkbox is checked, the activity list includes issue status changes and notes. If the **Changesets** checkbox is set, the list will also include repository commits and if the **Messages** checkbox is selected you will also see messages posted to forums (including topics, replies, and so on).

> Please note that issue events shown here are not the same as issue history entries shown on the issue page. The latter shows much more details and these details also are sent to watchers (in other words, having subscribed to issue changes you get more notifications).

In the earlier screenshot, it is not obvious which activity is for what event type. Different event types on this page have different icons and, thus, using this page more you will learn how to recognize the event type. Meanwhile let me tell you what events are shown on this screen.

The first entry for **Today** is news posted by **Wilson**. Below is the issue status change and note. All entries for **28 Jul** are files added under the **Files** tab. And an entry for **18 Jul** is a document added under the **Document** tab.

In addition you can subscribe to the activity feed by using the **Atom** link below the list.

Once you get used to this page you will love the listing as it's compact, easy-to-read and supports the filter—there is no easier way to check the latest events for project.

Global activities

There is also the global activity page that shows events on all projects (to which a user has access, of course). This page can be useful for employees who work on different projects. For example, company directors, who want to know what's happening on all projects. To get there, click on the **Projects** top-menu item and then the **Overall activity** link.

Configuring projects

Now we are going to discuss topics solely intended for Redmine project managers, that is, for users having permissions allowing them to edit project properties or properties related to projects. If you are the one who created the project, most likely, you have such permissions. Anyway, it's easy to check, if you see the **Settings** tab in the project menu, you can manage this project (or at least some of its properties).

So let's move to this tab now:

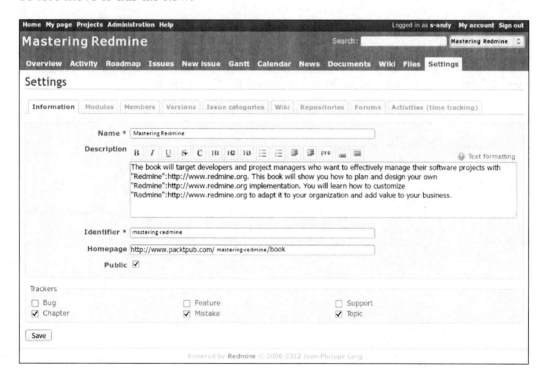

Under this tab, you see the project's settings menu, which also has tabs.

We will skip the **Issue category** tab as it has been discussed in the previous chapter, we will also skip the **Repositories** and **Forums** tabs as they have been reviewed along with the appropriate modules. We will not review the **Activities (time tracking)** tab as it's going to be reviewed in the next chapter.

Information

The first tab which gets opened automatically, the **Information** tab, contains generally the same fields that are found in the new project form.

Only users having the **Edit project** permission will be able to see this tab.

Modules

The second **Modules** tab also contains fields, which can be seen on the new project form. These fields allow you to choose modules for the project:

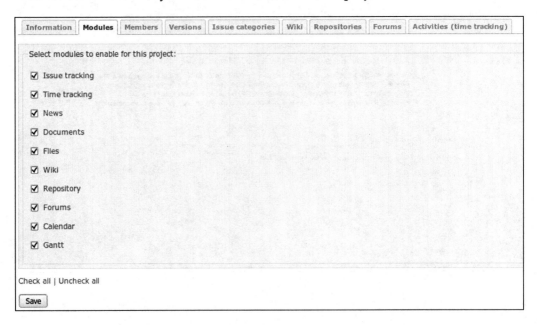

Using this tab, you can enable modules anytime you need them or when you are ready to populate the module's pages.

 Only users having the **Select project modules** permission will be able to see the **Modules** tab.

Members

The next tab is the **Members** tab, seen in the following screenshot:

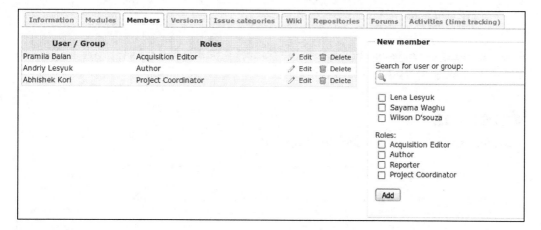

This is the tab where we add members to a project. Here we can also see the list of current members.

 To have access to this tab, a user must have the **Manage members** permission.

The **New member** block allows you to choose many users and many roles at the same time (a user can have several roles in a project). The user list will also contain group names, if Redmine has user groups defined. The search field can be used to filter users and groups by a part of their name, thus, if I typed so in the search field the user list would contain only **Wilson D'souza**. Selected users get added to the member list after you click on the **Add** button.

The user list inside the **New member** block contains only users which are not members of the project yet. In other words, to assign a different role to a project member, you need to click on the **Edit** link in this member's row. When you do this, the following form gets opened in place:

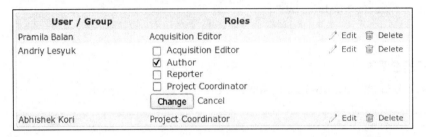

After applying changes or clicking on the **Cancel** link this form disappears and the member's row gets updated accordingly.

Versions

Now, let's see what's under the **Versions** tab:

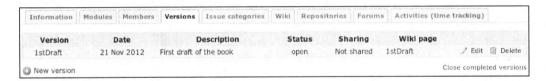

So here we manage project versions.

 If you don't have the **Manage versions** permission, you won't see this tab.

Project versioning is extremely important for software projects. Thus, in Redmine project versions can be used by issues (to specify in what version the issue is going to be fixed), project files can be uploaded to a specific version, the project roadmap shows versions, the calendar can show version dates along with issue dates, Redmine Wiki syntax supports version links, custom fields support **Version** type, and so on. In other words, by not adding a version, you literally limit the functionality that is available for your project in Redmine.

For this reason it is important to manage versions correctly. Let's check the new version form, which becomes available when you click on the **New version** link:

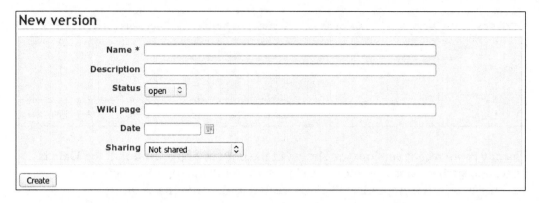

In the preceding screenshot, **Name** is actually the version number which can be just a string (such as **1stDraft** in my case). But it's not recommended to use strings for versions as you can end up with broken sorting for versions (which can be corrected using the **Date** field though).

The **Description** field is optional and should contain a very short description of what is special about this version, for example, **Maintenance release**. This description will be shown on the roadmap and on the version page.

The value of the **Status** field can be **open, locked**, or **closed**, where **locked** means that the project is in a *frozen* state, that is, all issues have been fixed but not tested. Thus, you can't change the **Target version** of an issue to a locked or closed version.

The **Wiki page** field contains a Wiki page name that describes the changes made in this version. The content of this page will be embedded into the version section on the roadmap page and into the version page. Such Wiki page should contain a changelog for the version.

 Remember about SEO when choosing the name for the associated Wiki page. Thus, you can use the "Changelog" word plus the version name, for example, Changelog-1-0-2.

When you save a version, the value which has been specified for the **Wiki page** field, becomes a link pointing to the associated Wiki page (see the **1stDraft** link in the previous screenshot). The same Wiki page also gets opened when you click on the **Edit associated Wiki page: 1stDraft** link on the version page.

Despite how it may seem, the **Date** field is not just used to show the due date of the release. In particular the value of this field affects the order of versions:

Version	Date	Description	Status	Sharing	Wiki page		
1.4.x	18 Jun 2012		closed	Not shared		Edit	Delete
2.2.x	29 Aug 2013		open	Not shared		Edit	Delete
1.0.x			closed	Not shared		Edit	Delete
1.3.x			closed	Not shared		Edit	Delete
2.0.x			locked	Not shared		Edit	Delete
2.1.x			open	Not shared		Edit	Delete

Usually more recent versions are shown at the bottom of the list but, if the **Date** is specified, such versions get moved to the top and others appear as newer versions. In other words, the empty **Date** field is treated as distant time in future.

 You should not mix versions with dates and versions without dates, especially versions with the same status. Otherwise, your version list will be disordered. However, you can use dates for old and current versions and leave them empty for future versions.

The value of the **Date** field is also used to determine whether the version is completed. But let's get back to this a little bit later in this topic.

The last field on this form, the **Sharing** field, accepts the following values which have the following meanings:

- **Not shared**: This version won't be shared. That is, it will be available only to this project.

- **With subprojects**: This version will be available to all subprojects of this project to any nesting level.

- **With project hierarchy**: This version will be available to all subprojects as well as to all parent projects of the current project (but not to other subprojects of parent projects). To be able to choose this option, a user must have the **Manage versions** permission for the parent project as well.

- **With project tree**: This version will be available to all subprojects of the current project as well as to all subprojects of all parent projects of the current project. It will also be available to all parent projects of the current one. Like for the previous option, to be able to set this option a user must have the **Manage versions** permission for the parent project.

- **With all projects**: This version will be shared among all projects which are hosted on this Redmine installation! As this is a very wide sharing method, this option is available only to administrators. You have to be extremely careful when you choose this option.

Any of these fields can be modified later by clicking on the **Edit** link next to the version in the version list. This link opens the same form that we have just reviewed. You can also remove the version by clicking on the **Delete** link.

Now let's speak about the **Close completed versions** link which can be found on the right-hand side under the version list. A completed version can be considered to be a not-yet-closed version which, however, meets all conditions to be closed. When reviewing the **Date** field from the version form I promised to get back to this field. That's here! The value of the **Date** field along with the number of open issues in the version are used to determine if a version is completed. If the date is in the past, and there are no open issues in the version, such a version is considered to be completed. So by clicking on the **Close completed versions** link, you just close all such versions.

Wiki

The last tab in the project's settings that we will review in this topic, is the **Wiki** tab:

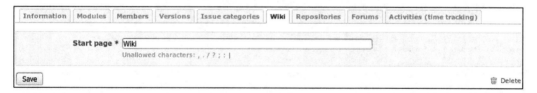

The value **Wiki** is the default name of the starting Wiki page in the project. Using this form you can change this name (for example, if you have prepared another Wiki page for the next release). After modifying this value, when users click on the **Wiki** tab in the project menu they will get the Wiki page with the name that has been specified here.

The **Delete** link in the bottom-right corner allows you to delete the start page. It not only deletes the Wiki page itself but also the start page name! After this, the **Wiki** tab in the project menu (not in the project's settings menu) disappears as the start page no longer exists as well as the name for the start page. Actually, I believe, the more gracious method to achieve the same is just by disabling the **Wiki** module.

Closing a project

Many a time, a company develops many small projects, in several years such a company ends up with a huge list of projects, the majority of which are not used anymore (no new issues, files, Wiki pages, no updates to forums, and so on). Removing such projects can be unacceptable as: some of them can be renewed in future, some can be forked and the data of the original project can still be needed for the fork, data of others can be needed for reference, and so on. Leaving such projects in the list can be also problematic as, in this case, the project list becomes unusable. This is when the **Close** link on the project **Overview** page comes in handy.

When clicked, and after confirmation, this link puts the projects into a read-only mode. In this mode, all the project information remains available, all read permissions are preserved, but nothing can be changed or added. Refer the following screenshot:

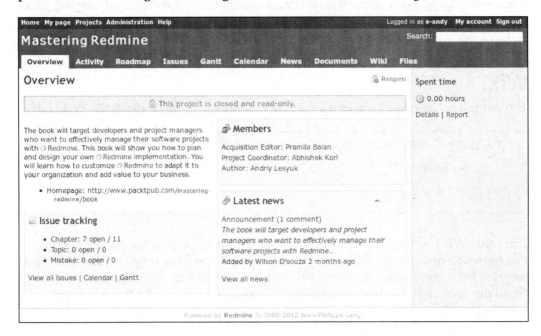

The overview page of the closed project contains the warning and the **Close** link turns into the **Reopen** link. Yes, the latter can be used to make the project active again. Also note that the closed project does not have **New issue** and **Settings** tabs anymore.

Only project members having the **Close / reopen the project** permission can make the project read-only or active.

The project list does not include closed projects by default.

Project maintenance best practices

As of now we have reviewed the functionality which is available for projects in Redmine. But, in my opinion, it's not enough to learn what functionality is available, it's much more important to learn how to use it properly. So the main thing that I would like to share with you in this chapter is my experience of what should be done and what should be avoided. Earlier, while reviewing different available functions, I was trying to give you some hints and advices. In this topic, I would like to list some best practices for better project maintenance. So let's get started:

- Specify the target version when you close an issue as it is used for the roadmap.

- Have a future version added to the version list. If you are unsure what version name or number this will be, name it Next version, you can always change the name later. If no future version is added a developer won't be able to select a value for the **Target version** field.

- Write the changelog for each released version using the the associated Wiki page functionality. Just the list of fixed issues, which is provided automatically, is not enough as this list is often huge, issue subjects are not intended to be clear enough for the changelog, and so on.

- Try to keep the done ratio of the issue accurate while you work on it. There are several reasons for doing this. First, customers may follow the issue and, in particular, its done ratio. Second, the grand total of issue done ratios is used to show the overall progress for the project version.

- Write news every time you make a release. Customers, who are waiting for a new release of your project, may subscribe to your news expecting to get one about the new release.

Custom queries

You should not expect your users to learn all the issue filter functionality and to configure it to their needs on their own. Where possible you should ensure that they feel comfortable while browsing your issue lists. This is not only about your customers but also, and especially, about your project members.

Let's review some examples of custom queries. Some of them, possibly, will be useful for you, others, I hope, will give you an idea about custom queries you may need:

Name	Filters	
	Field/Option	Condition/Value
My open issues	Status	`open`
	Assigned to	`"<<me>>"`
My open issues in the next version	Status	`open`
	Assigned to	`"<<me>>"`
	Target version	`"Next version"`
Issues watched by me	Status	`open`
	Watcher	`"<<me>>"`
Unassigned issues	Status	`open`
	Assignee	`none`
New features in the next version	Tracker	`Feature`
	Target version	`"Next version"`
Changelog for current stable version	Target version	`"Stable"`
	Sort	`Tracker`
Roadmap	Status	`open`
	Group results by	`Target version`
Issues grouped by assignees and sorted by priority	Status	`open`
	Group results by	`Assignee`
	Sort	`Priority`
Issues by trackers sorted by status	Group results by	`Tracker`
	Sort	`Status`

Project list

Let me explain in short the page where projects are listed. You should have seen this page already as it is where we find the **New project** link, the **View all issues** and the **Overall activity** links, which have been mentioned in this and the previous chapters:

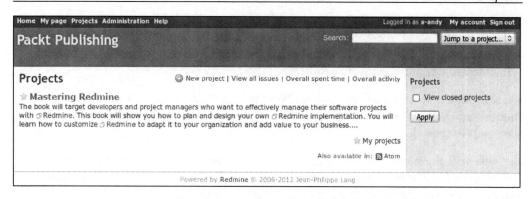

This page lists projects which are accessible for a user. The list includes shortened description of each project. If a project has a yellow star near the name, this means that you are a member of the project. On the sidebar, you see the form allowing you to show closed projects, which are not shown by default.

It's also possible to subscribe to the list of projects and be notified about new projects added. For this, just copy the **Atom** link and paste it into your favorite RSS aggregator.

Administrating projects

Redmine also has another list of projects, but this one is only for administrators and is available in **Administration | Projects** section:

Here you see all the projects that I have on my Redmine demo installation. This page has a very simple filter that allows you to filter projects by their status and by a part of the name. The **Clear** link can be used to clear this filter.

Available statuses for the filter are namely **all**, **active**, **closed**, and **archived**. If the status filter is set to **active** (which is default), the list won't include closed and archived projects. We have discussed what the closed project is, and you can read, what the archived project is, in a subtopic.

On this page, you can also see another **New project** link, which has also been mentioned in this chapter before. This link opens the same new project form that we have discussed.

But new things on this page are the **Archive** (and the **Unarchive**), **Copy**, and **Delete** links. I guess, there is no need to explain what the **Delete** link does (hint: it does, asking you for confirmation). Instead, let's talk about other links.

Copying projects

Let's see what happen when we click on the **Copy** link:

This form is very much the same as the new project form except it uses some values and states of the original project and has the additional **Copy** block.

In some circumstances, projects hosted in Redmine can be very similar. In such cases, with this **Copy** link, Redmine provides a way to create a project template and then copy it into new projects.

The **Copy** block allows you to choose which objects should be copied. The **Send email notifications during the project copy** option controls whether users should receive notifications about creation of new issues, forums, messages, wiki pages, and so on. You are unlikely to enable this option unless you want to spam them off.

To hide the project template from users, archive it.

Archiving

If you have finished a project and do not want it to appear in the project list anymore and be accessible at all, do you want to remove it? With all issues, all history, all comments and discussions, with all the documentation, and Wiki pages? If you do, you can use the **Delete** link. Otherwise, you should use the **Archive** link.

After being archived, a project disappears from the listings and its pages become inaccessible but still remain on the system. This way, when you change your mind, or just want to check something in the project, you will be able to unarchive it.

To make a project "read-only" use the **Close** link on the project overview page instead.

Summary

In this chapter, we have reviewed the functionality which you will use quite often while working with Redmine. The knowledge you have learned here should help you configure and maintain your own projects.

Nevertheless, the topics we have reviewed were not complicated and, probably, could be learned without reading a book. So the main goal was not to show you the basics of managing projects in Redmine, but also to show you things which you should consider when doing this. I also tried to share my experience about best practices when configuring and maintaining Redmine projects. I hope I have succeeded in this.

With each chapter, we learn more and more and you will probably wonder what else there can be in the next chapters? The very next one describes Redmine in its other role as a time tracking application.

6
Time Tracking

Some readers may wonder why time tracking functionality is going to be reviewed in a separate chapter. If time tracking is provided by a small project module, then why have we not reviewed it along with other modules in the previous chapter? Other project modules, except issue tracking, do not provide enough functionality to make users install Redmine for them or have way better competitors (for example, MediaWiki or DocuWiki for the Wiki module; Invision Power Board or phpBB for the forums module, and so on). On the contrary, the time tracking module is complete, competitive (considering the functionality provided by Redmine core and its other project modules), and often enough becomes the main reason for using Redmine. Thus, I, personally, first used Redmine as a time tracking application.

So, in this chapter, we will speak about time tracking with Redmine. We will also mention its other functionality, especially the issue tracking, as Redmine time tracking is based generally on issues. This is the first (and only) chapter which you do not need to emphasize on (if you do not plan to use time tracking). If, however, you decide to continue reading it, you will learn how to submit your time entries to Redmine, how to generate time reports, and what third-party tools you can use to improve your Redmine time-tracking experience.

In this chapter, we will cover the following topics:

- Using Redmine time tracking
- Defining activity
- Tracking time
- Checking spent time
- Generating reports

Using Redmine time tracking

Really, why Redmine should be chosen over other time tracking alternatives? The answer is because of the inclusion of other features that are not limited to issue tracking. Time-tracking applications rarely come alone, as the time tracking is a simple task and is unlikely to have many features. Thus, time tracking is also available in Trac, OrangeHRM, and so on.

Anyway let's see its benefits:

- In Redmine, time entries are associated with tasks, which are implemented using issues. This way, tasks can have detailed description of what should be done, can be shown on the Gantt chart, and much more.

- Due to the way issues are implemented, tasks can also have an estimated time which can be used to evaluate the speed of development, determine problematic tasks, and so on.

- Users can specify exactly what they were doing on the task, using the **Comment** field.

- Using the **Activity** field, administrators and project managers can categorize the time spent.

- Redmine allows adding time entries from SCM commit messages (described in details later).

- Spent time report is available (actually this is the only report available in Redmine).

- It can be a benefit or not, but Redmine supports only the hours value (which can be a float) and does not care about the start and the end times.

To enable the time tracking module for the project, make sure that the **Time tracking** checkbox is checked in project settings under the **Modules** tab.

To enable the time tracking module for new projects by default, go to **Administration | Settings | Projects**.

Defining activity

A task may need different types of work to be performed and completed, for example, a software feature needs to be designed, developed, and tested. Sometimes the information about the time that was spent for different types of work is very important, as it helps determining what types are more time consuming and therefore, allows to optimize the work flow. But, such information is especially useful if different types of work involve different hourly payment rates. That's what the **Activity** time entry field should be used for.

Of course, it should not be a user who names the activity. For this reason, Redmine allows adding activities only to administrators and choosing the activities that apply the project only to project managers (users having the **Manage project activities** permission).

Thus, administrators can add activities by going to **Administration | Enumerations | Activities (time tracking)**, as shown in the following screenshot:

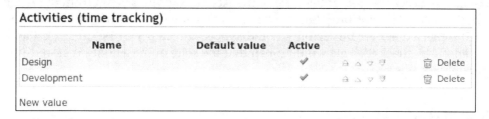

Each activity's enumeration item has a position in the enumeration list. To change the position, you can use the green arrow icons. An activity will be enabled for a project by default if the **Active** property is set, and it will be selected by default in the time entry form if the **Default value** property is set.

New activities can be added using the **New value** link. This link opens the form, which also appears when you click on the activity name, as shown in the following screenshot:

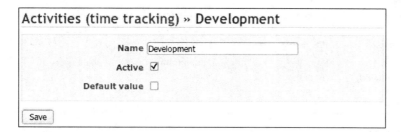

Activities available in **Administration | Enumerations** also appear in the project settings under the **Activities (time tracking)** tab, as shown in the following screenshot:

Here project managers can select the activities which will be available for the project. Those activities—the **Active** property of which is set—will be selected here by default. Clicking the Reset link will switch to default settings, that is, the **Active** checkboxes on this screen will become checked, if the corresponding activities are active in **Administration | Enumerations**, otherwise they will become unchecked.

The **System Activity** column can be a source of confusion. Check marks shown in this column indicate whether the state of the **Active** column is taken from the **Active** property in **Administration | Enumerations**. Thus, if we modify the **Active** column here, the check mark for this activity will disappear (even if we first uncheck it and save, and then check it). This would mean that the state of the activity is stored separately for this project.

Tracking time

The time entry form, which is used to add time entries to Redmine, can be accessed from several places. Thus, users get redirected to this form when they click the **Log time** link in the top-right contextual menu on the issue page:

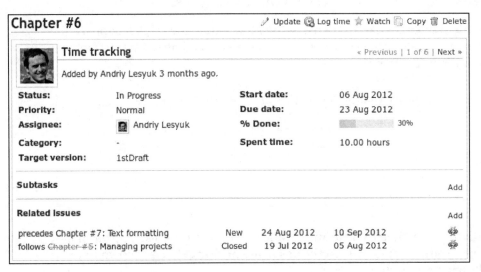

The same **Log time** link is also available on the spent time report page, which will be reviewed later in this chapter.

 To be able to log time, a user must have the **Log spent time** permission.

The time entry form can also be opened by clicking the **Log time** item in the drop-down menu, which can be invoked by right-clicking on an issue in the issue list, as shown in the following screenshot:

 The **Log time** menu item disappears if we select more than one issue.

Also, this form is partially available within the issue edit form, which is shown when we click the **Update** link on the issue page, as shown in the following screenshot:

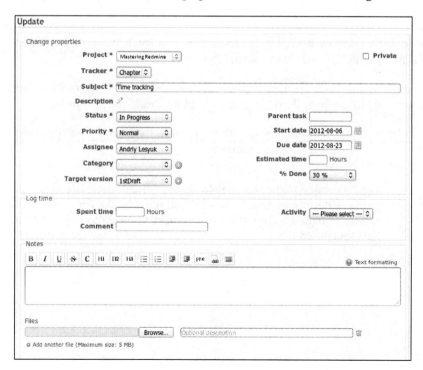

Bulk time entries

You can install the Bulk Time Entry plugin, which was originally authored by Eric Davis to make it possible to add several time entries at a time. This plugin adds the **Bulk time entries** item to the top-left menu which is shown on every page, `https://github.com/spilin/redmine-bulk_time_entry_plugin`.

The full-time entry form, that is, the form without unmodifiable values (such as project), looks like the following screenshot:

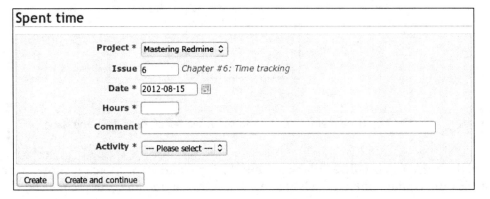

As you can see, the **Issue** field is optional, that is, you can add spent time directly to the project. This can be useful if, for example, you track time spent on meetings or similar stuff, which do not have associated issues.

The **Date** field in this form should contain the date when you spent time working on the issue and/or project. By default this field contains today's date.

The **Hours** field should contain the number of hours that you have spent doing the work. The value of this field can be decimal.

The float value in the **Hours** field should contain decimals after points, not minutes, that is, .00 - .99 and not .00 - .59. For example, to specify 1:30 (one hour and thirty minutes) ,you should put `1.50` into the **Hours** field.

While the **Comment** field is optional, in most cases, it's highly recommended to describe here shortly what exactly you were working on during those hours. In fact, this field distinguishes time entries in addition to the **Activity** field but this one, unlike the latter, is of free form. The comment is for your managers, so if they do not need such details, you can leave the **Comment** field empty.

> Avoid general comments, such as "Worked", "Tested", or similar. Good examples are "Researched why did the issue come up", "Implemented GetSomething() function", "Was writing the Time Tracking topic", and so on.

The **Activity** field in this form should be set to the type of work you were doing for the task. If you were doing various work, you should create separate time entries for each type.

> **Time Tracker plugin**
>
> The Time Tracker plugin originally authored by Jérémie Delaitre can simplify the process of logging time by adding **Start** and **Stop** links into the account menu (which is located in the top-right corner) , see a `https://github.com/martinllanos/redmine_time_tracker`.

When you have filled in the form, you can either click on the **Create** button and be redirected to the previous page, or click the **Create and continue** button and get this form again to add another time entry.

> **Time tracking from mobile**
>
> To track time from iPhone, you can use RedmineApp by going to `http://getredmineapp.com`. This is a full-featured Redmine client which also supports adding time entries.
>
> For Android phones, you can use the dedicated time-tracking client RedTime by going to `http://redtime.ubicoo.com`.

Tracking time using commit messages

When reviewing **Administration | Settings | Repositories** (we did it twice in *Chapter 3, Configuring Redmine* and in *Chapter 4, Issue Tracking*), I skipped part of the form. Refer to the following screenshot:

I skipped the **Enable time logging** and the **Activity for logged time** fields as at that time we knew nothing about time entries. So, let's see what we can do with these settings now.

If the **Enable time logging** option is checked, and the **Activity for logged time** field is set to some value, you can add time entries from repository commit messages. For example, if you run `$ svn commit -m 'Finished controller, refs #1554 @4:30'`, Redmine will add a time entry for the issue #1554 with the **Hours** field set to 4 hours and 30 minutes. This time entry will use the activity selected in the **Activity for logged time** field. The comment of the time entry will be "Applied in charset R" `changeset R`, where R is a revision number. The date of the time entry will be the date when the commit has been done.

A commit message, which adds a time entry, should have the following format:

```
refs #N @HM
```

Following are the parts of the format:

- `refs`: This is a referencing keyword, which is specified in the **Referencing keywords** field (it can be omitted, if the **Referencing keywords** was set to "*")
- `#N`: This is an issue number, for example, #1554
- `@HM`: This specifies the time spent. HM can be **1h30m, 5hours, 1hour5min, 20min, 1:30, 1.5h, 2, 8h**, and so on

Checking spent time

The time tracking module is one of the most deeply integrated project modules in Redmine. As a result you can find hours, which have been entered into time entries, in many places. So, under this topic, we will speak about how time entries are used and where they can be found.

>
> To be able to view time entries, a user must have the **View spent time** permission. Thus, to hide time entries from your customers, make sure that their roles (and at least **Non member** and **Anonymous**) do not have this permission.

This topic will be of interest mainly to managers. But other users, who enter time entries, will find some interesting information here as well.

> **Invoices plugin**
> The Invoices plugin of Kirill Bezrukov can be used to generate invoices using hours specified in time entries. But, note that you need the commercial PRO version for this, check the link http://redminecrm.com/projects/invoices.

Time spent for issues

If an issue has time entries, the grand total of all hours of all the issue time entries is shown on the issue page in the **Spent time** property, as shown in the following screenshot:

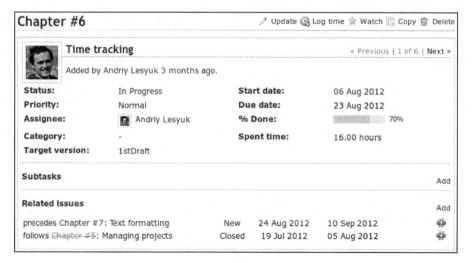

The number of hours (**16.00 hours**) here is a link. By clicking on this link, you will be redirected to the time report for the issue.

Time spent for versions

If an issue has the **Target version** field set, its time entries' hours will be included into the grand total which is shown on the version page, as on the following screenshot:

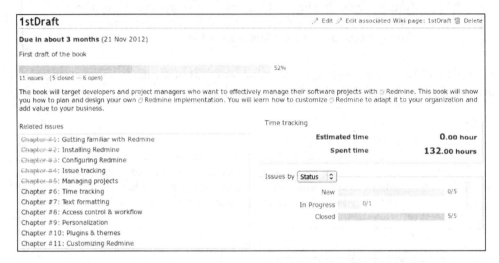

Here **132.00 hours** is just a text, and not link.

Time spent for projects

The grand total of all hours ever entered for the project is available on the sidebar of the project overview page:

I'm not sure whether one may need the grand total for a project, but you can find really useful links below it, which are available only here. These links point to the time report, which will be reviewed in the next topic. The number of hours on this page is not clickable.

Project activity

Time entries entered for a project can also be seen on the project activity list page, which can be accessed using the **Activity** tab. To see time entries on this page, you need to enable the **Spent time** filter on the sidebar either by checking the checkbox and clicking the **Apply** button or by clicking the **Spent time** link (the label near the checkbox).

Time entries are shown as project events on the following screenshot:

If you click the title of the event, which is **1.00 hour (Chapter #6 (In Progress): Time tracking)**, you will be redirected to the time report for the issue **#6**. Below the title, you see the time entry comment. Date and time here indicate when users have added the time entry and not when they worked on the issue.

Your time entries

Your latest time entries (considering the date you spent time on) can be also found in the **Spent time (last 7 days)** block on **My page** (if this block is enabled). **My page** and its available blocks will be discussed in *Chapter 9, Personalization.*

Generating reports

Redmine is known to lack reporting functionality but not in the case of the time tracking. And this is natural as the time tracking is useless without reporting.

From the previous topic, we have learnt that Redmine provides many links to the time report. Let's list them here (some links have already been mentioned):

- **Overall spent time** on the project list page can be accessed using the **Projects** item in the top left-menu and lists all visible time entries for all projects

- **Details** and **Report** links on the project overview page list all time entries for the project

- Number of hours on the issue page lists all time entries for an issue

- The title of a time entry event on the project activities page lists all time entries for an issue

So, generally, the time reporting is available at three nesting levels—on the global level (all projects and issues), on the project level (all issues), and on the issue level. Let's review here the report at the issue level (for **Chapter #6**), which I got by clicking on the hours number on the issue page:

The breadcrumbs in the top-left corner can be used to switch between the nesting levels. To the right-hand side from the breadcrumbs, you see the **Log time** link, which can be used to add new time entries.

The **Date range** filter supports two modes—you can either specify exact **From** and **To** dates or use predefined periods, as shown in the following screenshot:

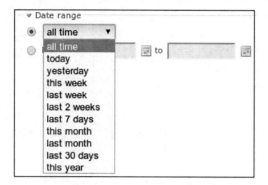

This page has two tabs—**Details** and **Report**; even though both tabs can be used to generate reports (that's why I named this page the time report page).

Let's review each tab.

Details tab

Under this tab, we get a list of time entries for the given period. This list is shown in a table with sortable headers (all besides the **Comment** column). Above the list, the grand total of hours is shown. Projects and issues links in the list point to the report pages for corresponding projects and issues. The rightmost columns contain icons that allow editing and deleting time entries (of course, users should have appropriate permissions to see these icons). Below the list, we see the **Atom** and the **CSV** links. The former can be use to subscribe to time entries and the latter can be used to export time entries.

As you might have noticed, rows of the list are selectable either by checking the checkboxes in the leftmost column or by clicking on rows (you can hold the *Ctrl* key to select more than one row). Right-clicking on selected row(s) invokes the drop-down menu, as shown in the following screenshot:

Using this drop-down menu, you can invoke the bulk time entries form, which allows changing several time entries at a time.

Report tab

Under the **Report** tab, we see a kind of report builder, as shown in the following screenshot:

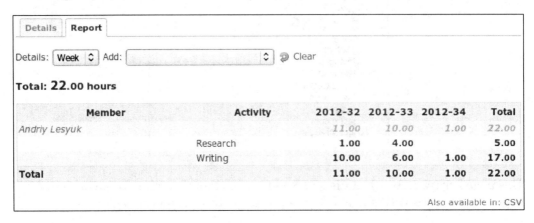

The **Details** property specifies what columns the report will contain. In my case, these are weeks (**2012-32**, **2012-33**, and so on, where **32**, **33** are week numbers). The time report supports years, months, weeks, and days in columns.

The **Add** property is more interesting. It allows you to choose up to three groupings. Thus, in the previous screenshot, the first grouping is **Member** and the second one is **Activity**. Groupings should be added in the same order as they appear in the report. Thus, first I added the **Member** group, and then I added the **Activity** group.

The following grouping properties are supported:

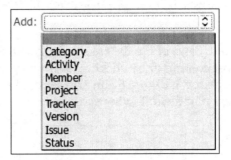

Here, the **Category** group stands for issue categories.

> The grouping list will also contain custom fields if you define them for issues. Custom fields will be discussed in *Chapter 11, Customizing Redmine*.

The resulting report can be exported using the **CSV** link.

> **Timesheet plugin**
>
> The Timesheet plugin originally authored by Eric Davis can be used to generate more flexible time reports , see at `https://github.com/spilin/redmine-timesheet-plugin`.

Summary

You don't have to work in some company to track time in Redmine, as you see it fits great for personal time tracking as well. Although Redmine time tracking is quite basic, it can be easily extended by third-party tools (including cell phone apps but not limited to them). I hope the knowledge you have gained reading this chapter will help making time tracking as comfortable as possible for you.

Till this moment, in the last three chapters, we spoke about three main roles of Redmine (one role per chapter). Along with these roles, we have also reviewed all the functionality of Redmine, which has been divided between roles and therefore, chapters. So, no more functionality to review, and no more special roles. So what's next? Having read all the previous chapters, we can claim that we have learnt Redmine. But, is it enough? Right now, we are at the level which is close to the advanced user, but we still do not know many things. For example, we know that we can use the Wiki syntax almost everywhere in Redmine. But, have we learnt the Wiki syntax? That's what we are going to do in the next chapter.

7
Text Formatting

As a developer, I can assure you of the importance of rich text formatting in user requests, especially in issue descriptions, for a good text comprehension. It is especially useful if the one, who is going to comprehend for example, an issue is dealing with a lot of such issues constantly. In practice, unfortunately, users often disregard rich formatting that ends up to result in bad readability and, sometimes, in distorted messages (when some symbols are treated as formatting markers). Therefore, I believe, the familiarity with the Redmine text formatting is essential for using Redmine. Luckily the formatting is not too complicated as it uses the Textile markup language. So in this chapter we are going to learn it.

The Textile markup language attempts to add rich formatting to the plain text while not breaking its readability. Thus, list items begin with * or #, italic text is enclosed in _ (underline), and so on. This way, if one writes text without any formatting markers, in most cases, such text should be rendered just fine. Moreover, due to "naturalness" of its syntax Textile is able to recognize the following:

- Paragraphs: They should start with new lines and after an empty line
- Quotes: The paragraphs that start with >
- Links: Links starting with `http://`

Textile also recognizes plain text, thus, also adding rich formatting to texts, which do not have any special Textile rules. In other words, Textile is very simple and easy to learn. At least, most of its syntax. However, this book is not aimed at simple things, which can be learned on your own, so here you will also find some complicated advanced topics as well.

 While it's possible to use the Markdown markup language with Redmine instead of Textile, in this chapter, we will review only the latter as Markdown formatter needs to be installed using a third-party plugin and Textile comes with Redmine.

In this chapter, we will cover the following topics:

- Formatting text in Redmine
- Wiki formatting syntax

Formatting text in Redmine

You might wonder why we reviewed the Wiki module in *Chapter 5, Managing Projects*, and not here. The answer is: The Wiki module and the text formatting are not the same. Thus, having disabled the Wiki module you do not disable rich formatting, it will still be available for issue descriptions, issue comments, news, project description, and so on. The Wiki module is just the module which uses the text formatting most intensively. However, the rich text formatting was implemented mainly for the integrated Wiki system (which is provided by the Wiki module) and, therefore, it is often named as the Wiki formatting (and that's the name I will use to refer to it further).

While it's unlikely you will use this possibility, the Wiki formatting can be disabled in **Administration | Settings | General** using the **Text formatting** option:

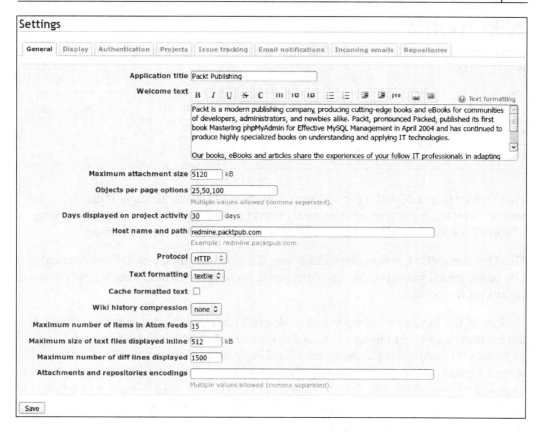

This option is used if you want to replace the Textile formatter with, for example, Markdown. For this, however, you will also need to install the Markdown Redcarpet plugin.

If this option is set to **none**, the Wiki formatting will be disabled for the whole Redmine. In other words, everything you put into a text area will be shown as it is, ignoring any formatting syntax. This, by the way, will also apply to the Wiki system, that is, Wiki pages will still be there but no Wiki syntax will be available for them. However, Redmine internal linking syntax (such as linking to issues, linking to Wiki pages, and so on), which will be covered further, will still be functioning! Otherwise the Wiki system would become completely useless, in particular, without support for links to other Wiki pages.

Wiki toolbar

Almost every text area for fields, that support the Wiki formatting comes with the Wiki toolbar:

This toolbar does not make the text area a WYSIWYG editor though, it just provides an easy way for pasting most commonly used formatting markers. A well working WYSIWYG solution for Redmine does not currently exist, as far as I know.

The **Text formatting** link to the right opens the short summary of Wiki syntax rules. The page, which gets opened, also contains links to more detailed documentation regarding the syntax.

Neither of the toolbar icons open any dialog, all icons just paste syntax markers into the current position in the text area. If the user selects text in the text area, clicking on icons will format the selected text accordingly, thus, if the user selects a part of text and clicks on the ᴮ icon, this text will be enclosed into * (bold marker). If the user selects several lines in the text area and clicks on the ≔ or ≡ icon, * or # (list markers) will be added to the beginning of each selected line accordingly.

The Wiki toolbar is really helpful at the beginning of using Redmine when users do not remember all the markers. After becoming a more experienced user, I believe, you will prefer typing syntax markers directly into the text area over clicking on the corresponding icons (at least I do). Also the Wiki toolbar does not contain all the available markers, so you won't be able to completely avoid typing them. For this reason and because we have not learned available syntax markers yet, we won't review these icons here. You can play with them on your own or get back to them later after having learned the formatting markers.

[

To check what an icon does you can hover the mouse cursor over it.
]

Preview

In most cases, forms with Wiki-syntax-enabled text areas also contain the **Preview** link:

This link can and should be used for checking, if the formatting is going to be rendered correctly, before submitting content to Redmine. After clicking on it, a preview of the content of the Wiki-syntax-enabled text area is rendered beneath the form.

If a not-yet-submitted content is using images, which have been attached to a not-yet-submitted related resource (for example, new issue), the preview won't be able to show these images as, in fact, they have not been uploaded to the server yet.

Always use the **Preview** link, if available, before submitting a content to the server. Do this, even if you are sure, that formatting markers are correct, or if you have not used any formatting at all, as the content can include some special symbols or sequence of symbols, which may be treated as formatting markers by core Redmine formatter or third-party extensions.

Of course, in most cases, you may change the content later, after submitting. However, if users have subscribed to the content they usually get the first submitted version and not the corrected one. Also, further changes can get logged into the resource change history (for example, issue history), this way flooding it.

Placing the linked images

As already mentioned (and as will be discussed further), the Wiki content can use linked images. Here the word "linked" means hosted on the same Redmine installation and, possibly, in the same resource (for example, issue), and embedded into the Wiki content using the Wiki syntax. Of course, the Wiki syntax allows us to use images hosted on external resources but in many cases this can be inadmissible, for example, for security reasons or for load speed. So let's see where you can place your linked images.

If the resource (for example, issue or Wiki page) you are writing content for has a possibility to attach files, attach your images to this resource. Thus, for issue comments, you can attach images to the issue.

But what if there is no way to attach files to the resource? This is the reason I wrote this topic separately. In such cases, some users attach images under the **Files** tab of the project's menu. I would not recommend to do this. Under the **Files** tab, your customers expect to see files for download, that is, installation packages, documentation, samples and so on. They may decide these images are somehow related to the project (for example, think of them as diagrams) and should be downloaded. Besides if images are placed here, it will create a confusion for the customer when they want to download project related files.

I believe, the best way is to attach such images to an especially created Wiki page, for example, "Linked-images" (see *Chapter 5, Managing Projects*, on how to create Wiki pages). On this page you can also describe its purpose and annotate images that are attached. If not referenced from other Wiki pages, this page will be available only on Wiki index pages such as **Index by title** and **Index by date**. If you have disabled the Wiki module, you can use a special closed issue instead.

Let's now speak about how to extract image URL. If you hover your mouse cursor over an attached file, you should see the link which ends with **/attachments/<id>/<filename>**. That's the URL you should use when referring to images from within the Wiki content! Use the relative URL (which starts with /, that is, `/attachments/<id>` or `/redmine/attachments/<id>` depending on whether your Redmine uses subdomain). Here `<filename>` is optional.

Wiki formatting syntax

Till now we spoke about how the text formatting is integrated into Redmine. We started the chapter by discussing this to avoid reviewing these issues later, when we will be learning the syntax rules. Therefore, now we can (and will) focus on the rules exclusively.

Basics

All Textile syntax rules can be divided into special rules (for example, ones which implement lists and tables) and the rest. So the rest actually includes not only the very basics but also the rules that are very simple and do not need a separate discussion. And these are the rules we are going to learn right now. Let's start with basic principles.

A Textile document is a plain text document. The new line symbol in Textile is treated as `<br />` tag in HTML, that is, the rest of the text after the new line symbol in the current paragraph starts on a new line.

A paragraph in Textile is separated from the previous and the next paragraphs by an empty line, that is, two new line symbols. Thus, the following text will be treated as a single paragraph:

```
Redmine is a flexible project management web application.
Written using the Ruby on Rails framework,
it is cross-platform and cross-database.
```

Alternatively, you can start each paragraph with `p.` (there should be a space after):

```
p. Redmine is a flexible project management web application.

p. Written using the Ruby on Rails framework,
it is cross-platform and cross-database.
```

But, again, paragraphs should be divided by an empty line. Otherwise `p.` in the second line will just be ignored (shown as it is in the first paragraph).

The `p.` marker stands for *paragraph* and is converted into the HTML `<p>` tag. In fact, it's the same, if we did not use `p.`, because Textile uses the HTML `<p>` tag for every paragraph, which does not have any other marker at the beginning of the line.

> The `p.` marker can be used to keep indents identical for all paragraphs in a document. Thus, for a code paragraph you can write it as follows:
> ```
> p. <code>...</code>
> ```

Similar to the `p.` marker `h1.`, `h2.`, `h3.`, `h4.`, `h5.`, and `h6.` markers get converted into HTML's `<h1>`, `<h2>`, `<h3>`, `<h4>`, `<h5>`, and `<h6>` tags accordingly. These markers can be used to add headings to your Wiki content. The following code snippet will help us see all the heading levels:

```
h1. First heading

h2. Second heading

h3. Third heading

h4. Fourth heading

h5. Fifth heading

h6. Sixth heading
```

The earlier code is rendered as shown in the following screenshot:

First heading

Second heading

Third heading

Fourth heading

Fifth heading

Sixth heading

Such headings not only have their own styles but also define Wiki document sections. Thus, sections that were created using h1. to h4. markers, can be edited separately using pen icons to the right. Headings down to the fourth level also get shown in the table of contents, which can be added to the document using the {{toc}} macro, which is explained later in this chapter.

In addition to basic blocks—such as paragraph and headings—Textile supports basic inline text styles. Thus, to make the text bold use *, to make it italic use _, and so on. For example, let us see how the following text will be rendered:

```
This is the difference between *strong* and **bold**.
Inline cite looks ??this way??.
Inline text can be +inserted+ or -deleted-.
This is the difference between _emphasize_ and __italics__.
Also Redmine supports ^superscript^ and ~subscript~.
```

The following screenshot shows how the text mentioned earlier will be rendered:

This is the difference between **strong** and **bold**.
Inline cite looks *this way*.
Inline text can be <u>inserted</u> or ~~deleted~~.
This is the difference between *emphasize* and *italics*.
Also Redmine supports ^{superscript} and $_{subscript}$.

The superscript and subscript styles should be separated by spaces from nearby words. Thus, code like supports^superscript^ will not work as there is no space between supports and ^.

Here you should have noticed an odd thing with strong and bold, and emphasized and italic styles. Yes, in most cases * and **, and _, and __ are the same (and look the same) besides they are converted to different HTML tags. A full list of HTML analogs is given in the following table:

Textile	HTML
...	<strong>...</strong>
...	<b>...</b>
??...??	<cite>...</cite>
+...+	<ins>...</ins>
-...-	<del>...</del>
_..._	<em>...</em>
__...__	<i>...</i>
^...^	^{...}
~...~	_{...}

Explaining the difference between <strong> and <b> tags is out of scope of this book and is related to HTML. Basically, <b> and <i> are just styles while <strong> and <em> set off the content.

Sometimes when writing documentation, you may need to use shorter names or phrases for something but still reserve the possibility to check the details. For such purposes, you can use footnotes and acronyms.

A **footnote**, to be more exact, is a number that can be specified inline using square brackets, for example, Some text[1] (there should be no space between the text and the footnote number). The text for the footnote should be specified separately, preferably, at the bottom of the document using fnX., where X is the footnote number. Like p. and hX., the fnX. marker should be on the start of the line. As this is a so-called block marker, each footnote line should be separated from the lines above and below it with empty lines.

Unlike footnotes, acronyms are specified wholly inline using parentheses. Their syntax is ABC(Text), where ABC is an all-caps word, which is going to be shown on the page, and Text is the text, which is going to be shown when the users hover their mouse cursor over the acronym. Like for footnotes, there should be no space between the acronym and the text.

Let us see how the following Textile code will be displayed:

```
In Redmine[1] Wiki pages can be exported to PDF(Portable Document
Format), HTML(HyperText Markup Language) and TXT(Plain text).

fn1. Flexible project management web application written using Ruby on
Rails.
```

The following screenshot shows how the earlier mentioned code will be displayed:

In Redmine[1] Wiki pages can be exported to PDF, HTML and TXT.

[1] Flexible project management web application writt HyperText Markup Language

You can also visually separate the content by adding - - - (three dashes), ***, or ___ between paragraphs (separated from paragraphs by empty lines). These markers will produce the horizontal line (made with the HTML <hr> tag).

The Textile processing of some part of the text can be disabled using the special <notextile> tag. For example:

```
<notextile>This text will be shown *as it is*.</notextile>
```

However, this does not apply to links, this applies only to formatting. Please note that in this case this text will be processed by HTML engine, but tags won't work inside <notextile>, these tags will still be escaped by Textile, that is, they will be shown as they are. The problem here is that new line symbols and empty lines won't be processed as well, so such text will be shown in a single paragraph.

Quotes

For applications like Redmine it's very useful to be able to embed quotes, especially for issue comments and forum messages. Luckily, Redmine Textile implementation allows to do this. Moreover, appropriate forms usually provide buttons for easy pasting quotes from original messages.

In Redmine quotes can be embedded in two ways.

- By default for pasting a quote Redmine uses the > marker at the beginning of the line (it's another block marker). This marker is especially useful because it supports nesting. Thus, you can write:

```
>> Initial message
> Reply to initial message
```

The following screenshot shows how the earlier mentioned example will be rendered:

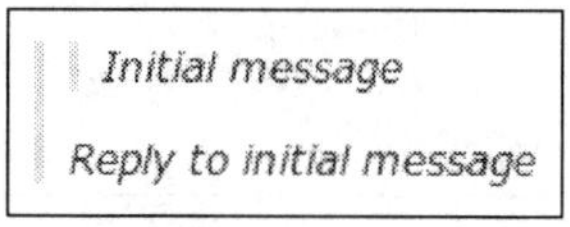

The > marker does not have to be separated from the previous line by an empty line. Furthermore, an empty line will only break the left gray line, which indicates that this is a quote.

- Another way is to use `bq.` marker. Generally, both produce visually identical results (because both use the HTML `<blockquote>` tag) but `bq.` does not support nesting. However, the `bq.` marker, like the `<blockquote>` tag, supports the `cite` parameter.

```
bq.:http://www.redmine.org Redmine is a flexible project
management web application. Written using the Ruby on Rails
framework, it is cross-platform and cross-database.
```

The syntax is:

```
bq.:cite ...
```

Here `cite` can be an absolute or relative URL or a named anchor (starting with #). This parameter is not displayed or anyhow used by browsers but can be used by search engines.

Lists

Redmine Textile implementation supports bullet and numbered lists. Bullet list items can be created using the * marker and numbered list items can be created using the # marker. Both should be placed on the start of the line and be followed by a space (unlike strong * marker which should be followed by a word).

Bullet and numbered lists can be nested. To add a nesting level, just add another marker at the beginning. Let's see how the following example will be rendered:

```
# The first item
## Nested item
### Next nesting level
# The second item
```

The following screenshot shows how the earlier example is rendered:

```
1. The first item
       1. Nested item
               1. Next nesting level

2. The second item
```

You can also mix types of nested lists, for example, check the following code:

```
# The first item
#* Nested item
#** Next nesting level
# The second item
```

Images

Images can be embedded into a Wiki content using the ! marker. The syntax of this marker is as follows:

```
!<options>.<image url><title>!:<href>
```

In the preceding syntax, `<options>.`, `(<title>)` and `:<href>` are optional.

Image URL can be absolute or relative. Thus, to embed an image attached to a different resource (which has been described at the beginning of this chapter) you need to write the URL, for example:

```
!/attachments/110!
```

Of course, users having access to the Wiki content should also have access to the resource the image is attached to.

Images from the current resource, that is, from the resource the Wiki content is connected to (for example, **Description** content, which is connected to issues), can be embedded just by specifying their file names, for example:

```
!9144_07_12.png!
```

In such cases Redmine is trying to find the file with the given name in the current resource's attachment list and uses the attachment if found.

The optional `<href>` parameter can be used to turn the image into a clickable link pointing to some URL, for example:

```
!redmine-logo.png!:http://www.redmine.org
```

The optional `<options>` parameter can be used to align the image relative to the text. Supported alignment options are `<`, `=`, and `>` which align the image to the left, center, and right correspondingly. For example, let's see how the following code is rendered:

```
!<.redmine-logo.png!
```

```
Redmine is a flexible project management web application. Written
using the Ruby on Rails framework, it is cross-platform and cross-
database.
```

The following screenshot shows how the earlier mentioned code is rendered:

Redmine is a flexible project management web application. Written using the Ruby on Rails framework, it is cross-platform and cross-database.

Resizing images

You can resize an image when it is displayed in the Wiki content using CSS `width` and `height` properties, for example:

```
!{width:64px;height:64px;}.<image url>!.
```

The `<title>` parameter can be used to specify the alternative text for the image, which will be displayed if there are any problems while loading the image (it's the analog of the `alt` attribute of the HTML `<img>` tag).

The alternative text may also be used by users' e-mail clients when the Wiki content is sent in e-mail notifications. So it's a good idea to always specify the title.

Links

Redmine's Textile supports two types of links—normal and internal.

Normal links

If the text contains links starting with `http://`, `https://`, `ftp://`, `ftps://`, `sftp://`, or `www.`, they will be recognized and rendered as links automatically. The same will be done with e-mail addresses, they will be rendered as mailto links.

Normal links can also be created using the following syntax:

```
"Anchor(Text)":link
```

Here, `Anchor` is the text, which is going to be displayed and be clickable, `Text` is optional link title, which will be displayed when users hover their mouse cursors over the `Anchor`, and `link` is the URL that the link will point to.

Internal links

Redmine Wiki formatting would be incomplete without support of internal links, especially, as has been noticed before, without Wiki links.

Redmine internal links are also known as Redmine links as, in fact, they are not part of Textile but are built on top of Textile and have been developed especially for Redmine.

Wiki links

It's essential for any Wiki system to support cross-page links as such links are the basis for the Wiki navigation. Otherwise the only way to find the page you are interested in, would be to use the Wiki index.

Cross-page links in Redmine's Wiki can be created using the following syntax:

```
[[Project:Page#NamedAnchor|Title]]
```

Everything besides `Page` is optional in the earlier syntax. Here `Page` is the name of the Wiki page, which is the last element of the page URL. For example, if the page URL is `http://www.redmine.org/projects/redmine/wiki/RedmineWikis`, the page name is `RedmineWikis`.

A free-form page name will also be converted to the valid URL path. Thus, `[[Free form page name]]` will link to page named `Free_form_page_name`.

It may be needed to link to the section on the Wiki page. Sections, which are created using `h1.` to `h4.` markers have named anchors that can be used for this (that is, we can link only to sections on the first level and down to the fourth level). A named anchor is generated from the heading title, so we can just use the heading title as `NamedAnchor`. For example:

```
[[Wiki#First heading]]
```

The NamedAnchor is used as a URL component, also known as the fragment identifier. As characters, which can be used in URL are limited, Redmine sanitizes named anchors on the Wiki page and the value you specify in the Wiki link. If, in some cases, you need to specify the already sanitized named anchor you can determine it by hovering your mouse cursor over the heading and then over the pilcrow which will appear to the right of the heading title, the named anchor will appear after the # sign in the URL (that is, as URL fragment) on the status bar.

You will rather rarely want to use the page name as a link text. To show a different text you should put it into the Wiki link as Title (after the | sign). For example:

```
See [[AnotherWikiPageName|this page]] for details.
```

If the page you want to link to, belongs to a different project you should prefix it with the project name or identifier as follows:

```
[[Mastering Redmine:Wiki]]
```

Don't hesitate to put cross-pages links in places where you think they would be useful. Remember that with Title parameter you can turn a part of the text into a cross-page link. Sufficient amount of such links will only improve your Wiki structure.

Project links

If projects that you host on your Redmine installation are somehow related, you may want to link some projects to others. For such cases, Redmine supports project links which have the syntax:

```
project:Name
```

Here project is the keyword defining the project link and Name is the project name or identifier.

Project links point to the project overview page and always use the project name as link text (this can't be changed).

In addition, project links can use the numeric project ID. For this case the syntax is project#ID. But as far as there is no way to determine the project numeric ID (besides digging the database), I don't think it's a very useful feature.

Version links

Linking to a version is a very useful feature and I, personally, use it quite often. Thus, it can be used in news when you describe new features of a new version, in issues if you want to specify which version is affected and so on. Version links point to the version page and always use the version name as link text. The syntax is:

```
version#ID
version:Name
```

In the preceding syntax, `version` is the keyword which tells that this is the version link, `Name` is the version name (can be enclosed into quotes) and `ID` is the numeric ID, which can be seen, for example, in URL of the version page (the last component).

To link to a version in a different project prefix it with the project identifier, for example:

```
redmine:version:2.0.3
```

Issue links

Most likely, you will use issue links even if you don't plan to. That's because their syntax is very natural and obvious. It's just `#X`, where, `X` is the issue number.

Resolving an issue is the process which sometimes involves not only the assignee but also users, customers, QA engineers, and so on. In this case, it is very useful to be able to refer to the particular note (history entry) in the issue instead of just the issue, especially if this note contains a comment explaining some details. In such cases use the syntax:

```
#X-Y
#X#note-Y
```

In the preceding syntax, `Y` is the history entry number, which can be seen on the issue page.

Unlike other links, issue links when rendered contain more details. See the following screenshot:

The issue **#6** here is already closed and, therefore, is stroked out. When users hover their mouse over an issue link the hint box is shown, which contains the issue subject and status.

Attachment links

While support for attachments in a resource can be used to store images, which will be used in the Wiki content of this resource, the main goal of attachments is actually different. Usually we store files in a Wiki page, an issue, a forum topic, and so on to let other users download them. In such cases somewhere in the Wiki content we refer to the attached files. Instead of just filenames and text like "attached to this page" we can use the syntax as follows:

```
attachment:filename.ext
```

This will produce the link to the attached file, which will trigger its download when users click on it. Instead of `filename.ext` use the filename of the attachment, enclose it into quotes if it contains spaces or other special symbols.

The file, you refer to in the Wiki content, should be attached to the resource this Wiki content is connected to. That is, you can't use the attachment links for project files.

News links

Sometimes when we write news we may need to mention previously posted news. For such cases we can use the marker as follows:

```
news#ID
news:"Title"
```

In the preceding syntax, `ID` is the numeric ID of news, which can be found in news page URL (the last component), and `Title` is the title of news (can be enclosed into quotes). When rendered news links always use the title as the link text.

You can also refer to news in other projects using the following syntaxes:

```
project-identifier:news#ID
project-identifier:news:Title
```

Document links

The very same can be done for documents:

```
document#id
document:"Title"
```

Here, ID is the numeric document ID, which can be found in URL of the document page, and Title is the document title.

To link to a document in a different project use the following syntaxes:

```
project-identifier:document#id
project-identifier:document:"Title"
```

Forum links

Linking to forums is very much the same:

```
forum#ID
forum:"Name"
```

Again, here ID is the numeric ID of the forum (you know how to find it) and Name is the name (title) of the forum.

 If you have only one forum it's not easy to determine its ID but it's still possible. Links to this forum (for example, new message link) contain boards/ID/, where ID is the forum ID

Forum links can be used, for example, to advise users where they can discuss their questions. While message links can be used, like issue notes, for pointing to the message with details regarding some issue.

Messages, also known as topics, are what users add into forums. A message can be referenced only using ID (while it has the subject it's not guaranteed to be unique). So the syntax for message links is as follows:

```
message#ID
```

In the preceding syntax, ID is the unique numeric ID of the message.

Unfortunately, the message ID is not shown in the message list and you need to determine it on your own:

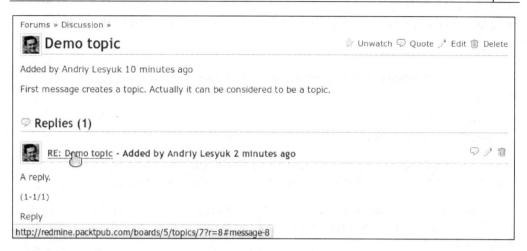

Here the message ID of the first (and only) reply is **8** as can be seen from the URL (shown on the status bar). The first message has ID **7** (it is actually the topic) and the numeric ID of the forum is **5**.

To link to forums or messages of other projects just prepend the project identifier like for other similar links.

Links to repository

Repositories support is one of the most powerful features of Redmine so it is not surprising that many repository related links are supported.

As you might know SCM systems were created to manage and track revisions. Each revision, which is also known as commit or changeset, brings changes to files, so a reference to the revision may be needed to let users know when and how files were changed. How to do this depends on the type of the revision ID, which, in turn, depends on the type of SCM.

For numeric revision IDs, for example, for Subversion revisions, you should use:

```
Repository|rX
```

In the preceding syntax, X is the numeric revision number and Repository is the repository identifier, which should be used if you have more than one repository in the project. That is, the Repository parameter is optional. For example:

```
r128
stable|r9868
```

For other revision IDs, for example, for Git revision, you should use the following:

```
commit:Repository|ID
```

In the preceding syntax, `ID` is the revision ID and `commit` is the keyword. For example:

```
commit:0e1a622a
commit:stable|9fde11f9
```

When rendered revision links, similar to issue links show the hint box with the commit message, when users hover their mouse cursors over the link.

In addition to just revisions, you may need to reference to particular files and even lines, for example, to show where you think the problem lies. In such cases, use the syntax as follows:

```
source:"Repository|Path@X#LY"
```

Here `Path` is the path to the file in the repository (not including the repository name), `X` is optional revision ID (numeric or not), `Y` is optional line number, and `Repository` should be used if it's not the default repository in the project. For example:

```
source:trunk/lib/redcloth3.rb
source:redmine|trunk/lib/redcloth3.rb
source:trunk/app/helpers/application_helper.rb@7248
source:trunk/app/helpers/application_helper.rb#L779
```

The file from the repository can be also downloaded. That is, you can create a link which will trigger the file download. To do this, use the following:

```
export:"Repository|Path"
```

All these links (revision, sources, and download) can be prepended with the project identifier if you want to reference revisions or files in a different project.

Code

Redmine would not be a good project hosting and issue tracking application without the possibility to embed the code into the Wiki content. The code can be syntax highlighted or not. It can be inline or in the block.

 Syntax highlighting in Redmine is implemented using the CodeRay library, see at http://coderay.rubychan.de

For the inline code enclose the text into the @ marker, for example:

```
@Redmine::WikiFormatting@
```

Alternatively, you can use the <code> HTML tag as follows:

```
<code>Redmine::WikiFormatting</code>
```

Both methods produce the same result and can be used inline. But the <code> tag also supports the programming language parameter:

```
<code class="Lang">...</code>
```

Here Lang should be replaced with the code language. Currently supported values, which can be used as a Lang parameter, include C, CPlusPlus (*C++*), CSS, Clojure, Delphi (*Object Pascal*), Diff (*used for viewing differences in Redmine*), ERB (*eRuby*), Groovy, HAML, HTML, JSON, Java, JavaScript, PHP, Python, Ruby, SQL, XML, and YAML.

Unfortunately Redmine syntax highlighting always adds line numbers that makes it nearly unusable inline. However, only the <code> tag supports the programming language and therefore it has a special usage in Wiki formatting.

We'll get back to this soon and now let's speak about how to embed the code as a block. It's enough just to add additional spaces before the text, for example:

```
The code block:

   module Test
     class Klass
       end
   end
```

Note the empty line before the code block. Alternatively you can use the <pre> HTML tag:

```
<pre>
...
</pre>
```

Both these methods produce the block of code.

And here is where we can use the programming language support of the `<code>` tag. As none of the block markers support the language and the code block is where we really want the code to be highlighted (and line numbers to be shown) we can combine them. For example:

```ruby
<pre><code class="ruby">
    def self.included(base)
        base.extend(ClassMethods)
        base.send(:include, InstanceMethods)
        base.class_eval do
            unloadable
            alias_method_chain :repository_field_tags, :add
            alias_method_chain :subversion_field_tags, :add
            alias_method_chain :mercurial_field_tags,  :add
            alias_method_chain :git_field_tags,        :add
            alias_method_chain :bazaar_field_tags,     :add
        end
    end
</code></pre>
```

The preceding code will be rendered as follows:

```
1     def self.included(base)
2         base.extend(ClassMethods)
3         base.send(:include, InstanceMethods)
4         base.class_eval do
5             unloadable
6             alias_method_chain :repository_field_tags, :add
7             alias_method_chain :subversion_field_tags, :add
8             alias_method_chain :mercurial_field_tags,  :add
9             alias_method_chain :git_field_tags,        :add
10            alias_method_chain :bazaar_field_tags,     :add
11        end
12    end
```

Tables

The main idea of Textile is to make the formatting code still readable even in the raw form. For this reason, perhaps, the | (the vertical bar) marker was chosen for building tables. Thus, you can write the code as follows:

```
|              |Heading 1|Heading 2|Heading 3|
|Row heading 1|    ?    |    ?    |    ?    |
|Row heading 2|    ?    |    ?    |    ?    |
|Row heading 3|    ?    |    ?    |    ?    |
```

The preceding code will be rendered as follows:

	Heading 1	Heading 2	Heading 3
Row heading 1	?	?	?
Row heading 2	?	?	?
Row heading 3	?	?	?

Very natural, isn't it? In practice, however, users usually skip spaces and the raw code looks less readable.

You might know that options for syntax rules are specified after the marker and before the dot. Yes, the | marker also supports options and thus, the _ option makes a cell a heading cell. So if we change the preceding code to the following:

```
|_.                |_.Heading 1|_.Heading 2|_.Heading 3|
|_.Row heading 1|      ?      |      ?      |      ?      |
|_.Row heading 2|      ?      |      ?      |      ?      |
|_.Row heading 3|      ?      |      ?      |      ?      |
```

We will get the output as seen in the following screenshot:

	Heading 1	**Heading 2**	**Heading 3**
Row heading 1	?	?	?
Row heading 2	?	?	?
Row heading 3	?	?	?

Unfortunately the more complex the rule is, the less readable is the raw text.

I, personally, can't imagine good tables support without the support of merging cells. In Textile, cells can be merged horizontally using the \x option, where x is the number of cells, and vertically using the /y option, where y is also the number of cells. Let's see how it works with the preceding example slightly shortened:

```
|_/2\2.                    |_\2. Common heading      |
                           |_.Heading 1|_.Heading 2|
|_/3.Common row|_.Row heading 1|      ?      |      ?      |
               |_.Row heading 2|      ?      |      ?      |
               |_.Row heading 3|      ?      |      ?      |
```

The following screenshot shows the result of the preceding code:

		Common heading	
		Heading 1	Heading 2
	Row heading 1	?	?
Common row	Row heading 2	?	?
	Row heading 3	?	?

If you think that the table rules miss some important options such as aligning, don't hurry to conclude, wait for the advanced syntax topic that we will cover later.

Macros

Everything we have discussed until this topic cannot be altered or extended (*or at least it's not easy, I mean Redmine API does not allow to do this*). Redmine, however, introduces macros, which can be utilized to extend the Wiki formatting.

A macro has the syntax as follows:

```
{{MacroName(Arguments)}}
```

Let's review macros which come with the core Redmine.

Table of contents

While technically it's not a macro it is reviewed here as it has a very similar syntax, which is:

```
{{toc}}
```

This marker, if it's the only one on the line and is separated by empty lines from other paragraphs, generates the table of contents as seen in the following screenshot:

First heading
Second heading
Third heading
Fourth heading

Optionally, the {{toc}} marker supports aligning. Thus, to align the table of contents to the right use {{>toc}} and to align it to the left use {{<toc}}.

Collapsed block

Sometimes we need to publish marginal information, which does not have high importance but still needs to be included in the content. The problem is that this information is going to occupy space on the page and, possibly, draw attention away from more important things. This is where the {{collapse}} macro can come to our help:

```
{{collapse(hint)
text
}}
```

This macro makes the text invisible by default. Instead it shows hint, clicking on it will unhide the text.

Thumbnail

We have already discussed how to embed images into the Wiki content. Thus, to show a smaller image on the Wiki page, which links to the full-size image attachment, we can write it as follows:

```
!{width:100px;}.image.png(Title)!:/attachments/download/N
```

The problem appears when the attached image is really huge. If using the ! marker, it gets transferred in the full size and is resized by the user's browser. So, to avoid slow load and to cache resized images on the server, Redmine adds the {{thumbnail}} macro:

```
{{thumbnail(image.png, size=100, title=Title)}}
```

In the preceding macro, image.png must be attached to the current resource, size specifies the size of the thumbnail, and title defines the title for the thumbnail.

Thumbnails not shown?

For generating thumbnails Redmine uses ImageMagick's convert tool, which does not get installed with ImageMagick libraries. To install this tool execute the following command:

```
$ apt-get install imagemagick
```

Include

If you need to copy some text into many Wiki pages, for example, disclaimer or rules, you can create a separate page with the recurring content and then include it into other Wiki pages. That's what the {{include}} macro is used for. Its syntax is as follows:

```
{{include(Project:Name)}}
```

Project is the project identifier and is optional here, it is needed only if you include the Wiki page from another project. Name is the name of the Wiki page to include.

Child pages

To assist in building, the Wiki navigation Redmine includes the {{child_pages}} macro, which has the syntax as follows:

```
{{child_pages(Name, parent=1, depth=2)}}
```

In the preceding syntax, Name is the name of the Wiki page, child pages of which should be listed. If Name is omitted Redmine will use the current Wiki page (if the macro is not executed from a Wiki page, an error will be raised). The parent option tells that the Wiki page itself should be included into the list (as the parent page). The depth option limits the depth level of child pages to list.

The following screenshot shows the sample output:

Hello world

This is a funny macro that is used for educational and testing purposes. It just outputs the given arguments.

```
{{hello_world}}
```

Macro list

If a plugin ships with a macro how do we know that it is available? That's where the {{macro_list}} macro can help, it just outputs short information about macros available in the particular Redmine installation.

The syntax is simply written as follows:

```
{{macro_list}}
```

If you use plugins that provide some macros it can be a good idea to list all available macros somewhere on Help or similar Wiki page.

Advanced syntax

Redmine Textile is much more powerful than it may seem at first glance. Its power lies in options which are supported by many syntax rules. While usually you won't need to resort to the advanced options sometimes some of them may seem to be essential for receiving the result we need.

Advanced options are usually specified between the marker and the . (dot) mark, which indicates the end of options. Thus, the following syntax can be used for table cells and blocks:

```
|(options).|
p(options). ...
```

For some markers like list ones, options should be specified right after the marker and before the space:

```
*(options) ...
```

Images and normal links also can use the advanced options:

```
!(options)image.png!
"(options)Anchor":http://www.example.com
```

Alignment

Some alignment options have already been mentioned but these were options specific to that rule. In addition to them, Redmine supports common alignment options as follows:

- <: Align to the left
- =: Align centrally
- <>: Justify
- >: Align to the right

For examples:

```
p<>. This paragraph will be justified.
bq>. This quote will be aligned to the right.
```

Some of the elements, for example, table cells, also support the vertical alignment options as follows:

- ^: Align to the top
- -: Align middle
- ~: Align to the bottom

For example:

```
|/3^. Cell value aligned to the top|
```

Padding

Block elements, such as paragraphs and cells, can be padded using (and) options. These options tell us how many ems of padding should be added to the left (for ( ) and to the right (for)) side correspondingly. The amount is specified using several parentheses. For example:

```
p(((). This paragraph will use padding.
```

For this paragraph the left padding will be set to three ems and the right padding will be set to one em.

Custom style and language

Using Textile we can do even more. For example, we can set the CSS class name for the element:

```
p(info). This paragraphs will use <p class="info">.
"(redmine-link)Redmine":http://www.redmine.org
```

Of course, such CSS classes should be defined in CSS files. But it's not a problem if the style you need does not exist in CSS rules as you can write CSS rules directly in Textile as follows:

```
"{color:red}Redmine":http://www.redmine.org
*{font-family:Tahoma} Tahoma font
```

Unfortunately, not all CSS properties are supported. Thus, supported CSS properties include namely `color`, `width`, `height`, `border`, and others which start with `border-`, `background` and ones that start with `background-`, `padding`, starting with `padding-`, `margin`, starting with `margin-`, `font`, `font-`, `text`, and anything that starts with `text-`.

Using Textile, you can also define the language for the element:

```
*[en] English
bq[en]. English quote.
```

Textile span

If you are familiar with HTML and CSS you should know the magic `<span>` tag. I call this tag magic because it is intended to be used especially for styling a part of the text if no other HTML tag fits better. This element is also supported in Textile and can be created using the `%` marker. For example:

```
Let's make %{color:red}this text red% and %{color:yellow}this one
yellow%.
```

The *span* element supports most of the advanced options described earlier.

Disabling element

What if we do not want the text `#1` to be rendered as the issue link? Almost every marker or element in Textile can be disabled using the `!` marker. For example:

```
!#1
!r128
![[Wiki]]
!{{toc}}
!{{macro_list}}
```

Table advanced syntax

Tables are the most complex elements in Textile, so it may become a headache to style all the cells properly especially if we use the advanced styles. For such cases, Textile supports batch styling.

To style the whole table we can use the `table.` marker. This marker should be the only one on a line and should precede the table markers. For example, to make the table border color red, we can do the following:

```
table{border-color:2px solid red}.
|_.Heading 1|_.Heading 2|
|     ?     |     ?     |
```

Similarly batch mode also exists for rows. Thus, to change the background color of the heading row to gray we do the following:

```
{background-color:gray}. |_.Heading 1|_.Heading 2|
                         |    ?      |    ?      |
```

Quick syntax reference

Here are syntax rules provided by the Textile markup language:

Block markers		List markers	
`p.`	Starts paragraph	`#`	Numbered list item
`h1.`	First-level heading	`##`	Nested numbered list item
`h2.`	Second-level heading	`*`	Bulleted list item
`h3.`	Third-level heading	`**`	Nested bulleted list item
`h4.`	Forth-level heading	`#*`	Nested mixed list item
`h5.`	Fifth-level heading	**Phrase markers**	
`h6.`	Sixth-level heading	`*...*`	Strong text
`bq.`	Quote block	`**...**`	Bold text
`>`	Quote	`??...??`	Citation
`>>`	Second-level quote	`+...+`	Inserted text
`fnN.`	Footnote text (see also [N])	`-...-`	Removed text
Inline markers		`_..._`	Emphasized text
`...[N]`	Footnote index	`__...__`	Italicized text
`ABC(...)`	Acronym	`^...^`	Superscript
Textile links		`~...~`	Subscript
`http://...`	HTTP link	**Image marker**	
`www....`	HTTP link	`!url!`	Image
`ftp://...`	FTP link	`!url(title)!`	Image with title
`mailto:...`	Email link	`!url!:http://...`	Image link
`"text":http://...`	Link with anchor	**Code**	
`"text(...)":http://...`	Link with title	`@...@`	Inline code
Tables		`<code>...</code>`	Inline code
`| ... | ... |`	Cells	`<pre>...</pre>`	Code block
`|_. ... |_. ... |`	Heading cells	`<code class="lang">...</code>`	
`|\N. ... |`	Cell merged horizontally	`<pre><code class="lang">`	
`|/N. ... |`	Cell merged vertically	`...`	
		`</code></pre>`	
Horizontal line markers		**Disabling formatting**	
--- or *** or ___		`<notextile>...</notextile>`	

Extensions for Textile provided by Redmine:

Redmine links

Wiki links

`[[...]]`	Link to Wiki page		
`[[...#section]]`	Link to section		
`[[...|text]]`	Link with anchor		
`[[project:...]]`	Link to other projects		
`[[project:...#section|text]]`			

Version links

`version#id`	Link by ID
`version:...`	Link by name
`project:version:...`	Link to other projects

Attachment links

`attachment:file`	Link to attachment

Project links

`project:project`	Link to project
`Project:"..."`	Link by name

News links

`news#id`	Link by ID
`news:"..."`	Link by title
`project:news:"..."`	Link to other projects

Forum links

`forum#id`	Link by ID
`forum:"..."`	Link by name
`message#id`	Link by ID
`project:forum:"..."`	Link to other projects

Issue links

`#N`	Link to issue
`#N-note`	Link to note
`#N#note-note`	Link to note

Repository links

`rN`	Link to revision
`commit:id`	Link to revision
`source:path`	Link to file
`source:path@rev`	Link to file in rev.
`source:path#LN`	Link to line
`source:path@rev#LN`	Link to line in rev.
`export:path`	File download
`repo|rN`	Link to revision
`commit:repo|rev`	Link to revision
`source:"repo|path"`	Link to file
`export:repo|path`	File download
`project:rN`	Revision in project
`project:commit:rev`	Revision in project
`project:source:path`	File in project
`project:export:path`	Download from project

Document links

`document#id`	Link by ID
`document:"..."`	Link by title
`project:document:"..."`	Link to other proj.

Macros

`{{toc}}`	Table of contents	`{{collapse(hint)...}}`	Collapsed block
`{{thumbnail(image.png)}}`		`{{child_pages}}`	Child pages index
`{{thumbnail(image.png, size=100)}}`		`{{child_pages(page)}}`	
`{{thumbnail(image.png, title=...)}}`		`{{child_pages(depth=3)}}`	
`{{include(page)}}`	Include Wiki page	`{{child_pages(parent=1)}}`	
`{{include(project:page)}}`		`{{macro_list}}`	List of macros

Advanced style options provided by the Textile markup language:

Advanced options (used inside other syntax rules)			
Alignment		**Padding**	
<	Align to left	(	Left padding
=	Align centrally	)	Right padding
<>	Justify	( )	Both paddings
>	Align to right	**CSS**	
^	Align to top	(css classes)	CSS class names
-	Align middle	{css-style}	CSS style rules
~	Align to bottom	[lang]	Language
Special markers (for styles)			
%options...%	Phrase options	table<options>.	Table options

Summary

I hope you did not get the feeling that Redmine Wiki formatting is too complicated? Even if you did, believe me, it's only the first impression. As you practice more, you will find it flexible and funny.

I'm quite sure that having learned this chapter you will be able not only to astonish your Redmine colleagues but also to be more intelligible in your posts, to mark more important information, and so on.

In the next chapter, we will learn how to improve the workflow of issues, how to adapt it to your methodology, and how to control the access to your Redmine installation.

Access Control and Workflow

8

You might expect to see the very major part of the administration area discussed in a single chapter, but that's not going to happen. In this book, I'm trying to review Redmine by functional parts and not by web interface sections. However, this is the chapter which discusses many sections of the administration area, as they are related to the access control and the workflow.

On the other hand, you might wonder why the access control and the workflow are reviewed in a single chapter? In terms of Redmine, the workflow is a set of rules for the issue life cycle, in particular, for issue status change. These rules take into account member roles and trackers (issue types). And these are, actually, member roles that define access permissions.

We will not just review many sections of the administration area but will also discuss them and their influence on the system functionality. So, this chapter is intended for administrators, however, it will be interesting for project managers as this chapter explains how to configure Redmine to ease and optimize the development process, in particular, the issue life cycle. Other users may also find this chapter useful, as here, they can learn what permissions they need to gain access to certain types of functionality.

In this chapter, we will cover the following topics:

- Roles
- Trackers
- Issue statuses
- Workflow
- Modifying workflow
- Practical example

Roles

Redmine roles define which permissions users have in projects. As you already know users can be added to projects as members. To do this, we select a user and a role. So, here, a role is a kind of membership type, that's why roles are also often called member roles.

Roles are system wide and can be managed in **Administration | Roles and permissions**, as shown in the following screenshot:

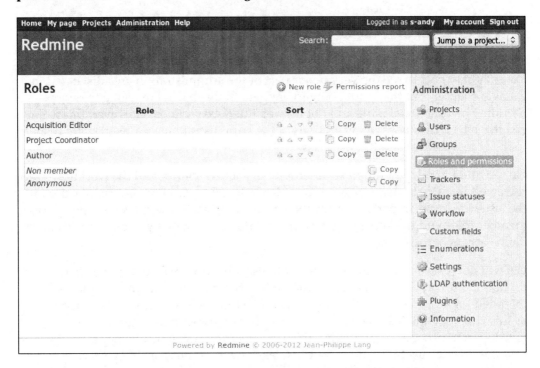

The order of roles—how it is presented on this page—is important as the same order is used for the forms, with which users select member roles. Therefore, this order can be changed using the arrows in the **Sort** column. Normally, you will want the order to be from the most privileged at the top to the less privileged at the bottom.

The italicized **Non member** and **Anonymous** roles are virtual ones, meaning they do not really exist in the database and thus, cannot be renamed, removed, their order cannot be changed, and so on (permissions can be changed for them though). The **Non member** role is used for users who are not members of the project and the **Anonymous** role is used for unauthorized (not logged in) users.

A role can be edited by clicking on the role name in this list. When you do this, you get the following form:

Roles » Acquisition Editor

Name * Acquisition Editor

Issues can be assigned to this role ☑

Issues visibility All issues

Permissions

Project
- ☑ Create project
- ☑ Select project modules
- ☑ Create subprojects
- ☑ Edit project
- ☑ Manage members
- ☑ Close / reopen the project
- ☑ Manage versions

Forums
- ☑ Manage forums
- ☑ Edit own messages
- ☑ Post messages
- ☑ Delete messages
- ☑ Edit messages
- ☑ Delete own messages

Calendar
- ☑ View calendar

Documents
- ☑ Manage documents
- ☑ View documents

Files
- ☑ Manage files
- ☑ View files

Gantt
- ☑ View gantt chart

Issue tracking
- ☑ Manage issue categories
- ☑ Edit issues
- ☑ Set issues public or private
- ☑ Edit notes
- ☑ Set notes as private
- ☑ Manage public queries
- ☑ Add watchers
- ☑ View Issues
- ☑ Manage issue relations
- ☑ Set own issues public or private
- ☑ Edit own notes
- ☑ Move issues
- ☑ Save queries
- ☑ Delete watchers
- ☑ Add issues
- ☑ Manage subtasks
- ☑ Add notes
- ☑ View private notes
- ☑ Delete issues
- ☑ View watchers list

News
- ☑ Manage news
- ☑ Comment news

Repository
- ☑ Manage repository
- ☑ Commit access
- ☑ Browse repository
- ☑ Manage related issues
- ☑ View changesets

Time tracking
- ☑ Log spent time
- ☑ Edit own time logs
- ☑ View spent time
- ☑ Manage project activities
- ☑ Edit time logs

Wiki
- ☑ Manage wiki
- ☑ View wiki
- ☑ Edit wiki pages
- ☑ Rename wiki pages
- ☑ Export wiki pages
- ☑ Delete attachments
- ☑ Delete wiki pages
- ☑ View wiki history
- ☑ Protect wiki pages

Check all | Uncheck all

[Save]

The **Issues can be assigned to this role** option controls if the role is assignable, that is, if members of this role appear in the value list for the **Assignee** issue field. This can be useful, for example, for a reporter or customer role, which you unlikely want to make assignable.

The **Issues visibility** option specifies which issues should be visible for members of this role. It accepts the following values:

- **All issues**: All issues, including private ones, are visible to the user.
- **All non private issues**: All issues, except private ones, are visible to the user.
- **Issues created by or assigned to the user**: Only issues, which are owned by the user, are visible. This means that an issue should be created by the user or assigned to the user to be visible.

However, the most interesting and important part of this form can be found under the **Permissions** label.

Permissions

Generally, Redmine access control is built on permissions, and all such permissions (if editable) can be found in this form. Thus, when a plugin adds a permission, it is also added here.

The permission list is split into blocks (**Project, Forums**, and so on); each block corresponds to a project module. Thus, when a plugin adds a project module and permissions for this module, you will see new block and new permissions in this block here. An exception is the **Project** block, which is not related to a project module and defines permissions for the project itself.

Redmine users can be divided into three types—unauthorized (not logged in) users (presented by the **Anonymous** role), authorized users but not members of the project (presented by the **Non member** role), and project members (other roles). Generally, permissions are defined for these three types and not all permissions are available for all the types. Thus, Redmine can't permit project creation to unauthorized users. Most of the permissions are defined for project members though.

 All these permissions are implicitly granted to the administrator.

So let's discuss each block and permission now.

Project block

The **Project** block, as has been mentioned earlier, holds permissions for the project. If a plugin provides any system permissions for accessing objects outside projects, for example, blog posts provided by the Redmine Blog plugin, such permissions will appear in this block as well. Refer to the following permissions:

- **Create project** permission is available for registered users and controls if the user is allowed to create new projects.

  As we know, to have permissions, the user should be associated with the role, and to be associated with the role, the user should be added to the project. So, how users can have the **Create project** permission if they have not been added to any project yet? The first project should be always created by the administrator. Normally, this will be the general company project named, for example, after the company name. You can add users, who you want to allow creating projects, to this project. Alternatively you can, of course, grant the **Create project** permission to the **Non member** role.

- **Edit project** permission controls if the project member can change project properties located under the **Information** tab in the project settings.

- **Close/reopen the project** permission controls if the project member is able to close or reopen the project, which can be done on the project overview page.

- **Select project modules** permission controls if the project member can manage project modules under the **Modules** tab in the project settings.

- **Manage members** permission controls if the project member is allowed to manage project membership under the **Members** tab in the project settings.

- **Manage versions** permission controls if the project member is able to add, edit, and delete project versions using the **Versions** tab in the project settings.

- **Create subprojects** permission controls if the project member is able to add subprojects to the project. Such project members should also have the **Create project** permission.

Forums block

The **Forums** block contains permissions for Redmine message boards, which are provided by the Forums project module and are available under the **Forums** tab in the project menu. Refer to the following permissions:

- **Manage forums** permission controls if the project member has access to the **Forums** tab in the project settings, where message boards can be created, edited, or removed.

- **Post messages** permission specifies if the user can add messages to the project message board. This also includes whether the user can reply to the message. This permission is available to all users including not logged-in ones.

- **Edit messages** permission controls if the project member can modify forum messages, including ones posted by other users. This permission will be useful for forum moderators.

- **Edit own messages** permission controls if the user can modify own forum messages. Granting this permission, you should always remember that the original text can be copied into replies as a quote, so this permission won't help in such cases. Generally, the **Edit own messages** permission, that is, editing, should be used only to correct typos. Certainly, this permission is available only to logged-in users.

- **Delete messages** permission specifies if the project member can delete forum messages, including messages of other users. This permission can be useful for spam moderation.

- **Delete own messages** permission controls if the user can delete own forum messages. Like with the **Edit own messages** permission when granting this one, you should consider that the message text can be copied into replies, or replies may be based on the message. This permission is available to registered users.

Calendar block

The **Calendar** block contains permissions that define access control for the calendar, which is available under the **Calendar** tab, if the Calendar project module is enabled:

- **View calendar** permission is the only permission in this block. This permission controls if the user has access to the **Calendar** tab of the project menu. Please notice that if the user does not have access to issues, the calendar will be empty or will contain only versions' due dates (if they were specified). This permission can be specified for all users, including not logged in ones.

Documents block

The **Documents** block holds permissions for accessing the **Documents** tab of the project menu, which is provided by the Documents project module. Refer to the following permissions:

- **Manage documents** permission controls if the user can create, edit, or delete documents. Users with this permission will also be able to attach files to documents as well as to remove attachments.

- **View documents** permission controls if the user can see documents and download their attachments. This permission can be granted to any user, including not logged in ones.

Files block

The **Files** block contains permissions for accessing the **Files** tab of the project menu. This tab is available only if the Files project module is enabled. Refer to the following permissions:

- **Manage files** permission specifies if the user is able to add or remove project files.
- **View files** permission is needed for the user to be able to download project files. This permission can be granted to any user, including not logged in ones. However, project files will still not be available for non members if the project is private.

Gantt block

The **Gantt** block holds permissions for accessing the **Gantt** tab of the project menu, which contains the Gantt chart. This tab is available only if the Gantt project module is enabled.

- **View gantt chart** permission controls if the user has access to the **Gantt** tab of the project menu. This permission is useful if the user has permissions to see issues, otherwise the Gantt chart will be always empty. The permission can be specified for all users, including not logged in ones.

Issue tracking block

The **Issue tracking** block holds permissions related to issue tracking. This is the largest and perhaps, the most important block. Permissions in this block influence not only the content under the **Issues** tab of the project menu but also every page, where issues are involved, and these are almost all project pages including the overview page, roadmap, calendar, gantt, and more. Issue-tracking functionality is provided by the Issue tracking project module. Refer to the following permissions:

- **Manage issue categories** permission controls if the project member can add, edit, or delete issue categories, which can be done under the **Issue categories** tab in the project settings menu—in addition, project members with this permission can add issue categories within the issue form.

- **View issues** permission is the most important permission as it controls if the user can see issues, that is, without this permission, the user won't see any issues in the project. So, in most cases, you will want this permission to be set. The permission is available for all users, including not logged in ones.

- **Add issues** permission controls if the user is able to add new issues. This permission is also available for not logged in users.

- **Edit issues** permission controls if the user is able to edit issues, including adding attachments. This permission is available for all users, including not logged in ones.

- **Manage issue relations** permission controls if the user can add or remove related issues, which can be done on the issue page. This permission is also available for not logged in users.

- **Manage subtasks** permission specifies if the user is able to add child issues to the issue, which can be done on the issue page. Such user should also have the **Add issues** permission. Like the latter, this permission is also available for not logged in users.

- **Set issues public or private** permission controls if the user is able to modify the **Private** flag of the issue. If this permission or the **Set own issues public or private** permission is set, the user will also be able to see the value of this flag in the issue list (by enabling the appropriate column), and filter the issue list by the value of this flag. The permission is available for not logged in users as well (for example, if an anonymous user reports a critical security issue).

- **Set own issues public or private** permission controls if the user is able to modify the **Private** flag of the issue, which was created by this user. Users with this permission will also be able to see the value of this flag in the issue list and filter the issue list by this value. The permission is available for all registered users.

- **Add notes** permission specifies if the user can comment issues. This permission also allows adding attachments to the issue. The permission is available to all users, including not logged in ones.

- **Edit notes** permission controls if the user can edit issue comments. This permission, however, does not allow to remove files that were attached to the issue along with the comment. The permission is available to all registered users and is useful for moderation.

- **Edit own notes** permission allows the user to modify own comments, that is, the comments that were created by this user. This permission, however, won't allow the user to remove files that were attached along with such comments. Permissions like this one should be used only for correcting typos, as the original text from the comment can be used in replies as a quote. The permission is available for all registered users.

- **View private notes** permission specifies if issue private notes are visible to the user. The permission is available only to project members.

- **Set notes as private** permission controls if the user can post issue private notes. Note that without the **View private notes** permission, such user won't be able to see own private notes. The permission is available only to project members.

- **Move issues** permission is used to determine whether the issue can be moved between projects by the user. In addition to this permission, such user must have the **Add issues** permission in both — the source and the target projects. Certainly, the permission is available for non members as well.

- **Delete issues** permission controls whether the issue can be deleted by the project member.

 However, in my opinion, issues should never be deleted. Each issue is assigned a unique ID and can be referenced from many places. When you delete an issue, its ID becomes unused. Besides, while most of associated objects are deleted as well, the issue can be referenced by links from, for example, Wiki pages which will become dead. Instead issues can and should be closed.

- **Manage public queries** permission specifies if the project member can add, modify, or delete public custom queries. Custom queries is a very powerful feature, and public custom queries can make the project more customer-friendly. However, too many public queries for the project can make this feature ineffective. So, this permission should be granted to users who know what to do with it.

- **Save queries** permission indicates if the user can save custom queries. Custom queries are available for all users, including not logged in ones, but only logged in users can save queries (if this permission is set).

- **View watchers list** permission specifies if the user can see who is watching the issue. This permission is available for all users, including not logged in ones.

- **Add watchers** permission is available for all users as well. This permission controls who is able to add watchers to the issue. For anonymous users, it can be useful if the user knows who is likely interested in the issue. However, when granting this permission, you should consider that watchers may get e-mail notifications on changes in watched issues. In other words, you are granting the permission for sending many e-mails to project members.

- **Delete watchers** permission specifies who will be able to remove watchers from the issue. This permission is available for all users, including not logged in ones as well. But, you will unlikely want to grant this permission to anyone besides project managers. The user, who is watching the issue, may expect to be notified about changes in the issue, so I don't think it's good if someone besides this user removes him/her from watchers.

News block

The **News** block contains permissions for accessing news, which are available under the **News** tab in the project menu — if the News project module is enabled for the project. News are visible to everyone, including not logged in users, and there is no permission to change this (besides disabling the News project module). Refer to these permissions:

- **Manage news** permission specifies if the project member is able to post, edit, and delete news in the project. The user with this permission will be also able to remove news comments (which is useful for spam moderation).

- **Comment news** permission controls who can comment news. This permission is available to all users, including not logged in ones. But, I would not recommend granting this permission to anonymous users, as in my practice, news are where spam goes most often.

Repository block

The **Repository** block holds permissions, which control access to repositories. Some of these permissions apply not only to Redmine (as a web application) but also to SCM servers, if the advanced repository integration has been configured (see *Chapter 3, Configuring Redmine*). Repositories are available under the **Repository** tab in the project menu if the Repository project module is enabled. Refer to the following permissions:

- **Manage repository** permission allows the project member to add, edit, and delete repositories. This permission also allows you to modify committer associations.

- **Browse repository** permission controls if the user can browse the content of the repository. If the SCM server has been configured to support the advanced integration, this permission also controls access to the repository on the SCM server. The permission can be set for all users, including not logged in ones.

 Thus, if your Redmine supports the advanced repository integration and you want anonymous users of your SCM server to have the read-only access to the repository, you should grant this permission to the **Anonymous** role.

- **View changesets** permission specifies if the user has access to the repository revision list and revision pages. For full repository browse access, you should set this permission along with the **Browse repository** permission. The permission is available for all users, including not logged in ones.

- **Commit access** permission has nothing to do with Redmine itself. This permission is used by the SCM server, if the advanced integration has been configured, to determine whether the write access to the repository should be given to the user. The permission is available for all users, including not logged in ones.

- **Manage related issues** permission specifies if the user can add or remove issues related to the revision, which can be done on the revision page. The permission is available for all users, including not logged in ones.

Time tracking block

The **Time tracking** block holds permissions used to control the access to the time tracking in the project. Refer to the following permissions:

- **Log spent time** permission specifies if the user is able to add time entries to the project. This also applies to the time entries added using commit messages. The permission is available to all registered users.

- **View spent time** permission controls if the user can see time entries of the project. This applies not only to the time report but also to the sum of spent hours on the project overview page, spent hours on the issue page, and so on. The permission can be set even to not logged in users.

- **Edit time logs** permission allows modifying time entries of any user in the project. This permission can be granted only to project members. Anyway, I doubt it's good to allow a user to modify time entries of other users.

- **Edit own time logs** permission allows the user to modify own time entries. This permission is available for all registered users.

- **Manage project activities** permission controls if the project member can enable or disable time-tracking activities for the project.

Wiki block

The **Wiki** block includes permissions for working with Wiki pages, which are available under the **Wiki** tab in the project menu (if the Wiki project module is enabled). These permissions do not apply to other Wiki syntax-enabled contents (for example, issue description).

- **Manage wiki** permission specifies if the project member has access to the **Wiki** tab in the project settings (do not confuse with the **Wiki** tab in the project menu). In fact, this tab allows you to specify the starting Wiki page name only.

- **Rename wiki pages** permission controls if the project member is able to move the Wiki page to a different parent page and/or change its name.

- **Delete wiki pages** permission controls if the project member is able to remove the Wiki page.

- **View wiki** permission is the permission which actually makes the Wiki page visible to the user. You should unset this permission if you want to hide Wiki from particular roles. The permission is available for all users, including not logged in ones.

- **Export wiki pages** permission controls if the user is able to export the Wiki page to PDF, HTML, or TXT. Unsetting this permission actually has no sense as users can always save the Wiki page using browser. The permission is available for all the users.

- **View wiki history** permission is also available for all users, including not logged in ones. As you know the Wiki page stores the history of changes, sometimes some sensitive data can get there, so it may be needed to hide previous versions of the page. This permission allows the user to see the full changes history, previous versions of pages, difference between versions, and who authored each line.

- **Edit wiki pages** permission specifies whether the user should be allowed to edit the Wiki page in the project. With this permission, users can also add attachments to the Wiki page. You can grant this permission to not logged in users as well. The Wiki system stores the full history of changes and allows to rollback the previous version if needed, so it's quite safe, in most cases, to grant this permission even to the **Anonymous** role.

- **Delete attachments** permission allows the user to remove attachments from the Wiki page. While Wiki stores the history of changes of the Wiki text, it does not store the attachments history, so this permission can be used to prevent removing important files by anonymous users. The permission is available to all users.

- **Protect wiki pages** permission controls if the project member can lock or unlock the Wiki page. Having all the project Wiki system editable by anyone, you can make some pages editable only by trusted users. All such trusted users should have this permission set (yes, the page protected by one user can be edited by another user, who has this permission as well).

Permissions report

Member roles are used to differentiate users by declaring sets of permissions. In other words, the goal of the role is not just to hold the set of permissions but also, often, to make sure that some of the permissions are not granted to other roles. In fact, the role name should not just be the same as the real-life position, but also it should reflect granted permissions. This way, it will be easier to manage Redmine, to determine which role should be given to the user, and so on. Thus, access to project settings may be granted to "Project manager" or "Project administrator", editing permissions to "Moderator" or "Content editor", and so on. It's ok to assign several roles to a project member. So, you can name roles by their goals and assign different roles to a single user.

In such cases, it would be hard to keep all the role names and goals in mind while editing permissions using the previously described role page. Perhaps, for this reason, in practice, experienced Redmine administrators prefer the **Permissions report** page instead, as shown in the following screenshot:

As you can see, on the **Permissions report** page permissions are listed in columns, the titles of which are role names. The green check marks in column and row titles can be used to check or uncheck all the permissions in the column or row correspondingly. Like on the role editing page, the report page is divided into blocks by project modules, where each block can be collapsed or expanded by clicking on the plus or the minus icon to the left-hand side from the block title.

On this page, you can also clearly see that some permissions are not available for all types of users. To remind you what has been mentioned, **Acquisition Editor**, **Project Coordinator**, and **Author** roles are for project members, the **Non member** role is for registered users but not project members, and the **Anonymous** role is for not logged in users.

Role Shift plugin

This small plugin can be used to silently replace the visible role permission set with the permission set of another role. The replacement roles are defined per project and can replace the **Non member** and the **Anonymous** roles. Go to this link—`http://projects.andriylesyuk.com/projects/role-shift`.

Trackers

In Redmine, issues can be of Bug, Feature, Support (which are created by default), or any other type, as these types are configurable. In this application, issue types are referenced as **trackers**.

Trackers play an important role in issue tracking. They define issue properties, conditions for issue status transitions, fields availability, and so on. Thus, a feature is unlikely to have the status **Fixed** and a bug is unlikely to have the status **Planned**.

Trackers can be managed, created, edited, or removed in **Administration | Trackers**. Refer to the following screenshot:

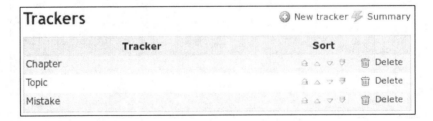

The order of trackers is also important as the same order is used when listing trackers in application forms. Most frequently used trackers or those, which you want to be used most often, should be on the top. To change the order of trackers, you can use green arrow icons.

The **Summary** link in the top-right corner opens the page:

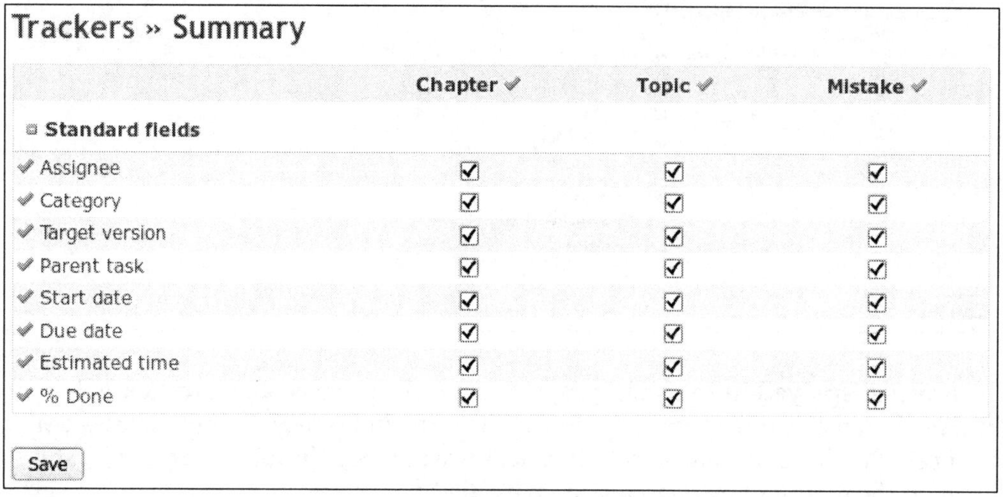

	Chapter ✔	Topic ✔	Mistake ✔
Standard fields			
✔ Assignee	☑	☑	☑
✔ Category	☑	☑	☑
✔ Target version	☑	☑	☑
✔ Parent task	☑	☑	☑
✔ Start date	☑	☑	☑
✔ Due date	☑	☑	☑
✔ Estimated time	☑	☑	☑
✔ % Done	☑	☑	☑

Trackers » Summary

Save

If you have any custom fields defined for issues, they will appear on this page as well, in the **Custom fields** block.

Here, you can select the issue field that should be available for the tracker. For example, the **Target version** field can be disabled for the "Support" tracker and so on. The green checkmark icons can be used to toggle all the checkboxes in the row or in the column.

Issue fields availability can be also configured on the tracker properties page, which is shown when we click on the tracker name on the **Tracker** list page:

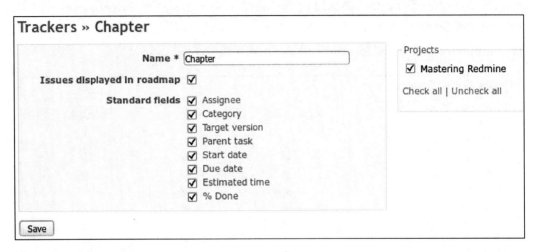

The **Issues displayed in roadmap** property controls if issues of this tracker get displayed on the roadmap page by default. The roadmap page though, allows you to choose the trackers to show, that is, trackers which are disabled here can be still shown in the roadmap by enabling them explicitly.

Keep your roadmap short and clear
Usually on the roadmap we show features and, by default, we do not show bug fixes, as they are less important for end users (they are important only for those who have faced them).

If you remember, the project properties page, which is available under the **Information** tab in the project settings menu, allows you to choose trackers that will be available in the project. Here, we have just another way to configure this—in the **Projects** block we can choose those projects the tracker will be available for.

You may want to change the name of the "Feature" tracker to something more common, that better describes your work. Thus, development of the system core can unlikely be named a feature development. For such cases, you can use the "Task" name instead.

Issue statuses

Can you imagine issues without issue statuses? We can say with confidence that issue tracking is useless without usage of issue statuses. Moreover, the more detailed are issue statuses, the more accurate is the workflow. But too many details can make the tracking process annoying. Therefore, I believe, choosing right issue statuses for your processes is extremely important for having a good experience with Redmine. In fact, this should be one of the first things you configure after deploying Redmine in your organization.

Issue statuses can be managed in **Administration | Issue statuses**:

Issue statuses					
Status	**Default value**	**Issue closed**	**Sort**		
New	✔		⬆ ⬈ ⬇ ⬊	🗑	Delete
In Progress			⬆ ⬈ ⬇ ⬊	🗑	Delete
Resolved			⬆ ⬈ ⬇ ⬊	🗑	Delete
Feedback			⬆ ⬈ ⬇ ⬊	🗑	Delete
Closed		✔	⬆ ⬈ ⬇ ⬊	🗑	Delete
Rejected		✔	⬆ ⬈ ⬇ ⬊	🗑	Delete

There should be the default issue status which is set when a user posts an issue. While in the web issue form, the user can select the initial issue status, such a possibility sometimes does not exist, for example, for issues created with e-mail messages. In this list, the default issue status, which can, of course, be only one, is marked with the checkmark in the **Default value** column.

Generally, an issue can be open and closed. Redmine can't guess this basic state by the issue status name, so each issue status also has the property indicating if this status closes the issue. In the status list, such issue statuses are marked in the **Issue closed** column. Redmine can have many statuses, which mark the issue as closed, for example, they can be **Closed** or **Rejected**, as on the screenshot, or **Won't Fix**, **Obsolete**, **Not Confirmed**, **Fixed**, and so on.

And, again, the order of issue statuses on this page is important and can be modified using the green arrows under the **Sort** column. The same order is used in issue forms and ideally, should reflect the completeness of the issue from the initial state (for example, **New**) till the final state (for example, **Closed**).

Issue statuses can be edited by clicking on their names. When you do this, the following form appears:

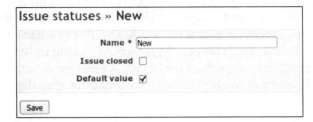

Generally, that's it regarding managing issue statuses. But, definitely not all regarding the issue tracking. As these are issue statuses, which define the life cycle of the issue and produce the workflow. It's just too complicated to be managed along with issue statuses, and therefore, it was placed into the separate administration section.

Workflow

Issue tracking is not just about keeping the list of issues, it's also about implementing the issue life cycle, which is also known as the **workflow**.

The Redmine issues workflow can be configured in **Administration | Workflow**:

Let's start with reviewing each tab.

Issue status transitions

The main goal of the workflow is to control the issue status, which can be set for the issue in certain conditions. Thus, instead of setting the **Open** status after the **In Progress** status (for example, when the issue was returned) we may prefer setting the special **Reopened** status. So, for this, we just let the **Open** status be set only after the **New** status is set and allow setting the **Reopened** status after the **In Progress** status (this way when checking the issue status, we will always know if the issue has been returned). These are the things which can be configured under the **Status transitions** tab.

Issue status transitions can be configured only per role and tracker. So, in the **Role** field we choose one of available roles, and in the **Tracker** field we choose one of trackers.

Some issue statuses may be not used by certain trackers (for example, the **Fixed** status and the **Feature** tracker), so to simplify the form Redmine allows you to skip such issue statuses. This, of course, cannot be done without the possibility to change as we need a way to utilize new statuses, which, of course, won't be used by trackers yet. So, to show all the available issue statuses uncheck the **Only display statuses that are used by this tracker** option.

And after clicking the **Edit** button, we get the following form:

✔ Current status	New statuses allowed					
	✔ New	✔ In Progress	✔ Resolved	✔ Feedback	✔ Closed	✔ Rejected
✔ New	☐	✔	✔	✔	✔	✔
✔ In Progress	✔	☐	✔	✔	✔	✔
✔ Resolved	✔	✔	☐	✔	✔	✔
✔ Feedback	✔	✔	✔	☐	✔	✔
✔ Closed	✔	✔	✔	✔	☐	✔
✔ Rejected	✔	✔	✔	✔	✔	☐

▹ Additional transitions allowed when the user is the author
▹ Additional transitions allowed when the user is the assignee

Save

In the left-hand column we see initial issue statuses, and in rows we see possible target statuses. In other words, this table defines if the status in the left-hand column can be changed to other statuses in the row. If the checkbox is checked, the change can be made.

For user convenience, the background color of the cell, the checkbox of which was initially selected, is green. This way you can check what was modified before submitting changes.

The table is divided into three blocks. The top block specifies common settings and two other blocks, which are collapsed by default, can optionally contain modifications to the common settings. Common settings apply to all users of the current role and to all issues with the tracker. The next block is for cases, in which the user is the author of the issue, that is, the issue was created by this user. And the last one applies to the cases, when the issue is assigned to the user.

There is no need to duplicate common settings in other blocks, as other blocks can only enable issue status transitions. Disabled transitions in additional blocks are just ignored.

Issue fields permissions

Since Version 2.1.x of Redmine the **Workflow** section has the additional **Fields permissions** tab, which can be used to make issue fields read-only or to require them for some trackers. This tab uses the same parameters form.

 Switching between **Status transitions** and **Fields permissions** tabs preserves the configuration of the form.

Clicking on the **Edit** button shows the following screenshot:

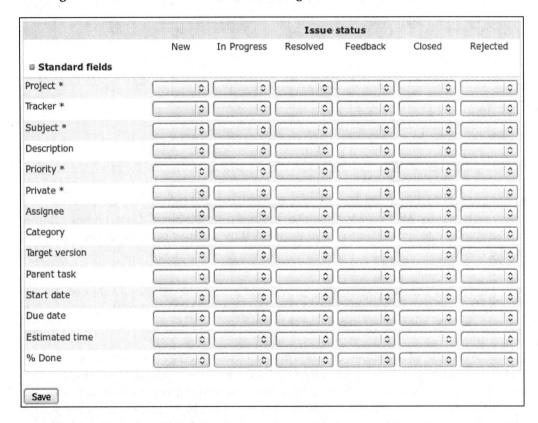

Each listbox in this form allows to choose the **Read-only** option. If this option is chosen for the field, the user with the corresponding role won't be able to change the value of this field, if the issue is of the corresponding tracker.

If you have defined custom fields for issues, they will appear in this form in the additional **Custom fields** block.

Fields, which are required by default, are marked with the red asterisk here. Fields, which are not required, have the additional **Required** option. If this option is selected for the field, it will become required for users with the corresponding role, if the issue is of the corresponding tracker.

 You can also remove fields, which are not required by default, for particular trackers using the **Summary** link in **Administration | Trackers**.

Like for issue status transitions, if fields permissions were set before, they are loaded with backgrounds of corresponding cells set to appropriate colors:

Here, the gray color stands for the **Read-only** option, and the red color stands for the **Required** option.

Quick functions

The workflow page also has the contextual menu with links in the top-right corner, which we did not review. I skipped this menu, because at that moment we did not know enough to understand what are they for.

The **Edit** link redirects to the same page, that gets opened, when we click on the **Workflow** item in the administration menu. So, this menu item is generally used to get back to the form from other workflow views.

Copying configuration

The **Copy** link can be used to quickly copy configuration from one role and tracker pair to another. This feature can be used if, for example, you mistakenly changed the wrong pair. Anyway, as you have seen, the workflow configuration is quite complex and utilizes many checkboxes and listboxes, so many of you may find this link useful for different purposes (another option is if you forgot to copy configuration on creation, but we will speak about this later). Refer to the following screenshot:

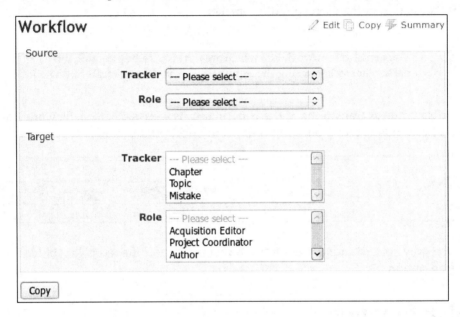

For user convenience the form supports selecting several target trackers and roles.

Summary link

The **Summary** link redirects to the page containing aggregate data:

	Acquisition Editor	Project Coordinator	Author	Non member	Anonymous
Chapter	28	13	13	✖	✖
Topic	30	13	13	✖	✖
Mistake	30	13	13	✖	✖

Those numbers represent the number of enabled permissions per role and tracker. ✖ means that no permissions are enabled.

While these numbers are, generally, useless each number and ⊠ is a link redirecting to the corresponding form. So, the summary page can be used for a quick access to permissions editing.

Modifying workflow

Configuring the workflow is one of the most complicated tasks in Redmine. And the proper configuration of issue status transitions is more significant and important than configuring fields permissions. So, before doing this I would recommend to draw the diagram of issue status transitions, which you plan to implement in Redmine, and discuss it with your team. This way, you will minimize the risk of the need to modify the workflow later. However, I believe, you can't fully avoid modifications as the workflow should be an adaptive system and can still change.

Modifying the workflow is not so complicated, but it is risky. Wrong setting can allow more than users need or limit them, if they need more. You have already seen all the configuration screens and the amount of elements, so you would probably agree that it's easy to miss something when you add new role, tracker, or issue status. Therefore, under this topic, we will speak about basic principles you should follow when adding new objects to the workflow.

Adding roles

Member roles can be added using the **New role** link, which can be found in the contextual menu in the top-right corner of the **Administration | Roles and permissions**. Clicking on this link opens the following form:

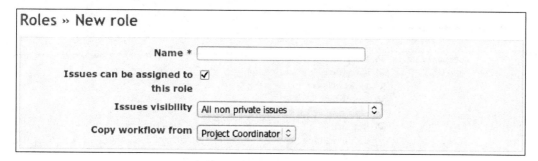

This form also contains **Permissions**, but I did not include them in the screenshot.

The new role form is very much like the role edit form, which was discussed earlier, but with the new **Copy workflow from** form. This option allows to choose the role, the workflow settings of which (that is, issue status transitions and fields permissions, but not role permissions) for all trackers will be copied into the newly created role.

So let's compile the list of things you should do when creating a new role, to make this process easier and faultless:

- For the **Copy workflow from** option choose the existing role, issue status transitions, and fields permissions of which are most close to the settings you want to have in the new role

- If you forgot to specify the value for the **Copy workflow from** option, use the **Copy** link to clone these setting to the new role

- Use green arrow icons to move the new role to the appropriate place in the role list

- Use the **Permissions report** link to adjust permissions for the new role

Adding trackers

New tracker can be added using the **New tracker** link, which is located in the top-right contextual menu on the tracker list page in **Administration | Trackers**. This link opens the following form:

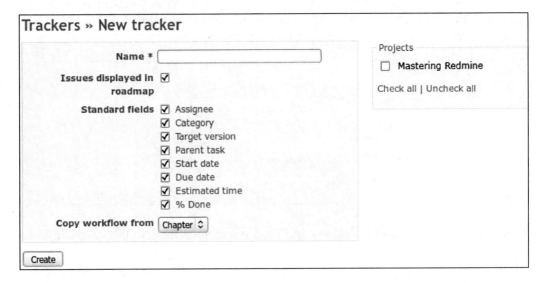

This form is almost identical to the tracker edit form. Like the new role form, this form also has the **Copy workflow from** option, which has exactly the same meaning—if a tracker is selected for this option, all workflow settings for all roles of the selected tracker will be copied into the new tracker.

 However, the workflow does not include fields availability settings, which can be specified during tracker creation using this form or later using the **Summary** link.

So, to avoid mistakes and misconfiguration when creating new tracker, try to follow this principles:

- Using the **Copy workflow from** option select the tracker, settings of which are most close to the ones you would like to set for the new tracker
- Configure fields availability using either the creation form or, maybe even better, using the **Summary** link
- Choose projects, for which you want to activate the new tracker, using the creation form
- Using the green arrow icons in the tracker list move the new tracker to the appropriate position

Adding issue statuses

New issue status can be added using the **New status** link in **Administration | Issue statuses**. This link opens the following screenshot:

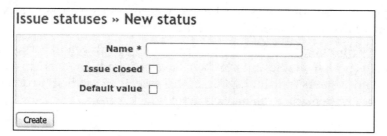

Have you noticed the difference? No **Copy workflow from** option is available this time. Issue addition is not going to be such easy. This form is exactly the same as the one used for editing issue statuses.

The workflow for the issue status can unlikely be copied as, usually, new statuses are placed somewhere between existing statuses (for example, *New — New status — In Progress*) that definitely needs to be configured manually. In practice, however, users often forget about the need to add the new status to the workflow that ends up with confusion and lack of understanding of why the new issue status is not visible in issue forms and in the workflow. Unfortunately, Redmine's interface and approach to this issue do not help much.

So, let's try to define some principles which can help make this process easier:

- Using green arrow icons in the issue status list move the new status to the appropriate position (keep closed statuses at the bottom).
- Print, write down numbers, or make a screenshot of the content of the summary page, which can be accessed using the **Summary** link in **Administration | Workflow**.
- In **Administration | Workflow** select any role and any tracker.
- Uncheck the **Only display statuses that are used by this tracker** option, otherwise the workflow won't show the newly added status.
- Reconfigure the workflow taking into account the new status. Do this for authors and assignees as well if applicable. Don't forget, also, about fields permissions.
- Using the **Copy** link in **Administration | Workflow** copy the just configured workflow to other role-tracker pairs, but only to those ones, which should have similar workflows.
- Adjust workflows you have just copied settings to (if needed).
- Repeat the previous five items for every group of role-tracker pairs, which should have similar workflow settings.
- Use the **Summary** link in **Administration | Workflow** and earlier saved data to check if all relevant numbers have changed. These are just numbers of allowed status transitions, but, in this case, they can help to determine if changes were made to all necessary role-tracker pairs.

Practical example

I can't think about any better way to demonstrate the workflow configuration than reviewing some real-life practical example. As Kanban Agile methodology is most popular, nowadays, let's see how to configure the workflow to satisfy Kanban task rotation practices.

Before configuring the workflow, it is always helpful to draw the issue life cycle diagram.

Kanban does not have any strict requirements to the board and column names, so here we'll use the following issue statuses, which should correspond to real-life column names on the Kanban board (except the **New** status, which should be set on creation, and means is to be reviewed):

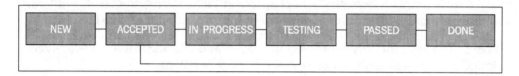

Assuming there is only one tracker and three roles: "Project manager", who reviews new issues and closes ready ones, "Developer" and "Tester". The following minimal settings should be applied in Redmine:

	NEW	ACCEPTED	IN PROGRESS	TESTING	PASSED	DONE
Project manager						
NEW		√				√
PASSED						√
Developer						
ACCEPTED			√			
IN PROGRESS				√		
Tester						
TESTING		√				√

Of course, this is a very basic example, but you can use it as the starting point.

Redmine Backlogs plugin

If you are using Agile development in your team, you may find the Backlogs plugin useful. Go to http://www.redminebacklogs.net.

Summary

In practice, Redmine users rarely configure the workflow and many of them just use the default settings, which come with Redmine. Some users add new roles, trackers, and issue statuses, but do not utilize the full power of the workflow. Instead, they just allow all trusted users to change any status to any other. My guess is that it is due to the high complexity of the Redmine interface which is responsible for managing the workflow. Therefore, I hope that in this chapter I've succeeded to clarifying how to embrace this important feature. Nevertheless, I'm quite sure that project managers, who have read this chapter, will feel more comfortable with Redmine now and will be able to transform it into a very helpful assistant.

The next chapter is not only for project managers and administrators, it's for every Redmine user, as it describes how to make it more personal.

9
Personalization

Some readers might want to start reading this book with this chapter as it looks like an introduction into using Redmine. But, I believe, it's not an introductory chapter. Usually, you first get used to the place and then unpack your boxes. Unpacking your boxes and making Redmine your "home" application is what, actually, this chapter is about.

This is the first time we speak about Redmine from a user's perspective:

- What can users do to improve their experience with Redmine?
- How can users get quick access to the needed functionality?
- How can users be sure that they won't miss important updates?

These are only some of the questions that will be answered in this chapter.

While the previous chapter was intended mainly for project managers and administrators, this one is intended for all users. For project managers and site owners, this chapter also gives an idea of what users need in order to have a better experience with Redmine.

In this chapter we will cover the following topics:

- Automatic account creation
- Gravatar
- Personal page
- Getting updates
- Personalizing issue list

Automatic account creation

The fact that we review the account creation process in this chapter seems pretty confusing. After all, the majority of readers, I believe, have already created accounts or own the default one, which is "admin" (*I want to believe, that the former "admin"*). However, under this topic we will review not the ordinary registration, but account creation, which does not actually involve filling in any registration form. So this topic is not intended for new comers, instead it will be of interest for site owners and administrators.

In case you did not know, many users try to avoid registering on every new site. There are many reasons for this:

- They don't trust the site and do not want to share their e-mail addresses, passwords, and so on
- They do not want to remember another username and password and do not want to use the same credentials, they are using on other sites
- They see no weighty reasons for creating an account on the site, and so on

 The last mentioned reason gives a hint towards the solution — make sure your potential users do know the benefits of registering on your site.

But, Redmine can make account creation easier and liberate from the need to remember a new password. It supports at least two technologies for this — OpenID and LDAP.

OpenID

OpenID is an open standard for authentication, which involves the OpenID identity provider as an authentication server. Thus, users do not store the password on the Redmine server. Instead OpenID users get redirected to the OpenID provider, where they authenticate and get returned back authenticated if successful.

The great thing is that the OpenID provider can be any Internet host and this protocol is supported by industry giants such as Google and Yahoo, which means that you can authorize using, for example, your Google account in Redmine. The drawback of this authentication solution is that you need to specify the URL of the OpenID provider.

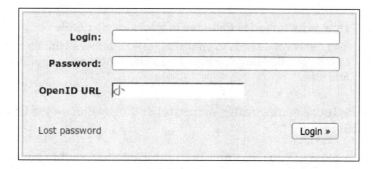

 Google OpenID URL is `https://www.google.com/accounts/o8/id`.

After putting the URL into the **OpenID URL** field the user clicks on the **Login** button and gets redirected to the OpenID provider. Then the provider usually asks for credentials of the user in the provider's system. After users login, or if users are already logged in, the provider asks to confirm that they really want to grant Redmine access to their profile. In the following screenshot, check how Google does this:

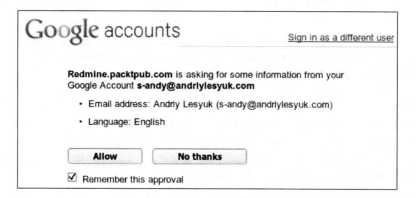

In particular, to create the user's profile, Redmine will need the full name and e-mail address. Redmine won't ask for or store the password and won't be provided with the password! The newly created user will have the same username the user has in the OpenID provider's system.

How to unauthorize Redmine in your Google profile?

You can revoke access to your Google account for Redmine in your Google profile using **Account | Security | Authorize applications and sites**.

Depending on Redmine settings after successful authorization on the OpenID provider you will be:

- Asked to activate your Redmine account using data sent to you by e-mail, if the **Self-registration** option in **Administration | Settings | Authentication** is set to **account activation by email**.

- Asked to wait for your new account to be manually approved by the Redmine administrator, if the **Self-registration** option is set to **manual account activation**.

- Logged into your new Redmine account, if the **Self-registration** option is set to **automatic account activation**.

- Asked to fill in some additional data for your new account (the password and the username among them), which actually indicates that there was a problem in Redmine's OpenID stack, which did not allow you to use the OpenID provider to login.

At the time of writing this topic, the native Redmine OpenID support does not work, at least for Google, so you may need the OpenID Fix plugin available at http://projects.andriylesyuk.com/projects/openid-fix.

The fact that any host can be an OpenID provider, of course, can become the reason for not using OpenID (or for using it along with manual or e-mail account activation). For example, if you use Redmine as a corporate project management application. But don't be in a hurry to get upset!

Do not require users to enter OpenID URL

Entering and remembering or copying and pasting the OpenID URL each time the user logs in whittles down the benefits of this authentication method. Luckily Jorge Barata Gonzalez created the plugin, which allows you to pick up the URL from the "selector" containing the most popular OpenID providers, including but not limited to Google, Yahoo, AOL, LiveJournal, WordPress, and so on. See the following Github page for more information:

https://github.com/mconf/redmine_openid_selector

LDAP

LDAP is the open protocol for accessing active directory services. Such services are commonly used for storing usernames and passwords and, therefore, LDAP, as a protocol is used for authentication. Most known directory services servers are OpenLDAP and Microsoft Active Directory and, yes, using LDAP you can connect Redmine to the Microsoft AD domain.

> In addition, directory services can be used for storing other user profile properties like Language but Redmine is limited in supporting this (for example, there is no way to select LDAP attributes for user custom fields).

Unlike OpenID, to support a directory server, administrators must manually add the server into Redmine using **Administration | LDAP authentication | New authentication mode**. Moreover, Redmine allows you to add many LDAP servers, each of which will be tried when a new user logs in. If the **On-the-fly user creation** option is checked for the server, Redmine will create the account for the user on the first login but will still use the password stored on the server.

The login process for LDAP users (unlike OpenID) does not differ from the login process of local users.

User/Group synchronization

Ricardo Santos created the LDAP Sync plugin, which can perform user and group synchronization. See the following Github page for more information:

`https://github.com/thorin/redmine_ldap_sync`

Gravatar

Gravatar is a very popular avatar image service (the name "gravatar" stands for "globally recognized avatar"). It uses the very simple algorithm for storing avatars. The client application (Redmine, in this case) sends the request with the hash of the user's e-mail to the service and the service returns the associated image. If no image is associated with the hash, Gravatar returns one of default avatars (see *Chapter 3, Configuring Redmine*).

Using avatar will help to visually identify your data (issues, comments, activities, and so on) among other users' data in Redmine.

This simplicity made it to be chosen as the profile picture source in WordPress and StackOverflow. With custom plugins, the support for Gravatars can be added to Drupal, Joomla, SugarCRM and more. This means that if you set the Gravatar for Redmine, you will also have it automatically in WordPress, StackOverflow, some Drupal sites, and so on.

In practice, however, usually more than a half of Redmine users do not make use of Gravatar. Maybe because Redmine has no statement for ordinary users anywhere about the possibility of adding an avatar using Gravatar? So, let's review how to do this in this topic.

 If you already use Gravatar you can safely skip this topic.

First, go to `https://gravatar.com/site/signup` and register using the e-mail address you have specified or are going to specify in your Redmine account.

After successful registration and e-mail confirmation you will be redirected to the e-mail addresses configuration screen as shown in the following screenshot:

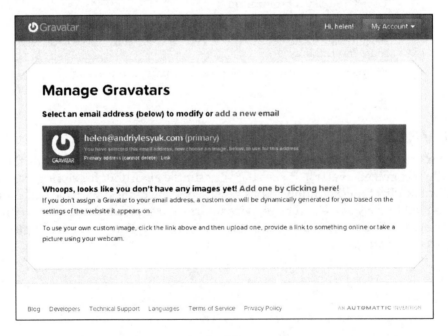

As you see from the preceding screenshot, you can register many e-mail addresses and manage them with single Gravatar account.

If you click on the **Add one by clicking here** link or go to **My Account | Add an image**, you'll be given the option to select the square area, which will be used for the avatar, and crop the picture as shown in the following screenshot:

After clicking the **Crop and Finish!** button you will have to choose the rating of the avatar image as shown in the following screenshot:

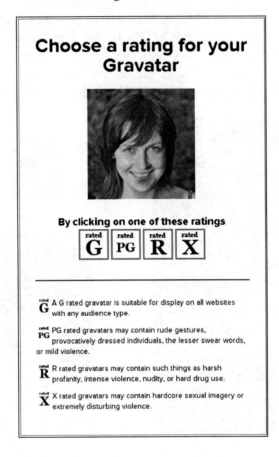

Usually you just choose **G** here by clicking on the appropriate box. You really should not use images with rude gestures, nudity, hard drug use, or sexual content for your Redmine avatars.

After selecting the rating, what I believe is just a formal step, the avatar becomes associated with the e-mail address and is ready to use.

Now, if you come back to Redmine, you see the new avatar near the name as shown in the following screenshot:

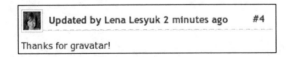

This avatar now gets shown almost everywhere, where the link to your profile is rendered.

Local Avatars plugin

While Gravatar is a universal solution sometimes you may need to have avatars stored locally, for example, if your corporate network has a limited Internet connection. In such cases you may use the Local Avatars plugin originally authored by Andrew Chaika and available at `https://github.com/alminium/redmine_local_avatars`.

Personal page

Perhaps you have already noticed **My page**, where you are redirected to after successful login (unless you were redirected to the login form from some other page)? If not, this page can be accessed by using the **My page** link in the top-left menu as shown in the following screenshot:

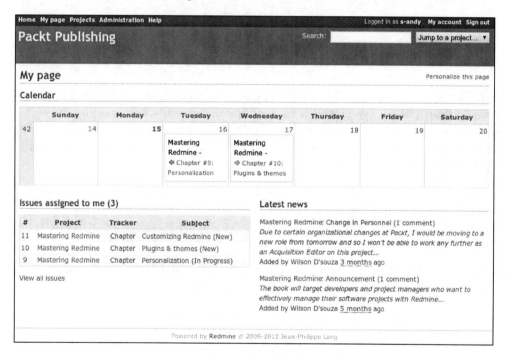

The idea of this page is to assemble all the information related to the user in one place, so that they can quickly move to the page of interest. But, as you already know, there is a lot of information the user can be interested in. Therefore, this page comes with the **Personalize this page** link.

After clicking on this link, the personalization screen opens as shown in the following screenshot:

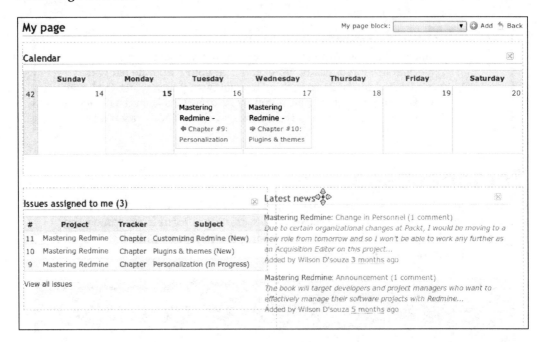

On this screen, each block of the personal page turns into a draggable and removable block. To drag a block, we just click its header and move it while keeping the mouse button clicked, (for example, I moved the **Latest news** block in the preceding screenshot). Any block can also be removed by clicking the ⊠ icon in the top-right hand corner of the block.

You should have noticed that the page is divided into three sections—top-wide section, left section, and right section. Each section is outlined by the dashed line. We can move blocks between these sections. We can also change the order of the blocks in the sections by moving them inside it. A section can be empty.

Besides removing blocks, we can add them in by using the **My page block** drop-down list as shown in the following screenshot:

These are the names of all the available blocks. You can add each of them to your personal page (but only once). To do this, select the block name and click on the **Add** link—the block will appear in the top-wide section, where you can move it from another section, if you want.

Now let's review what information these blocks provide.

 Plugins can add custom blocks, so you can see other block names on your installation.

Issues assigned to me

This block contains the list of issues, which were assigned to the user as shown in the following screenshot:

Issues assigned to me (3)			
#	Project	Tracker	Subject
11	Mastering Redmine	Chapter	Customizing Redmine (New)
10	Mastering Redmine	Chapter	Plugins & themes (New)
9	Mastering Redmine	Chapter	Personalization (In Progress)
View all issues			

The list is limited to 10 issues but the **View all issues** link allows you to move to the issue list containing all such issues. The list is ordered by the priority and the last update time.

Watched issues

The **Watched issues** block is very much like the **Issues assigned to me** block:

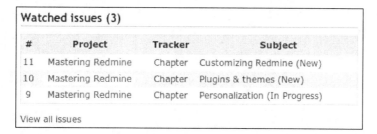

Watched issues (3)			
#	Project	Tracker	Subject
11	Mastering Redmine	Chapter	Customizing Redmine (New)
10	Mastering Redmine	Chapter	Plugins & themes (New)
9	Mastering Redmine	Chapter	Personalization (In Progress)
View all issues			

The difference is that the block lists issues that are watched by the user and sorted by the update time only.

Spent time

If you use Redmine for time tracking, you may find this block useful.

Spent time (last 7 days)			
Total: 12.00			
Activity	Project	Comment	Hours
14 Oct 2012			*5.00*
Writing	**Mastering Redmine** - Chapter #9: Personalization		5.00
13 Oct 2012			*2.00*
Writing	**Mastering Redmine** - Chapter #9: Personalization		2.00
12 Oct 2012			*1.00*
Writing	**Mastering Redmine** - Chapter #9: Personalization		1.00
11 Oct 2012			*2.00*
Research	**Mastering Redmine** - Chapter #9: Personalization		2.00
10 Oct 2012			*1.00*
Writing	**Mastering Redmine** - Chapter #9: Personalization		1.00
09 Oct 2012			*1.00*
Writing	**Mastering Redmine** - Chapter #9: Personalization		1.00

It lists the time entries of the user for the last 7 days. As you can see, time entries can be edited or deleted here.

Documents

The **Documents** block lists up to 10 documents from the projects that the user is a member of, as shown in the following screenshot:

```
Documents

Chapter 8. Access control & workflow

28 Sep 2012 02:55 pm

Chapter 7. Text formatting

10 Sep 2012 02:54 pm

Chapter 6. Time tracking

23 Aug 2012 02:54 pm

Chapter 5. Managing projects

05 Aug 2012 02:54 pm

Chapter 4. Issue tracking

18 Jul 2012 05:00 pm

Chapter 2. Installing Redmine

30 Jun 2012 05:00 pm

Chapter 3. Configuring Redmine

22 Jun 2012 05:00 pm

Chapter 1. Getting familiar with Redmine

12 Jun 2012 02:43 am
```

The list contains recently added documents.

Reported issues

This block contains issues which were created by the user. In fact, this is the only place where you can quickly find issues, reported by you, and, therefore, I personally use this block quite often.

You can also create an issue list custom query to list issues reported by you.

#	Project	Tracker	Subject
11	Mastering Redmine	Chapter	Customizing Redmine (New)
10	Mastering Redmine	Chapter	Plugins & themes (New)
9	Mastering Redmine	Chapter	Personalization (In Progress)
8	Mastering Redmine	Chapter	Access control & workflow (Closed)
7	Mastering Redmine	Chapter	Text formatting (Closed)
6	Mastering Redmine	Chapter	Time tracking (Closed)
5	Mastering Redmine	Chapter	Managing projects (Closed)
4	Mastering Redmine	Chapter	Issue tracking (Closed)
3	Mastering Redmine	Chapter	Configuring Redmine (Closed)
2	Mastering Redmine	Chapter	Installing Redmine (Closed)

Reported issues (11)

The list is ordered by the update time.

Latest news

This block contains 10 latest news items from the projects, the user is a member of, as shown in the following screenshot:

Latest news

Mastering Redmine: Change in Personnel (1 comment)
Due to certain organizational changes at Packt, I would be moving to a new role from tomorrow and so I won't be able to work any further as an Acquisition Editor on this project...
Added by Wilson D'souza 3 months ago

Mastering Redmine: Announcement (1 comment)
The book will target developers and project managers who want to effectively manage their software projects with Redmine...
Added by Wilson D'souza 5 months ago

Calendar

The **Calendar** block is the personal user's calendar for the current week.

Calendar

	Sunday	Monday	Tuesday	Wednesday	Thursday	Friday	Saturday
42	14	15	16	17	18	19	20
			Mastering Redmine - ◈ Chapter #9: Personalization	Mastering Redmine - ➡ Chapter #10: Plugins & themes			

Like the **Calendar** tab, this calendar contains important events on projects that the user is a member of.

Getting updates

Unless you check Redmine on a regular basis, once a day or even more frequetly, it's easy to miss important information like a new issue assigned to you, new data for an issue, changes in Wiki documentation, a new reply in the topic thread, and so on. Not everything is available on a single page (such as **My page**) and there can be too much information on other pages to analyze (such as the **Activity** tab).

Therefore, in this topic we will speak about how to be notified about changes made in objects of interest.

Notification settings

Personally I find it convenient to be notified using e-mail as you get this kind of notifications when you are ready for it (that is, you check for new messages and expect them to be there). Users usually check their mail boxes once a day or even more often anyway, there are plenty of different tools for checking e-mails (all these are benefits referenced further). It is possible to control what notifications you will get in Redmine in your e-mail client (for example, using filters) — these are only some of the benefits of e-mail notifications. The only problem with them is that they must be configured properly to be effective — too narrow configuration can prevent the important information from being sent and too wide a configuration can make you lose interest in reading each message.

So let's start with discussing how to configure notifications. Click on the **My account** link in the top right-hand side menu — you'll get the account page with the **Email notifications** box:

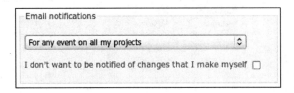

Let's review all the available notification options:

- **For any event on all my projects**: This option is selected by default. If you choose it, you will get all the notifications for all the events (for example, Wiki page change, thread reply, issue comment, and so on) on all projects, you are a member of. Practise shows that's really too much! So you're unlikely to want to leave this option selected.

- **For any event on the selected projects only...**: When you choose this option, the list of your projects appears below the drop-down list. In this list you can select which projects you want to receive notifications for, for all events. This is a kind of limited previous option in this list. For projects, which you have not selected here, Redmine will use the next option in this list.

- **Only for things I watch or I'm involved in**: If you choose this option, you are going to be notified about events in objects you watch, you created, or are assigned to you. This is, perhaps, the best choice. But if you choose it, do not forget to watch objects you are interested in but which were not created by you or are not assigned to you.

- **Only for things I am assigned to**: If you select this option you'll be notified about events on objects you watch or which are assigned to you. As in Redmine, only issues can be assigned to users, which means that only issues related notifications will be sent (except, of course, watched objects).

- **Only for things I am the owner of**: If you select this option, you'll be notified about events on objects you watch or have created.

- **No events**: This option disables notifications (including watched objects, what actually makes watching useless).

Getting no notifications while they are enabled?

Ask administrators if they have configured e-mail sending in Redmine. Refer to *Chapter 3*, *Configuring Redmine* to know more about this.

Did I mention that I personally would not set e-mail notifications to the **For any event on all my projects** option by default? This is not the only weird default value. Thus, the **I don't want to be notified of changes that I make myself** option is disabled by default, that means that, for example, if you add a comment to an issue, you'll also be notified about it. In my opinion, this is one of the first options that should be changed in your account right after registration.

None or only some of the notifications you expected to get?

For example, you are getting notifications for watched issues but not for watched topics. In this case, most likely that administrators disabled the **Message added** option in the **Email notifications** tab at the **Administration | Settings**. Ask them to check if the appropriate options are enabled.

Watching

The best way to ensure that you'll be notified about changes in an object is to watch the object. Watching an object is simple — just click on the **Watch** link in the top-right contextual menu (of the content area).

If you watch the object, the link title turns into **Unwatch**.

 Currently users can watch issues, news, Wiki pages, forums, and topics.

News feeds

The **Only for things I watch or I'm involved in** option is quite reasonable but what if we want to be notified about new issues? We can watch issues, but not new ones. In this case, should we switch to the **For any event on all my projects** option? No, luckily there is one more way to get such notifications, news feeds.

If an object or a listing has such a link, you can subscribe to it using a news feeds aggregator, for example, Google Reader.

Currently you can subscribe to project list(s), news, issue list(s), issue comments, activities, forum list(s), topic list(s), time entries, and revisions.

Personalizing issue lists

Redmine is an issue tracking application, which means that the majority of its users deal with issues and, therefore, with the issue list. So having your issues organized is extremely important for good performance. That's where custom queries can help again.

Custom queries are described in detail in *Chapter 4, Issue Tracking*. Some samples of are also reviewed in the *Project maintenance best practices* section in *Chapter 5, Managing Projects*. So here is a time to mention them again (which proves how good is this feature).

Let's review some examples of custom queries, which you can use to create specific issue lists in the following table:

Name	Filters	
	Field/Option	**Condition/Value**
My open issues	Status	open
	Assigned to	is "<<me>>"
Issues I work on	Status	is "In Progress"
	Assigned to	is "<<me>>"
My overdue issues	Status	open
	Assigned to	is "<<me>>"
	Due date	more than days ago "0" days

Name	Filters	
	Field/Option	Condition/Value
My issues which are due soon	Status	open
	Assigned to	is "<<me>>"
	Due date	in less than "0" days

You can subscribe to the customized issue list using the **Atom** link. Moreover, you don't need to save the custom query to be able to subscribe to it (just click on the **Apply** link and use the rendered **Atom** link).

Summary

I guess, now you understand, why this chapter is one of the last? In fact, it's intended for readers who know Redmine well. Thus, to customize the issue list users need to know how to work with custom queries; to configure and troubleshoot notifications users need to know what options should be set in the administration area; to customize the personal page users need to be familiar with the data shown in the blocks, and so on.

Perhaps, it could be a good chapter to end the book with, but Redmine is not a tool with certain list of features. It has a great special feature, which makes its feature list measureless—it has plugin API. There are a lot of plugins for Redmine with very different functionality—from adding a feature to turning Redmine into a completely different project. In the next chapter, we will review what plugins are; how to find plugins you need; and other related issues. If you are not an administrator of Redmine, do not hurry to skip the next chapter as there we will also review some interesting plugins.

10
Plugins and Themes

I have always liked playing with plugins, not only as a user, but also as a developer. My first written plugin was one for the Apache HTTP server. When I was working on it, I was amazed by the power the plugin API gives to developers. So, since then, I tried to include the plugin engine into every solution I develop.

When I started to learn the Redmine plugin API, I was amazed even more. Honestly, I can't say that I love Rails or am a fan of it, but the plugin API of Redmine is definitely the thing. Unlike other plugin APIs I've seen before, it's not just an API. The Redmine plugin API is based on Rails engine API (Rails just uses a different name for plugins), so it includes Redmine API and Rails API. Also, the API is based on Ruby, which is a very powerful metaprogramming language and provides unsurpassed means for patching code at runtime. This makes the Redmine plugin API absolutely unlimited, that is, you can do almost anything with it.

Certainly, there are a lot of different plugins for Redmine. While Redmine itself is quite functional without plugins, most likely you will find many plugins that you will want to make use of. But, here the first problem appears—it's not easy to find the working plugin for a certain version of Redmine. Also, the official plugin list misses some interesting ones. Therefore, in this chapter, we will learn how to find plugins and will review some of them.

In addition to plugins, we will pay a little attention to Redmine themes, as the theme is what makes an application look different (similar to plugins, we will also review themes that, I want to share with you).

So, who is this chapter for? This chapter is not only for administrators, who can install plugins, but also for project managers and other users, who can use plugins and can ask administrators to install them.

In this chapter, we will cover the following topics:

- Looking up plugins
- Installing a plugin
- Plugins review
- Themes

Looking up plugins

There is a plugin registry on the Redmine official website, which can be used to find the plugin you need (by the way, this registry is implemented using another plugin, which was written by Jean-Philippe Lang especially for the website). However, if you used it to find, for example, the Git Hosting plugin, you would fail (at least at the time of writing this topic). You would get similar result for some other popular plugins as well. The plugin registry relies on plugin authors. Some authors, for some reason, ignore the registry, whereas others abandon their plugins and let volunteers continue using them, and the volunteers feel rightful to register them on their own behalf. I'm sure, there are other reasons as well. This led to the incomplete plugin list (and to writing this topic).

> **Forum dedicated to plugins**
>
> In addition to the plugin repository, www.redmine.org provides a forum dedicated to plugins, where you can discuss plugins, ask for help, request custom plugin development, and so on. Go to http://www.redmine.org/projects/redmine/boards/3.

The official plugin registry was introduced relatively recently, so, I believe, it just needs time (and probably, some improvements) to become a reliable source of information about plugins. Meanwhile, we need to show resource to find some plugins, and what is also important is to find their versions, which will work with our Redmine version. That's what we will talk about under this topic.

Official registry

The official Redmine plugin registry should be your primary source of information for searching plugins. It's not ideal, and not all the plugins or their versions are registered there, but it was designed to maintain the plugin list; it supports Redmine versions and allows you to filter plugins by version. It also has a legible structure and so on.

This registry can be accessed through the following URL:
`http://www.redmine.org/plugins`:

This page contains five recently registered plugins. And on the sidebar, you see 10 recently released plugins, that is, new versions of those which were registered recently.

You can subscribe to the new plugin list using the **New Plugin** a RSS link.

To search the plugin list, just type keywords into the **Search** box in the top-right corner. But, note that you need to do this while being on the plugin list page, or alternatively, you can just select the **Redmine plugins** checkbox in the search form, as shown in the following screenshot:

We can also browse the plugin list by clicking on the **Browse all Plugins...** link in the bottom-left corner. After doing this, we'll be redirected to the complete plugin list sorted alphabetically, as shown in the following screenshot:

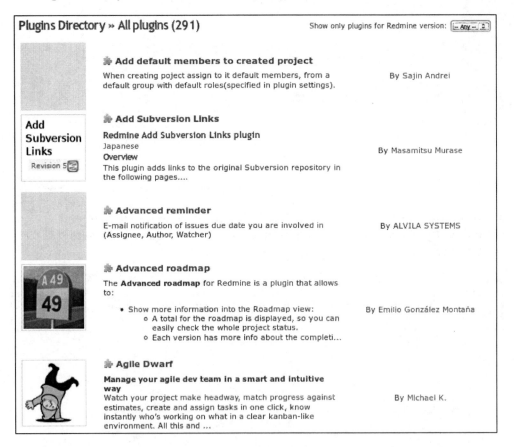

Note the drop-down list in the top-right corner; we can use this element to filter the plugin list by a certain Redmine version. But remember that some plugin versions may be not registered in the official repository yet (you can try finding recent versions on Github though, read the next topic on how to do this).

Subscribing to new versions of the plugin

On the plugin page, in the bottom-right corner, you can find the **Atom** link, which can be used to subscribe to new versions of a certain plugin.

Github

Redmine was written using Ruby on Rails, such as Github. Github is a project hosting and collaboration service, which is loved by open source developers mainly due to its social networking capabilities. Thus, Ruby on Rails code is now hosted on Github. For these reasons, this great service is loved by rubists. So, it would not be a surprise that most Redmine plugins can also be found on Github.

In other words, Github can be a secondary source of the information for searching Redmine plugins. So, let's see how we can search there.

To search Redmine plugins, you should use the following URL: `https://github.com/search`.

Refer to the following screenshot:

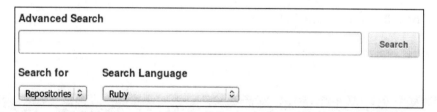

In this form, select **Repositories** for the **Search for** field and **Ruby** for the **Search Language** field. After that, you can put your keywords into the search box along with the `Redmine` keyword (and maybe, `plugin`).

Search results will include all repositories, which match your keywords, including original ones and forks (copies). Therefore, it can be hard to find the fork of a Redmine plugin, which is compatible with the version of Redmine you are using. It can be hard but is still possible.

Limiting results by the last push date

You can search Github by the last push date using the `pushed:` keyword. For example, use the query `Redmine plugin pushed:[2012-09-16 TO *]` to find all repositories, which were modified after the release of Redmine 2.1.0 (which was on 16th September, 2012).

Thus, if we searched for the Ultraviolet plugin, which is believed to work with Redmine up to version 1.3.x in the official repository (at the time of writing), we most likely would encounter some of its forks, as shown in the following screenshot:

This is the fork of Andy Bailey (**neosonic**). Below the repository name, you see the source repository (after **forked from**), which is also the original repository of Chris Gahan (**epitron**), the original author of the plugin.

The source repository can also be forked. The original one is the one which is not forked from any other repository (in most cases, if the original code is hosted on Github).

To find the most recently updated plugin, which theoretically should support the most recent version of Redmine, we need to open the network graph. This graph can be made available by clicking the number of forks (**14** on the previous screenshot).

Refer to the following screenshot:

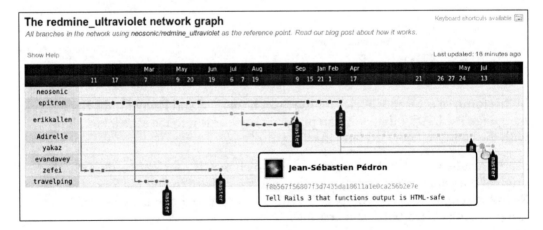

On this graph, spots are commits (code changes). We need to find the latest commits, therefore, we drag the graph by clicking on it, moving the mouse cursor to the left-hand side. The latest commits were made on approximately 13th July by Jean-Sébastien Pédron.

Hovering our mouse cursor over the spot shows brief information about the commit, which includes the author, the hash, and the message. In this particular case, the commit was made to support Rails 3, which is required by Redmine 2.x. So, it looks like the repository of **yakaz** contains the version of the plugin that, we need. To move to this repository just click on the spot.

> Plugin forks on Github are made by volunteers, who make changes required by them or their organization. So, most recent commits do not automatically mean support for recent versions of Redmine. Always read commit messages to get an idea of what are changes are for. Also note that the authors of forks are not necessarily good at programming (as well as original authors). Therefore, their forks can be buggy. It's also a good idea to always read the Github's README file, which is shown on the repository start page, as this file can contain some information about the code state and known issues.

Installing a plugin

After finding the plugin and before using it, we need to install it. The installation procedure may differ for some plugins, but all of them have common steps, which we will review in this topic. Anyway, before going with the steps reviewed, here, you should check the plugin documentation to ensure you won't miss anything.

> This topic is intended for administrators, who have access to the file system of the server, on which Redmine runs. Also plugin installation may require root access.

Redmine plugins usually come in archived files. Usually, these archives have a single directory, which should be copied into the `plugins` directory of Redmine (that is, into `/opt/redmine/plugins` if you installed Redmine into `/opt/redmine`).

What if the plugin directory is missing or seems to have an invalid name?

The plugin should come with a init.rb file in the main plugin directory (therefore, if this file is in the root, the plugin directory is missing, and if it's in one of the subdirectories, the plugin directory is the corresponding subdirectory). And a **init.rb** file should have the following line:

```
Redmine::Plugin.register :plugin_name do
```

Here, plugin_name is the name of the plugin, and the plugin directory must have exactly the same name.

If the plugin requires migration, that means that some changes must be made to the Redmine database in order for the plugin to work-we need to execute the following command on the Redmine server:

```
$ rake redmine:plugins:migrate RAILS_ENV=production
```

If you are not sure whether migration is required, just execute this command anyway.

Database migration files come in the db subdirectory of the main plugin directory, so if a such directory is there and contains files, migration is needed.

Now to activate the plugin, you need to restart Redmine using the following command (this command may differ for your installation):

```
$ sudo service apache2 reload
```

That's, actually, all you need to do to install an ordinary plugin.

You can check if Redmine sees the plugin by going to **Administration | Plugins**.

Uninstalling a plugin

I assume, that you will want to try many plugins to decide which one best fits your needs (unfortunately, some plugins do not provide enough information to make the decision without trying them). So, in this case you will need to learn how to uninstall plugins correctly.

Do not play with plugins on the production server! Set up a test server (can be a virtual machine) for this purpose.

First, we need to roll back the database changes, which were made during the installation. Thus, to remove the `plugin_name` plugin we need to execute:

```
$ rake redmine:plugins:migrate NAME=plugin_name VERSION=0 RAILS_
ENV=production
```

Of course, you need to execute this command only if the plugin comes with migration scripts. However, it is safe to do this even if it does not.

The rest of the uninstallation is simple.

Now remove the plugin directory (named after `plugin_name`) in the `plugins` subdirectory of the Redmine root directory (which is `/opt/redmine`, if you installed Redmine into this directory).

After that, just restart Redmine (the command depends on the Linux distribution that you use to run Redmine):

```
$ sudo service apache2 reload
```

Plugins review

When I was compiling the outline for this book, I had a choice to describe third-party plugins. Can Redmine be used without plugins? Sure, they can be used. Therefore, I decided not to mix the core Redmine review with the plugins review. Is Redmine thorough without plugins? I'm not sure whether it is. I haven't seen Redmine installation without plugins. Yet if you can extend your installation with features you might need, why not do this? Therefore, I mention appropriate plugins in the topics they are applicable for.

While checking forums, blog posts, articles, answers to questions, and similar stuff, you will find what plugins are most popular and most useful. Therefore, I could not decide which popular plugins to review. So, taking into account that you might encounter them anyway (as they are popular), I decided not to review them. That is, I decided to choose plugins for review not by their popularity.

The main criterion for selecting plugin for review is that they should be useful, but should not be prominent or usually searched for. Thus, here we will speak about plugins, which, I believe, are essential to install, for example, the Exception Handler, which will notify you of errors in Redmine. Also, we will speak about some really cool plugins, which you are unlikely to search for, for example, Mylyn, which makes it possible to integrate Redmine with Eclipse.

In other words, let's discover what amazing stuff can be done with plugins. But, let's start with some essential ones.

So, under this topic, we will review:

- Meta
- Exception Handler
- Mylyn Connector
- Screenshot Paste
- Lightbox
- Code Review
- Niko Cale
- Stuff To Do

Meta

There were times when HTTP meta tags were widely used by search engines. Thus, the meta description was used to describe the page in search results. Since then, search engines have become smarter and usually generate the description, which includes search keywords. But, the meta description, as well as meta keywords, are still used and have a huge meaning for SEO.

But, it's not only a matter of search engines, meta the description, and meta keywords are used everywhere. For example meta description is used by social networks to show more information about the page.

So, from this point of view, Redmine makes a big mistake using just "Redmine" for the meta description and "issue,bug,tracker" for meta keywords for all pages. As a results, when we add a Redmine-powered page to a social network, the post looks like the following screenshot (example for Facebook):

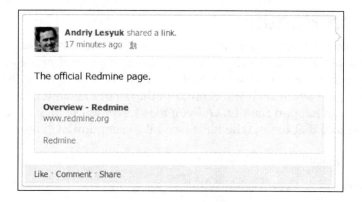

That's why I believe the Meta Tags plugin is essential for Redmine-powered sites, which can be accessed publicly, that is, pages which can be crawled by search engines and added to social networks by users.

 You can find the Meta Tags plugin at `http://projects.andriylesyuk.com/projects/redmine-meta`.

The Meta Tags plugin adds Meta description and keywords to the start page, the project overview, the issue pages, the news pages, and the Wiki pages. In addition, it provides API for adding content for these Meta tags from within Redmine view files.

So, with this plugin, when we add a Redmine page to social networks, the post looks like the following screenshot (example for Facebook):

Exception Handler

There is no perfect software; every application in some circumstances can give an error. Here, we talk not about a check, which results in an error message but about exceptions, which occur when the application cannot handle the situation. As mentioned, we can't avoid such situations, but that's not the matter; the matter is that such situations can happen silently, and you may never know they have happened as you can't be sure that users, who have faced the exception, will report it to you.

This becomes especially important, if we use:

- The most recent version of Redmine
- Some third-party plugins or their most recent versions
- Custom plugins, developed especially for Redmine

As too new or not a very well-tested software is known to fail. Luckily, Redmine writes all such exceptions to its logfiles. But, if your Redmine installation is heavily loaded and/or administrators do not check all logfiles regularly, you can still easily miss them.

The solution comes from the now-former Redmine core developer, Eric Davis, who developed the Exception Handler plugin. This plugin catches the unhandled exception, generates the report, and sends it to the specified e-mail addresses.

> You can find the up-to-date fork of the plugin maintained by Ricardo Santos at `https://github.com/thorin/redmine_exception_handler`.

The very first thing which needs to be done after this plugin installation is configuring the e-mail addresses at which we want to receive notifications. To do this, go to **Administration | Plugins**, and click on the **Configure** link to the right-hand side of **Redmine Exception Handler plugin**.

Settings: Redmine Exception Handler plugin

Email recipients	
Separate multiple email addresses with commas	you@example.com, another@example.com
Sender address	Application Error <redmine@example.com>
Subject prefix	[ERROR]
Email format	text ▼
	Test Settings by triggering a fake exception (will open in a new window)

Apply

After completing the form, you may check whether notifications can be sent to the specified e-mail addresses using the **Test Settings by triggering a fake exception** link.

Now you will always know when Redmine fails. And, unless you are able to check Redmine logfiles regularly and carefully, I believe, this plugin is essential to have installed.

 This plugin requires the `tinder` gem – `gem install tinder`.

Mylyn Connector

This plugin will be of interest only for users of Eclipse IDE.

Eclipse comes with a very interesting task management concept, in which a task becomes an interface customization unit. Thus, when the user select a task, Eclipse remembers all actions the user performs and hides the rest. This helps to concentrate on the task. This concept is provided by the Eclipse plugin called Mylyn.

In addition, Mylyn is able to work with different task repositories using **connectors** (connectors are small plugins allow us to connect Mylyn with third-party task repositories). Thus, by default, Eclipse comes with the Bugzilla connector, but official Eclipse sites also include connectors for JIRA, Trac, Mantis, Hudson, Microsoft TFS, and much more.

Thanks to Sven Krzyzak such a connector exists for Redmine as well. This connector connects (excuse the tautology) to the Mylyn Connector plugin, which was also originally developed by Sven. Both plugins (for different systems though) let Eclipse users see, use, and manage Redmine issues straight from Eclipse.

> You can find the Redmine Connector plugin for Eclipse at `http://sourceforge.net/projects/redmin-mylyncon`
> You can find the up-to-date fork of the Mylyn Connector plugin for Redmine, which is maintained by Daniel Munn, at `https://github.com/danmunn/redmine_mylyn_connector`.

In Eclipse, go to **Help | Install New Software...** and type the following URL into the **Work with** field `http://redmin-mylyncon.sourceforge.net/update-site/N` (or click on the **Add...** button and add this URL there). Then install **Mylyn Connector: Redmine** and optionally **Mylyn Connector: Redmine – Redmine-Plugin-Support**, which will appear in the area below.

After installing the connector in Eclipse, open the **Task List**, click on the down arrow next to the new task icon and select the **Add Repository...** menu item:

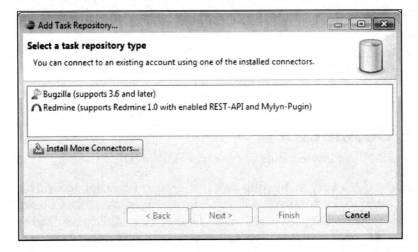

In the list of available connectors you should see **Redmine**. Select it and then click on the **Next** button. The following dialog box (seen in the screenshot) should open:

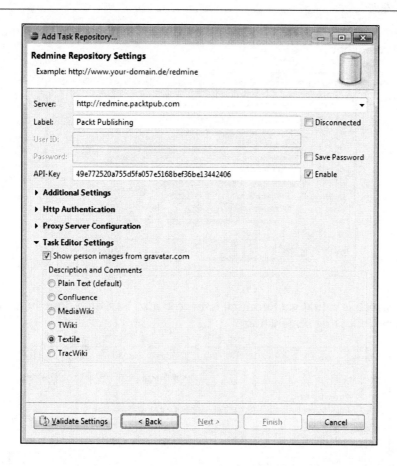

In this dialog, you should specify the parameters required for connecting to
Redmine. The dialog supports **User ID** and **Password** but I highly recommend
you to use **API-Key** instead, which can be found on your **My account** page.

After completing the dialog, you will need to click on the **Validate Settings** button,
after that the **Finish** button will become clickable. Clicking on the **Finish** button will
send you to the query edit dialog.

 The Redmine Connector plugin for Eclipse requires Java 6.

Now, when you open the **Task List** you should see something similar to the following screenshot:

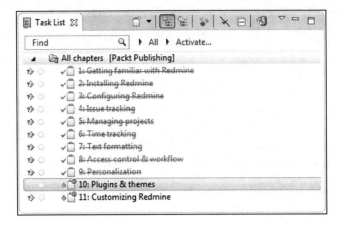

Each task, which is actually a Redmine issue, can also be edited directly from Eclipse as seen in the following screenshot:

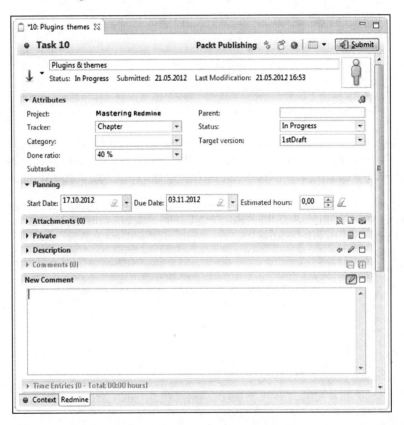

In fact, using Eclipse we can now do with the issue everything that is possible in Redmine.

 The Mylyn Connector plugin requires the `libxml-ruby` gem:

```
$ sudo gem install libxml-ruby
```

Also the plugin requires Redmine REST API to be enabled, which can be done in **Administration | Settings | Authentication** using the **Enable REST web service** option.

Screenshot Paste

As Redmine is an issue tracking application, it's no wonder that the majority of files attached to issues appear to be screenshots. Most Redmine users are used to pressing the *Print Screen* button, saving the screenshot into a file, clicking on the **Browse...** button in the issue form, and then submitting the screenshot.

I guess, few users know that Jean-Philippe Lang, the author of Redmine, created the Screenshot Paste plugin, which is intended to assist this routine. This plugin allows you to paste the screenshot from the clipboard directly into the issue form.

 You can find the up-to-date rework of the plugin, authored by Emmanuel Gallois, at `https://github.com/undx/redmine_screenshot_paste`.

If this plugin is installed, the following new element gets added to the issue form:

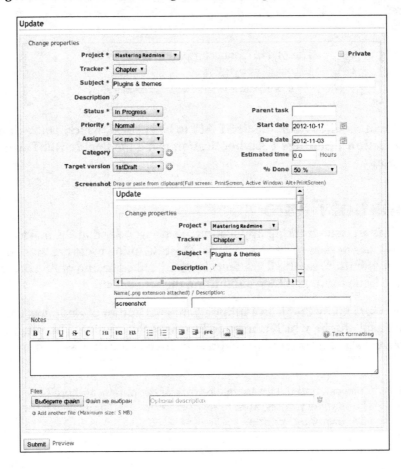

After submitting this form, the new screenshot gets added to the issue as an attachment.

 This plugin requires Java to be available in the user's browser.

Lightbox

Since Version 2.1.x, Redmine can show attached images as thumbnails if the **Display attachment thumbnails** option in the **Administration | Settings | Display** tab is enabled. However, when we click on the thumbnail, it opens in the current window in place of the issue page, so afterwards we need to go back.

In previous versions even the thumbnails were not visible (we could only see the file links) unless the particular Redmine installation used the Lightbox plugin, which was originally authored by Genki Zhang.

 You can find the up-to-date fork for the plugin, maintained by Ricardo Santos, at `https://github.com/thorin/redmine_lightbox`.

This plugin uses jQuery to show the attached image in a nice lightbox, when users click on the thumbnail. In addition to images, the plugin can also show the PDF documents and Flash applets. But the most beautiful thing is that it does this without leaving the current page:

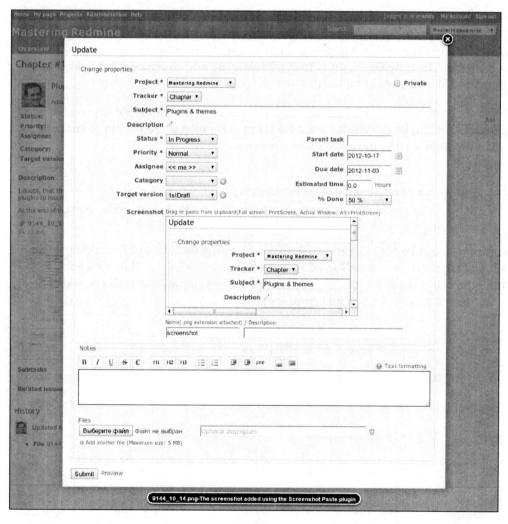

So to close the lightbox, we can click on the ⊠ icon in its top-right hand corner. If the issue has several images attached, clicking on the image in the lightbox moves it to the next image or PDF or Flash in the issue attachment list.

Code Review

Code review is an important part of the software development process, which can help to find serious vulnerabilities before the application gets released. It is especially important, if the development team includes new inexperienced members. Of course, there exists plenty of tools for automated code review and analysis but not everything can be automated and sometimes even a quick look at the code of an experienced developer can prevent the vulnerability from appearing in the production.

At the later phases of the software development process, the code review implies examining code commits, which can be easily seen in Redmine using its repository browser. Redmine revision pages include all the details regarding changes made in the code. The only thing left is to create an issue and describe what the reviewer found and why it should be fixed.

Tools such as Redmine are intended to automate everything, what is possible and acceptable, to make the work easier. So Haru Iida created the plugin to simplify issues creation during the code review process.

> You can find the Code Review plugin :
> https://bitbucket.org/haru_iida/redmine_code_review

This plugin can be considered to allow commenting each line of the code committed. But, in fact, reviewers are allowed to "attach" issues to lines and describe their thoughts about those lines within these issues. Such issues can be bugs, requests for checks or refactoring, or just comments:

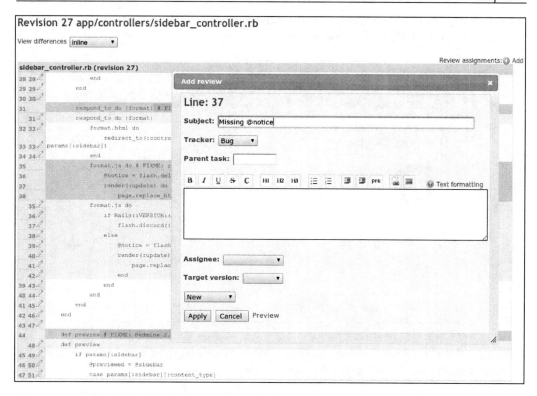

Thus, to add an issue for a line, users just need to click on the pen icon near the line number (note that only additions can be commented). After this the pop-up window with the simplified issue form appears.

If the line has been commented, then near the pen icon, we will also see the comment icon as seen in the following screenshot:

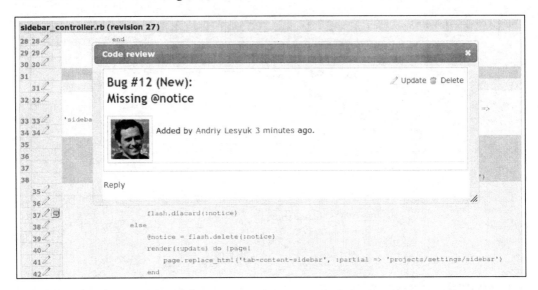

Clicking on this icon will pop-up the small issue window, which will contain the comment and links allowing you to move to the issue page:

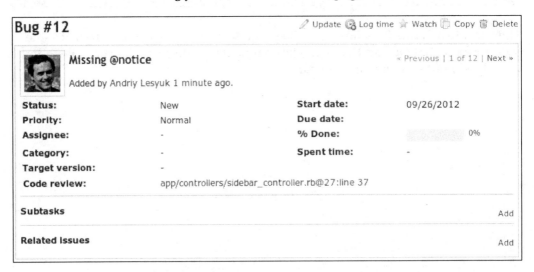

As you see from the screen, issues, created using the Code Review plugin contain the additional field **Code Review** with a short link to the related line.

All code reviews that are issues created for code lines, become available under the **Code Reviews** tab of the project menu:

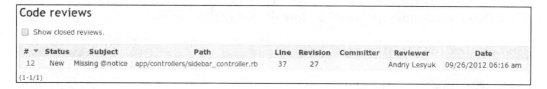

Additionally, the plugin allows you to request the code review for the commit or changes in the file. In this case an issue, which includes the details about the revision and, optionally, the file, gets created.

 The plugin has many dependencies—use `bundle install` to install it.

Niko Cale

It's hard to overvalue motivation. When you are motivated, you are able to do much more, and much better, and it feels good to get pleasure of doing the job. Employees cannot be motivated effectively if they hate the job! Apparently, a demotivated employee is more disposed towards producing bad code and bugs.

We all know Agile. What this methodology is missing is evaluating the motivation of an employee. So, as a workaround Akinori Sakata suggested using Agile to track the mood of employees. His idea is well known as the **Niko-Niko** Calendar (Japanese "niko niko" means something like a "smiley").

The implementation of the Niko-Niko calendar for Redmine was originally authored by Yuki Kita, who named it the Niko Cale plugin.

 You can find the up-to-date fork of the plugin, which is maintained by Yoshitani Mitsuhiro, at `https://github.com/luckval/redmine_niko_cale`.

This plugin adds the ability for users to specify their overall mood during the working day. This can be done using the **Today's feeling** link, which appears between the username and the **My account** link at the top-right user menu. The following screenshot shows the **How do you feel?** window:

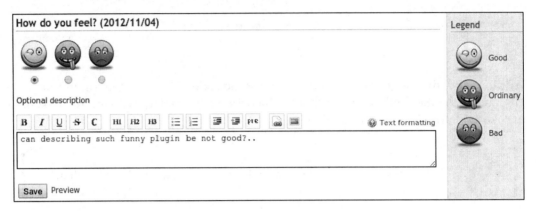

Users can choose between **Good**, **Ordinary**, and **Bad**. Optionally, they can also add a comment describing the reason for the feeling they selected.

The **Today's feeling** information should be specified at the end of the working day (just before leaving). After it has been specified, the **Today's feeling** link disappears from the menu. The specified feeling gets added to the user's profile as seen in the following screenshot:

The emoticon seen on the page directs you to the feelings page:

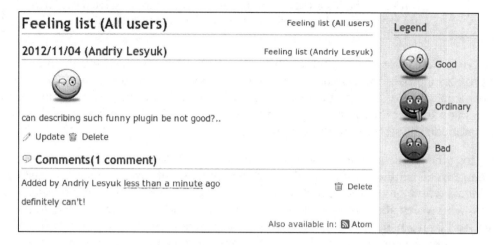

Here feelings can be modified and deleted. Also, on this page, other employees can comment on feeling.

This is how mood can be added to Redmine. All moods specified by employees appear on the Niko-Niko Calendar, which can be found under the **Nico-Cale** tab in the project menu:

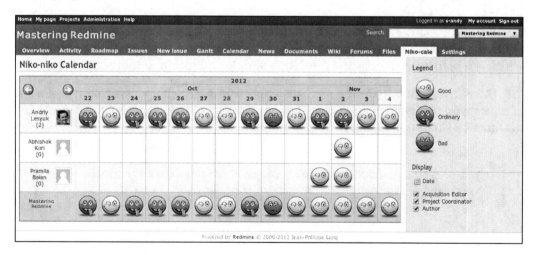

In order for the **Nico-Cale** tab to be shown, you need to enabled the **Nico Cale** project module in project settings under the **Modules** tab.

The **Niko-Cale** tab opens the actual Niko-Niko Calendar, which shows the mood for all project members and calculates the overall mood for the project team. The green arrow icons allow you to move through calendar periods and the filter on the sidebar allows you to filter the calendar by member roles. Hovering the mouse cursor over the emoticon shows the comment, if supplied.

Like for other Agile practices, the effectiveness of the Niko-Niko Calendar depends on employees' frankness. If properly used, this practise allows discovery of existing problems where other Agile practices fail. Thus, employees, who have too much work, who worry about the result, who get mobbed, and so on, are unlikely to use the **Good** icon when reporting their mood. The practice shows, that often enough the only unhappy employee in the team can appear to be not just depressed but to be the one, who knows more about problems and who is willing to speak about them. In other words, the Niko-Niko Calendar (and the Niko Cale plugin) can be used effectively to discover issues at the early stages and to find out the guy, who will speak about them frankly.

Stuff To Do

When one has many issues, it can become quite complicated to prioritize tasks and not to miss or delay more important ones. While Redmine offers custom queries, which can help here, there is the need for a simple and intuitive solution.

Eric Davis, the former Redmine core developer and a quite busy person (at least a lot of issues were assigned or related to him, thus, I also added a couple), implemented the Stuff To Do plugin aimed to help organizing users' task lists.

 You can find the Stuff To Do plugin at `https://github.com/ande3577/redmine-stuff-to-do-plugin`.

This plugin adds the **Stuff To Do** item to the top-left menu. This menu is much like the **My page**-that is, it contains the user personalized data.

In a few words, this page contains the user's tasks. It is divided into three blocks:

- **What's available**: It contains a list of issues assigned to the user
- **What I'm doing now**: It contains a list of issues that the user is currently working on (not by the status)
- **What's recommended to do next**: It contains a list of user's next tasks

Issues can be dragged from one block to another (in the preceding screenshot, I'm dragging the **Chapter 10** task to the **What I'm doing now** block). Thus, dragging the issue from **What I'm doing now** and **What's recommended to do next** actually removes the issue from the to-do list and moving the issue from the **What's available** block adds the issue to the to-do list. **What I'm doing now** and **What's recommended to do next** may contain a limited number of tasks that is, five for the first block and ten for the second one. As soon as an issue in the **What I'm doing now** block gets closed, the first issue from the **What's recommended to do next** block automatically moves to **What I'm doing now**. The order of issues in both these blocks can be changed manually just by dragging them.

 Contrary to the expectations the **What's available** block does not include issues with the **In Progress** status automatically—all issues should be dragged here.

If I dragged the **Chapter 11** task to **What's recommended to do next**, it would be added to the **What I'm doing now** block. This is because the plugin does not allow the issue to appear in the **What's recommended to do next** block, if there are less than five issues in the **What I'm doing now** block. Unfortunately, currently this can't be configured.

The plugin also allows privileged users to manage other users' to-do lists.

Themes

Redmine themes are just CSS files, which often come with images. That is, Redmine's support for theming is very basic. However, this makes installing Redmine themes very easy.

Installing themes

All Redmine themes are represented as directories in the `public/themes` subdirectory of the Redmine root directory (which is `/opt/redmine`, if you used the tutorial from this book to install it). Thus, by default Redmine comes with two directories in `public/themes`, `alternate` and `classic`, these are **Alternate** and **Classic** Redmine themes correspondingly.

So to install a new theme, you need to create a directory for it in `public/themes`. The name of the theme can, actually, be anything (you can use the name recommended by the theme author or think out your own). The only requirement is that it must be in lower case.

After you have created a directory for the theme put all theme, files into it. Thus, the theme must come with at least `stylesheets/application.css`, but it also can contain images in the `images` subdirectory, and so on.

Individual per-user themes

Haru Iida created a plugin which lets users choose a different theme (which, of course, should be installed in their profiles): `http://www.redmine.org/plugins/themechanger`.

As soon as all theme files are copied to the new theme directory, restart Redmine using the command (can be different):

```
$ sudo service apache2 reload
```

After this, go to the **Administration** | **Settings** | **Display** tab and select the theme in the drop-down list for the **Theme** field and click on **Save**.

That's it! Enjoy.

Themes review

Here faced a dilemma once again—what Redmine themes should I choose to review? I have chosen those that I personally like more, and which to my knowledge, are most popular.

When choosing a theme, you actually have a choice: what existing site do you want your Redmine to look like? Because public themes, especially nice looking ones, are used widely and often. So, if you can find it substantiated, better order the special theme for your site.

Basecamp

This theme was created by Peter Theill. It is a Redmine port of 37signals' Basecamp theme:

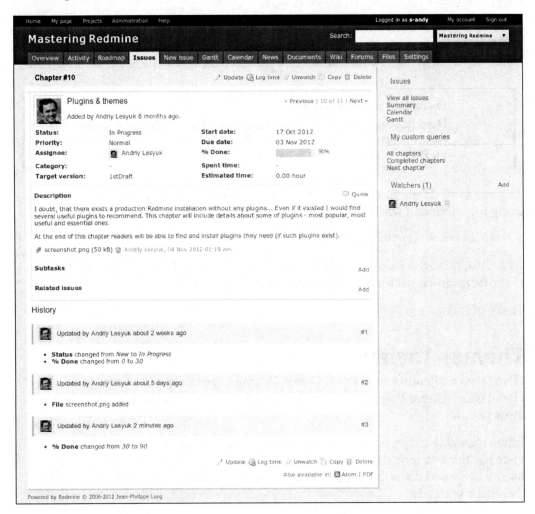

[The theme can be downloaded at `http://www.theill.com/stuff/redmine`.

Modula Mojito

This theme was originally authored by Eero Louhenperä from Modula:

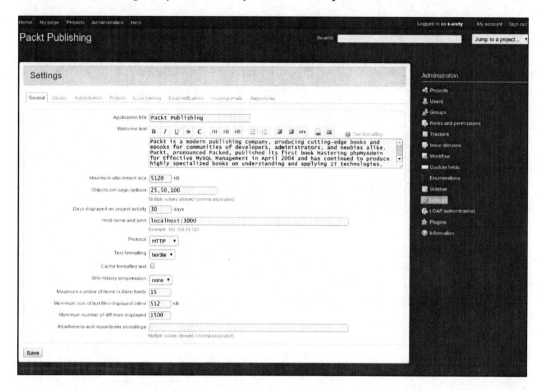

Later the maintenance of the theme was taken over by Steven Jones from Computerminds Ltd and it can be found at `https://github.com/computerminds/modula-mojito`.

A1

This theme was created by Kirill Bezrukov. It is based on the Ronin theme:

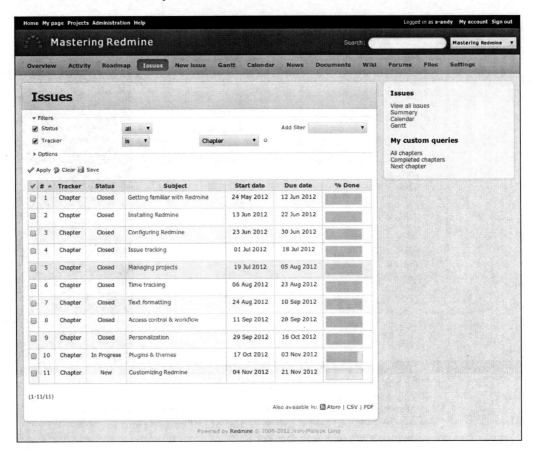

 This theme can be downloaded at http://redminecrm.com/projects/a1theme.

Highrise

This theme was also created by Kirill Bezrukov. It is based on 37signals' Highrise CRM theme. The theme comes in two versions—one with the project menu on the left sidebar and one with the project menu as tabs (ordinary case):

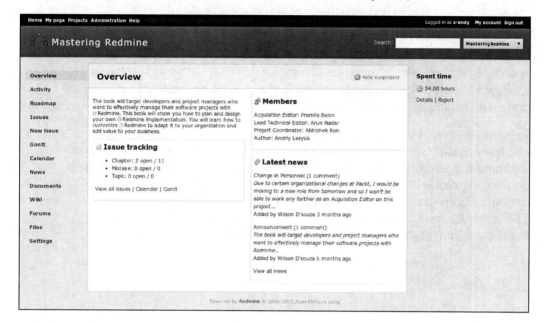

Both versions can be downloaded at `http://redminecrm.com/projects/highrisetheme`.

Summary

In this chapter I wanted to share my experience of searching functional Redmine plugins, as I personally find it quite complicated. Most likely, you won't be able to avoid using plugins as much of the power of Redmine can be found in them. In other words, I wanted you to feel easy finding and installing the plugins that you'll need.

To demonstrate what can be done with plugins we have also reviewed some of them. Of course, we have ignored many interesting, useful, and popular ones. But the goal was not to review such plugins (as otherwise this chapter would be too huge) but to draw your attention to some of them to show what interesting things can be done with others, and so on.

I assume that you have searched for and found plugins, that you will use, and have already chosen and installed a theme, which will be the face of your Redmine installation. In fact, you just did the basic customization, which gets done by everyone who uses Redmine. The next chapter is about advanced customization—it describes how to turn Redmine into a specific website. Therefore, the next chapter is rather for project managers, site owners, Redmine administrators, and server administrators.

11
Customizing Redmine

Have you noticed that the previous two chapters were about what can be called *customization*? That's natural because after we have learned an application, we would want to make it better fit our needs. Thus, personalization is the customization made by users for themselves using only the permissions they have. Installing plugins is the customization done by server administrators (don't confuse this with the Redmine administrator). But there was also another customization described – the configuration of Redmine, which was reviewed in *Chapter 3, Configuring Redmine.* While these were actually three chapters, all of them miss another customization level. All these chapters describe quite common things, which get done by everyone, who installs Redmine. These things are enough for corporate installations. But there are also advanced things, which become necessary, for example, if we want to use Redmine for a public forge site.

In such cases we usually want to have our own look and feel (theme), to add custom content to different pages, and so on. During this customization phase users usually ask experts for help. Thus, sometimes they want to develop plugins to implement different ideas but plugins, actually, are not always needed. Also, during this phase users often customize Redmine by themselves and, usually, do this incorrectly. So, what the right way is to customize Redmine, what we can do without developing custom plugins, and so on, are the topics we will speak about now.

In this chapter we will cover the following topics:

- Custom fields
- Customizing with Textile
- Customizing theme
- Customizing with plugins

Custom fields

I believe custom fields support is essential for any issue tracker or similar application. And, luckily, Redmine implements this feature very well. Thus, custom fields can be defined for issues, projects, versions, users, and so on (as well as for some objects provided by third-party plugins). Custom fields enrich these objects by allowing you to add properties, which are missing. They can also be used in filters, forms, and so on. To a great extent, custom fields let you change the way Redmine looks and behaves. This makes them a tool for advanced customization. This and the fact that they are supported for many object types make them appear in this chapter.

In fact, custom fields are the least unusual technique we will review in this chapter. Yet users rarely make use of them. My guess is that they feel they will be too complicated, but, actually, they are not. So let's go.

[Be sure to plan the usage of custom fields and avoid adding custom fields, which are going to be rarely used, as too many custom fields can confuse your users.]

Custom fields can be managed using the **Custom fields** section in the **Administration** menu, as shown in the following screenshot:

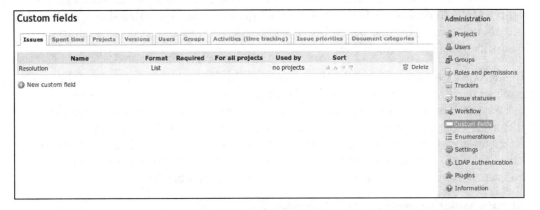

This section contains tabs, which correspond to different customized objects. Under each tab we can see the list of custom fields (by default they are all empty). We will review each tab (that is, customized Redmine core object) later. Now let's see what happens if we click on the **New custom field** link:

Custom fields » Issues » New custom field

Name *	[ ]
Format	[Text ▼]
Min - Max length	[0] - [0]
	(0 means no restriction)
Regular expression	[ ]
	(eg. ^[A-Z0-9]+$)
Default value	[ ]

Trackers
☐ Chapter ☐ Topic ☐ Mistake ☐ Rewrite

Required ☐
For all projects ☐
Used as a filter ☐
Searchable ☐

[Save]

This form is for issue custom fields (as we invoked it under the **Issues** tab). The form for other objects (which can be invoked under other tabs) differs, but most elements remain the same.

Thus, the first top block defines properties of the custom field and does not differ for different customized objects, but does differ for different custom field formats (this will be reviewed next). The following is an explanation about the properties of the custom field, which are shown in the preceding screenshot:

- **Name** is the only required property, which should contain the easy-to-understand and intelligible name of the custom field. This name will be shown in object forms and on object properties pages.

- **Format** field allows you to select the format of the custom field. As custom field formats introduce changes to the properties form, we will separately review them next.

- **Min – Max length** fields specify the minimal and maximal size of the custom field value.

- The value of the **Regular expression** field will be used to verify the custom field value. This is a very useful property as it allows you to ensure, that users will specify proper values for the custom field. Unfortunately, you need to be familiar with regular expressions to be able to use this property. Still I highly recommend you learn them.

- The **Default value** field can be used to specify the default value for the custom field.

Changing the way custom field values are displayed

The Extended Fields plugin can be used to define template files for certain custom fields (by format or by name). This way you can render boolean values as check marks, Twitter usernames as "Follow me" buttons, and so on. See `http://projects.andriylesyuk.com/projects/extended-fields/wiki/Custom-fields-view-customization`.

Custom field options

The second block contains custom field options. The **Trackers** option is exceptional and is only available for issue custom fields (this option allows you to select issue trackers, for which the custom field will be available). Other options get represented as checkboxes (not all available options are shown in the preceding screenshot).

The following table presents the availability of custom field options for customized objects:

Customized object	Required	Visible	Editable	For all projects	Searchable	Used as a filter
Issues	✓			✓	✓	✓
Spent time	✓					
Projects	✓	✓			✓	✓
Versions	✓					✓
Users	✓	✓	✓			✓
Groups	✓					✓
Activities (time tracking)	✓					
Issue priorities	✓					
Document categories	✓					

Required

The **Required** checkbox is available for all customized objects. It specifies whether the value for the custom field should be required.

 For issues you can have more flexible control over whether the custom field should be required on the **Fields permissions** tab of the **Workflow** section in the **Administration** menu.

Visible

The **Visible** checkbox controls whether the value of the custom field should be displayed on the object properties page (for example, the project overview page or the user profile page). That is, if this checkbox is not checked, the value of the custom field will be visible only in the edit mode (for example, in project settings or in the user account).

Editable

The **Editable** checkbox determines whether users can see and edit the value of the custom field. This checkbox is currently available only for the user object. Thus, custom fields of users with this checkbox unchecked are available only for administrators (under **Administration | Users**, and not in user accounts).

For all projects

The **For all projects** checkbox specifies whether the custom field should be available for all projects. This checkbox can be currently used only by issues. If this checkbox is unchecked for the custom field, project managers will still be able to enable the custom field for the particular project in project settings (Custom fields block in **Information | Custom fields**).

 Also do not forget to enable the custom field for trackers, which are available in the project.

Searchable

The **Searchable** checkbox tells if the value of the custom field should be checked to contain the search string, when users search for the customized object. This checkbox is available only for projects and issues as only these objects (out of all supported customized objects) are available in the Redmine search form.

The Redmine search form becomes available when we type the search string into the textbox in the upper-right corner and press *Enter*, or when we click on the **Search** label, as shown in the following screenshot:

The Redmine search form looks like the following screenshot:

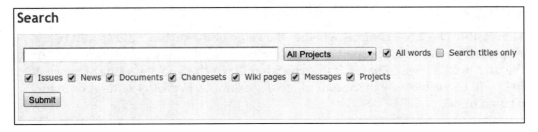

In other words, when we search for something in issues (that is, the **Issues** checkbox is checked in the search form), Redmine also searches in values of custom fields, for which the **Searchable** checkbox was checked.

Used as a filter

The **Used as a filter** checkbox allows the custom field to be used in custom queries. That's natural for issue custom fields but the checkbox is also available for projects, versions, users, and groups. Have a look at the following screenshot:

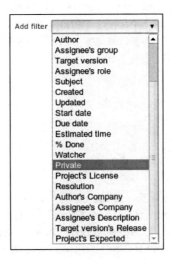

All filters under **Private** are custom fields and only (meaning that others are for other customized objects) the **Resolution** field is for issues. So as you see, project, user, version, and group custom fields are shown here with the appropriate prefix (**Project's, Author's, Assignee's,** and **Target version's**).

This way custom fields with the **Used as a filter** checkbox checked can be used in custom queries.

Custom field formats

Sometimes we need the custom field to store just a string, other times we want it to store a date or a Boolean value. Therefore, custom fields support the **Format** property, which can also be named the data type.

Text

Custom fields of the **Text** type hold just strings, that is, a sequence of any characters.

 To require the string to be of a particular format you can use the **Regular expression** property.

Long text

The **Long text** format is very much like the **Text** format except that it gets rendered as a text area when edited and not as a textbox like the latter. Despite possible expectation, this format does not support the wiki formatting.

Integer

Custom fields of the **Integer** format accept only integer values. However, minimal and maximal size, and regular expression can still be applied to custom fields of this format (for example, to allow only positive values).

Float

Custom fields of the **Float** format accept float values. Such custom fields can have minimal and maximal size, and regular expression as well.

List

In many cases custom fields are needed to ask users just to select a pre-defined value. For example, the project licence—from the list of available licences, the resolution type—from the list of resolution types, and so on. In all such cases it is more user friendly to render a drop-down list with values to select from. This is what can be done with the **List** format.

Due to the specificity of this format the block for entering custom field properties looks different (it gets changed, when you select the **List** format):

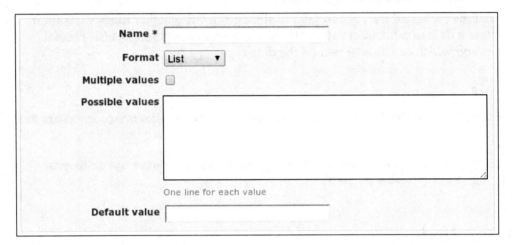

We see the following two new properties in the preceding screenshot:

- **Multiple values**, which specifies whether users will be able to select several values at a time.
- **Possible values**, where we specify strings, from which users will need to select the value for the custom field. Each possible value should be on its own line.

Copy and paste the value for the **Default value** property from the **Possible values** text area to avoid typos.

Date

The **Date** format can be used to get a date value using a custom field. The input element for this format is rendered along with the calendar icon, as shown in the following screenshot:

Clicking on the calendar icon invokes the calendar pop-up menu, assisting in choosing the date.

The custom field properties block for the **Date** format also differs:

Boolean

The **Boolean** format can be used if the custom field needs to accept just "Yes" or "No". As Boolean values are very simple, the properties block for custom fields of this format look like the following screenshot:

Unlike all other formats for the **Boolean** format the **Default value** property is rendered as a checkbox.

User

The input element for custom fields of the **User** format is rendered as a drop-down menu containing the list of project members. In other words, this format can be used to allow choosing a project member as a value for the custom field (can be used for, for example, second assignee, associated tester, or code reviewer).

This format is available only for issues, time entries, versions, and projects.

The custom field properties block for this format includes the **Multiple values** checkbox, as shown in the following screenshot:

If this checkbox is checked, the custom field will allow choosing several users at a time.

Version

The **Version** format is similar to the **User** format. The input element for this format is also rendered as a drop-down list containing project versions. Also similar to the **User** format the properties block includes the **Multiple values** checkbox.

 This format is available only for issues, time entries, versions, and projects.

Customized object types

Not all Redmine objects can have custom fields. Those which can, are available as tabs in the **Custom fields** section under **Administration**. In fact, every "customized" object introduces its own way of using custom fields. So, that's what we will speak about under this topic.

Issues

Redmine is primarily an issue tracker, therefore, it's no wonder that custom fields support for issues is the most advanced. Thus, issue custom fields have the additional **Trackers** option (see the screenshot at the beginning of this chapter); they can be enabled for all projects (using the **For all projects** checkbox) or for certain projects only (in project settings); their states (**Read-only** or **Required**) can be managed per issue status in the **Workflow** section under **Administration** along with core issue fields; they can be used in custom queries and more.

Issue custom fields can be specified or modified in the issue form, their values are shown on the issue page.

 Instead of requiring users to enter the issue custom field (using the **Required** checkbox), you can define conditions, on which the custom field will become required, on the **Fields permissions** tab in the **Workflow** section under **Administration**. Thus, to create the **Resolution** custom field we can make the custom field read-only for all issue statuses except **Closed**.

Spent time

Custom fields can be added to time entries as well. Values of such custom fields can be specified or edited in the time entry form. Unfortunately, this form is also the only place, where we can see these values.

Projects

Project custom fields are usually used to collect more details about the project. Values for these custom fields can be specified under the **Information** tab in project settings. If the **Visible** checkbox for the custom field is checked, the value of the field will be displayed on the project overview page under the description (and under the home page, if the last has been specified).

Versions

A project can have any number of versions; project versions can also have custom fields. Values for version custom field can be specified in the version form, which becomes available when we click on the **New version** link or the **Edit** link under the **Versions** tab in project settings. Values of version custom fields can be viewed on the roadmap and on the version page, as follows:

Here **Release** is a version custom field and **New features** is its value.

Users

In my opinion the default Redmine user profile is too scant, as it provides no fields to share any data with other Redmine users. Thus, this data could be Facebook, Twitter accounts, phone number, phone extension, company, position, and much more. Luckily the user object can be customized with custom fields.

For corporate installations, especially in large organizations, it is a good idea to create such user custom fields, for example, "Position", "Team", "Department", "Room", and so on.

Values of user custom fields can be edited in user accounts (**Administration | Users**) by administrators or in user profiles (the **My account** link) by users, but only if the **Editable** checkbox for these custom fields is checked. If the **Visible** checkbox for the user custom field is checked, it also gets shown on the user page, as follows:

Andriy Lesyuk

- Email: s-andy@andriylesyuk.com
- Company: Kayako, Inc.
- Company website: www.kayako.com
- Personal website: www.andriylesyuk.com
- Facebook: andriy.lesyuk
- Twitter: AndriyLesyuk
- Registered on: 09/20/2012
- Last connection: 11/16/2012

Projects

- Mastering Redmine   (Author, 09/20/2012)

Groups

User groups can also have custom fields, for which values can be specified in the group edit form (which can be accessed by clicking on **Administration | Groups**). Unfortunately, group custom fields are not shown anywhere else (however, issues can be filtered using them – see the **Used as a filter** option that we discussed previously).

Activities (time tracking)

Time tracking activities are, actually, "enumerations". **Enumerations** are Redmine objects, which allow storing list-style values. Activities such as other enumerations, also support custom fields. These custom fields can be edited or viewed in the enumeration edit form, which can be invoked in **Administration | Enumerations**, and under the **Activities (time tracking)** tab in the project settings, where per-project values for these custom fields can be specified.

Issue priorities

Issue priorities are also enumerations and also support custom fields. Values of issue priority custom fields can be edited and viewed only in the enumeration edit form (**Administration | Enumerations**).

Document categories

Document categories are also enumerations and they also support custom fields. Values of document category custom fields can be edited and viewed only in the enumeration edit form (**Administration | Enumerations**) as well.

Customizing with Textile

We have already reviewed the wiki formatting and Textile in *Chapter 7, Text Formatting*; then why are we coming back to it again? I was formerly asked to create a custom plugin to improve the layout of the Redmine start page (available through the **Home** link) with buttons, links, sections, and other similar stuff. My answer was, you don't need a plugin to do that.

Textile is a very simplified HTML. Of course, it can't be used to create full-featured HTML pages, but for many things it can appear to be sufficient. However, to achieve the necessary results you, most likely, will need to use the most advanced Redmine Textile features. Also, similar to HTML, you can't just learn how to create a good look and feel—you can only get the idea. You will need to inject your own creativity to get what you need. Therefore, under this topic we will review some interesting customization examples, which should help you understand the technique.

Wiki pages as tabs in the project menu

The wiki Extensions plugin, created by Haruyuki Iida, allows adding wiki pages to the project menu as tabs (configured per project). You can find more information on this at `http://www.r-labs.org/projects/r-labs/wiki/Wiki_Extensions_en`.

Things we will discuss here will look tricky and, perhaps, you will ask, why should we prefer this technique over writing a plugin? The anwer is, Textile formatting will survive the upgrade of Redmine, while a plugin, most likely, will need to be updated.

Using HTML code in wiki pages

Arlo Carreon created the wiki HTML Util plugin, which can be used to embed HTML, CSS, or JavaScript code directly into a wiki page. You can find more information at `https://github.com/mexitek/redmine_wiki_html_util`.

Warnings and other boxes

Redmine core CSS classes can also be utilized to build information boxes in the wiki content, for example:

```
p(conflict). A warning message.

p(box). Rendered as a box.
```

This is shown as follows:

> ⚠ A warning message.

> Rendered as a box.

Icons for text

If you want to put an icon before a text, you can, for example:

```
You can insert "(icon icon-fav)a link with an icon":http://www.
andriylesyuk.com or even %(icon icon-checked).not a link%...
```

This Textile code will be rendered in the following way:

> You can insert ⭐ a link with an icon or even ✔ not a link...

Here we use Redmine icon CSS classes and utilize the Textile SPAN element (using %).

Table-based layout

In modern web design everyone prefers building the page layout using DIVs and not old-style HTML tables. But in Textile we don't have enough control over DIVs. However, we can still use tables:

```
table{border:none}.
|{border:none}.eBook: %{color:#bbb}£18.99%|{border:none;padding:1em}.%
{font-size:1.5em}£15.19%
save 20%|{border:none}.!http://www.packtpub.com/sites/all/themes/
packt_new/images/addtocart.gif!:http://www.packtpub.com/mastering-
redmine/book|
|{border:none}.Print + free eBook + free PacktLib access to the
book: %{color:#bbb}£49.98%|{border:none;padding:1em}.%{font-
size:1.5em}£27.89%
save 44%|{border:none}.!http://www.packtpub.com/sites/all/themes/
packt_new/images/addtocart.gif!:http://www.packtpub.com/mastering-
redmine/book|
```

This tricky code produces the following result:

eBook: £18.99	£15.19 save 20%	**Add to Cart**
Print + free eBook + free PacktLib access to the book: £49.98	£27.89 save 44%	**Add to Cart**

In this example we defined CSS styles for the table (table{border:none}.) and its cells (for example, |{border:none;padding:1em}.) and, again, utilized the HTML SPAN element (for example, %{color:#bbb}£49.98%).

Customizing themes

A common scenario of customization is when users first choose the theme for Redmine and then slightly modify it to fit their needs. As a result such users lose the possibility of upgrading the theme in future (as it now contains their changes).

Suppose we want to customize the Redmine **Alternate** theme. Instead of modifying the themes files under the `public/themes/alternate` directory, let's create a new theme based on this one. To do this let's create the `packtpub` subdirectory for our theme (this will be its name) in the `public/themes` directory. In the newly created directory create the `stylesheets` subdirectory and the `application.css` file in it.

Now add the following CSS code into this file:

```
@import url(../../../themes/alternate/stylesheets/application.css);

#top-menu { background-color: #040404; }
#header { background-color: #8db1c9; }
#main-menu li a { background-color: #404040; }
```

Here the first line loads CSS from the **Alternate** theme so we need to include only the difference into our customized one.

Customizing with plugins

The most advanced customization can be accomplished by writing a custom plugin. With a plugin you can customize literally anything in Redmine. Of course, to write a full-featured plugin you need to be familiar with Ruby, Rails, Redmine API, JavaScript, HTML, CSS, web development concept, and so on. But who said, that you need a full-featured plugin?

As you know, a plugin's files are kept in a separate directory named after the plugin and located in the `plugins` subdirectory of the Redmine root. This way when Redmine gets upgraded, the plugin's files remain untouched. On the other side, many users put their customizations into Redmine core files, which get overwritten on upgrade. So why not put customizations into a plugin?

The Redmine plugin API is quite flexible and you allows to: overwrite any core view file without touching the original one; to add custom content to different views; load additional CSS style sheets, and so on. Therefore, a plugin can be used as a tool for customization. In fact, you do not need to write any complicated Ruby code to do this—just use small code snippets to activate different plugins capabilities. That's what we will learn in this topic.

Of course, to be able to customize Redmine's look and feel you need to be familiar, at least, with HTML. Familiarity with CSS is optional but will be very useful.

Writing a simple plugin

To be able to make use of the plugin capabilities we need to create a simple plugin first. Luckily, it's really simple.

Before proceeding, we need to choose a name for our plugin. Thus, for my website www.andriylesyuk.com, which runs Redmine too, I chose the name `andriy_lesyuk`. So, for this demo plugin I will choose just `packtpub`.

> Name your customization plugin after your organization or site name. Use alphanumeric characters and dashes.

So now we will create a directory for our plugin in the `plugins` subdirectory of the Redmine root directory, which is `/opt/redmine` in my case. So the full path for the plugin will be `/opt/redmine/plugins/packtpub`.

After this, in the newly created directory, we will create the `init.rb` file (the entry point for the plugin) and put the following code in it:

```
require 'redmine'

Rails.logger.info 'Starting Packt Publishing Plugin for Redmine'

Redmine::Plugin.register :packtpub do
    name 'Packt Publishing customization'
    author 'Andriy Lesyuk'
    author_url 'http://www.andriylesyuk.com'
    description 'The demo of the customization using the plugin.'
    url 'http://redmine.packtpub.com'
    version '0.0.1'
end
```

In place of `:packtpub` write your plugin name (keep the colon at the beginning). What should be changed in the rest of the code, I believe, is quite clear.

When done, after restarting Redmine you should see your plugin in **Administration | Plugins**, as follows:

Plugins

Packt Publishing customization

The demo of the customization using the plugin.   Andriy Lesyuk   0.0.1
http://redmine.packtpub.com

Of course, this plugin does nothing (besides putting itself into the plugin list), but that's all for now.

Customizing view files

Redmine is using the **Model-View-Controller (MVC)** architecture, where "view" files store the layout information. Most of the content of these files is just HTML code (the rest is eRuby, JavaScript, and so on). All views are located under the app/views path of Redmine. Any view can be overwritten just by copying the original view file into the appropriate path under the plugins app/views. So, let's now see how this works by reviewing one of the most common customization tasks, adding a logo to the layout.

First we need to create a directory for images in our plugin. This must be the assets/images directory. After creating it put the logo image into this directory.

When done, create the app/views directory in the plugins root and copy the app/views/layouts/base.html.erb file there from Redmine preserving the directory structure (thus, the full target location in my case is plugins/packtpub/app/views/layouts/base.html.erb).

Now open the base.html.erb file (the copy) and find the following line of code in there:

```
<h1><%= page_header_title %></h1>
```

This code renders the title of the page. Before this line, add the following line of code:

```
<%= image_tag('packtpub.png', :plugin => 'packtpub', :style => 'float:
left; padding-right: 1em;') %>
```

Here packtpub.png is the name of the image file and 'packtpub' is the name of the plugin.

 Alternatively, the logo can be added using CSS (for example, by creating a custom theme). To do this you can specify the background image for #header. However, the #header area should not already have the background image, which can be set, for example, by theme. The advantage of this method is that the customization, most likely, won't need to be updated after upgrades.

After saving changes, restarting Redmine, and reloading any Redmine page you will get something like the following screenshot:

Track changes you make to copies of Redmine core files, as you may need to replicate them, if Redmine core files get modified with an upgrade.

> The Plugin Views Revisions plugin of Vitaly Klimov allows you to bind the modified view file with certain Redmine version, thus, making it active only until an upgrade (this way preventing Redmine from crashes). More information can be found at http://www.redmine.org/plugins/redmine_plugin_views_revisions.

Using hooks

Redmine comes with "hooks" support. Hooks can be used to inject custom content into some pre-defined places in certain Redmine views. If possible, it is better to use hooks to add the content to the view instead of copying and modifying the view file, as for hooks you need to provide only the custom content and they are not affected by upgrades. Let's see how this works in another real-life example—let's add login instructions to the login page.

To be able to use hooks we need to add the hook listener to the plugin. To do this create the lib directory in the plugins root and place the packtpub_hook.rb file in it (you can use anything in place of packtpub in the filename). Now add the following code to the newly created file:

```
class PacktPubHook   < Redmine::Hook::ViewListener

    render_on :view_account_login_top, :partial => 'packtpub/login'

end
```

Here the name of the class, which is PacktPubHook, reflects the filename. :view_account_login_top is the hook, which gets called on the login form, and the :partial option contains the path to the custom content view file.

Now we need to create the file, which will contain the custom content. So first we will create the `packtpub` directory in `app/views` and then place the `_login.html.erb` file in it (note `_` at the beginning of the filename—it is required). Now put your custom content, which can be just HTML, into the newly created file.

And finally we need to register our hook listener. To do this just add the following line of code to the `init.rb` file (under `require 'redmine'`):

```
require_dependency 'packtpub_hook'
```

Here `packtpub_hook` is the filename of the hook listener without extension.

Now when you restart Redmine and go to the login page, you should see something like the following screenshot:

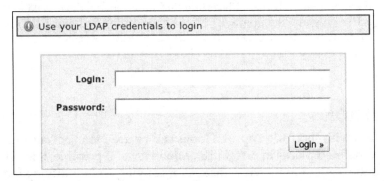

The warning above the form is added using the hook.

The following table lists some other hooks, which can be interesting for you:

Hook	Location
`:view_welcome_index_left`	Bottom of the left column (the start page)
`:view_welcome_index_right`	Bottom of the right column (the start page)
`:view_account_login_bottom`	Below the form on the login page
`:view_layouts_base_content`	Below the content on each page
`:view_projects_show_left`	Bottom of the left column (the project overview page)
`:view_projects_show_right`	Bottom of the right column (the project overview page)
`:view_issues_new_top`	Above the form on the new issue page

A full list of hooks can be found at `http://www.redmine.org/projects/redmine/wiki/Hooks_List#View-hooks`.

Summary

If the Redmine installation is not customized, it's a demo. Even Redmine.Org is customized (the ad on the sidebar, the plugins registry, and so on). All users prefer to customize the software they are using. Usually, Redmine users at least install some third-party plugins and a theme. But, in fact, all just mentioned can be described as installation and configuration. The real customization is what has been described in this chapter!

Some readers will, perhaps, never need what has been described here though (but, I believe the chapter was still interesting for them). But those who will, will be able to save time and money by doing the customization properly.

Index

Symbols

A

B

view documents permission 235
Documents module 138, 139

E

Editable checkbox 315
edit issues permission 236
edit messages permission 234
edit notes permission 236
edit own messages permission 234
edit own notes permission 237
edit own time logs permission 239
edit project permission 233
edit time logs permission 239
edit wiki pages permission 240
e-mail integration
    about 72
    e-mail fetching, IMAP/POP3 used 83, 84
    e-mail fetching, web service used 81, 82
    e-mail notifications configuration,
        configuration.yml used 72, 74
    e-mail notifications configuration, web
        interface used 74-76
    e-mails, receiving 78
    e-mails, sending 72
    incoming e-mail format 78-81
    reminding e-mails, configuring 77, 78
Email notifications box 272
Emission email address option 75
engines 8
Enumerations 323
Exception Handler plugin
    about 288
    settings 288
    URL 288
export wiki pages permission 240

F

Feature tracker 108
FHS (Filesystem Hierarchy Standard) 41
Files block
    about 235
    manage files permission 235
    view files permission 235
Files tab 140
finnlabs 21

Float format 317
footnote 205
For all projects checkbox 315
Forums block
    about 233
    delete messages permission 234
    delete own messages permission 234
    edit messages permission 234
    edit own messages permission 234
    manage forums permission 233
    post messages permission 234
forums module 151

G

Gantt block
    about 235
    view gantt chart permission 235
Gantt tab 156
gem tool 43
General tab, administration settings
    about 65
    cache formatted text 65
    tips 66
Github
    about 281
    Redmine plugins, searching 281, 283
    URL 281
Github Hook plugin 90
global activities 167
global configuration 158, 159
Globally Recognized Avatar. See Gravatar
Gravatar 67, 261, 262
Gravatar image
    Identicons 67
    Monster ids 67
    Mystery man 67
    Retro 67
    Wavatars 67

H

Highrise theme
    about 309
    download link 309
    versions 309
Homepage field 162

Thank you for buying
Mastering Redmine

About Packt Publishing

Packt, pronounced 'packed', published its first book "*Mastering phpMyAdmin for Effective MySQL Management*" in April 2004 and subsequently continued to specialize in publishing highly focused books on specific technologies and solutions.

Our books and publications share the experiences of your fellow IT professionals in adapting and customizing today's systems, applications, and frameworks. Our solution based books give you the knowledge and power to customize the software and technologies you're using to get the job done. Packt books are more specific and less general than the IT books you have seen in the past. Our unique business model allows us to bring you more focused information, giving you more of what you need to know, and less of what you don't.

Packt is a modern, yet unique publishing company, which focuses on producing quality, cutting-edge books for communities of developers, administrators, and newbies alike. For more information, please visit our website: www.packtpub.com.

About Packt Open Source

In 2010, Packt launched two new brands, Packt Open Source and Packt Enterprise, in order to continue its focus on specialization. This book is part of the Packt Open Source brand, home to books published on software built around Open Source licences, and offering information to anybody from advanced developers to budding web designers. The Open Source brand also runs Packt's Open Source Royalty Scheme, by which Packt gives a royalty to each Open Source project about whose software a book is sold.

Writing for Packt

We welcome all inquiries from people who are interested in authoring. Book proposals should be sent to author@packtpub.com. If your book idea is still at an early stage and you would like to discuss it first before writing a formal book proposal, contact us; one of our commissioning editors will get in touch with you.

We're not just looking for published authors; if you have strong technical skills but no writing experience, our experienced editors can help you develop a writing career, or simply get some additional reward for your expertise.

JIRA Development Cookbook

ISBN: 978-1-849681-80-3   Paperback: 476 pages

Develop and customize plugins, program workflows,
work on custom fields, master JQL functions, and
more - to effectively customize, manage, and
extend JIRA

1. Extend and Customize JIRA--Work with
   custom fields, workflows, Reports & Gadgets,
   JQL functions, plugins, and more

2. Customize the look and feel of your JIRA User
   Interface by adding new tabs, web items and
   sections, drop down menus, and more

3. Master JQL - JIRA Query Language that enables
   advanced searching capabilities through
   which users can search for issues in their JIRA
   instance and then exploit all the capabilities of
   issue navigator

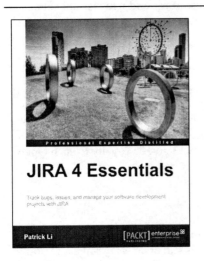

JIRA 4 Essentials

ISBN: 978-1-849681-72-8   Paperback: 352 pages

Track bugs, issues, and manage your software
development projects with JIRA

1. Successfully manage issues and track your
   projects using JIRA

2. Model business processes using JIRA
   Workflows

3. Packed with step-by-step instruction,
   screenshots, and practical examples

Please check **www.PacktPub.com** for information on our titles

Mastering phpMyAdmin 3.4 for Effective MySQL Management

ISBN: 978-1-849517-78-2   Paperback: 394 pages

A complete guide to getting started with phpMyAdmin 3.4 and mastering its features

1. A step-by-step tutorial for manipulating data with the latest version of phpmyadmin

2. Administer your MySQL databases with phpMyAdmin

3. Manage users and privileges with MySQL Server Administration tools

4. Learn to do things with your MySQL database and phpMyAdmin that you didn't know were possible!

FreeSWITCH Cookbook

ISBN: 978-1-849515-40-5   Paperback: 150 pages

Over 40 recipes to help you get the most out of your FreeSWITCH server

1. Get powerful FreeSWITCH features to work for you

2. Route calls and handle call detailing records

4. Written by members of the FreeSWITCH development team

Please check **www.PacktPub.com** for information on our titles

Lightning Source UK Ltd.
Milton Keynes UK
UKOW01f0304010314

227358UK00004B/85/P